The Fundamentals of
Sports Media and Sponsorship Sales
Developing New Accounts

David J. Halberstam

THE FUNDAMENTALS OF SPORTS MEDIA AND SPONSORSHIP SALES:
DEVELOPING NEW ACCOUNTS.

Library of Congress Control Number: 2015911219

ISBN: 9780692488393

Halby Group, Inc.
http://halbygroup.com/

Cover design by Ingenious Tek Group

First Printing

Contents

Dr. Bernie Mullin graces the title with a stirring narrative that captures the importance of developing new business. Dr. Mullin is one of the few sports executives who have achieved glittering success on both sides of the business: as an academician, serving as a pioneering professor at the University of Massachusetts, and as a practitioner, holding lofty positions at NBA headquarters and later as president of the Atlanta Hawks. Mullin's foreword addresses the importance of growing sponsorship revenue in the coming years by regularly landing new corporate partners.

David Halberstam comments on recent action, stymieing cold callers, (e.g., JPMorgan and Coca-Cola shutting down voicemail). Yet, he points out, it is more difficult to stifle the determined seller who finds alternative ways to get through to prospects. Halberstam acknowledges some of the pioneers of sports sponsorship sales and the early leaders who set the stage for spiraling success.

The stage is set by recognizing the contribution of sellers to the growth of the American economy and the critical role that cold callers play every day. Yes, there's some fun cold calling and there's certainly an unequaled sense of satisfaction when nailing down a new piece of business, but be prepared for the painstaking daily grind that the effort requires. Cold calling comes in a variety of forms, from hard core selling to Dodgers' announcer Vin Scully knocking on doors in the neighborhood to collect charity. Because sports sponsorships and media rights are projected by PricewaterhouseCoopers to enjoy healthy growth in the next decade, hungry sellers will be in demand for the foreseeable future.

Chapters:

Before you embark, ask yourself if you have the stomach and desire, the nose of where to go to chase business, and whether you are committed to the critical organizational requirements needed to succeed?

How do you go about getting interviews and being relevant in the job market? How do you prepare for an interview? Where do you seek a job, and how do you differentiate yourself from others? What not to do when pursuing a job. Inspirational, successful and unique stories of job seekers are also reviewed.

Committing to good organizational practices early in sales careers is essential because account activity is fluid. This important chapter provides detailed instruction on how to remain vigilantly on top of things. The benefits of CRM (customer relationship management) now being used by so many sales organizations are also addressed.

How to train your mind, eyes and ears to glean leads. Learn to match core competencies of the product you're selling with prospects' needs. The importance of reading, from the local business pages to *Barron's*. Think creatively and practically. How to identify new industries nationally that potentially suit sports sponsorships. What new local businesses moving into your area will benefit from a partnership with your local team?

Never pick up the phone or send an email before you're prepared. What to do before reaching prospects. Because clients want to buy from experts, not sellers, how to use social media to grow your credentials. Examples of account preparation from companies like FedEx, Microsoft, Discover Card and others.

What to say, how to say it. Be mindful of your goal: you're trying to get a face-to-face appointment. Suggested techniques and exercises. Critical importance of listening. Breaking barriers of unwillingness and dealing with silence on the other end of the phone.

Prepare psychologically. What to include, what to bring with you, how to dress and what to do if the prospect isn't there when you show up. How to command a room. How to motivate a room and galvanize a group of functionaries.

Dealing with the emotional roller coaster. Overcome adversity on tough days. Understand that failure and rejection are a prelude to success.

Not allowing setbacks to temper your enthusiasm. A sampling of the many who've overcome rejection, from Oprah Winfrey and Frank Gehry to Michael Jordan and Christopher Columbus, from Dr. Seuss and Gil Hodges to FedEx and ESPN.

From the pope to Yogi Berra, from President Clinton to Commissioner David Stern, from Benny Goodman to Warren Buffett and from Phil Jackson to Peyton Manning, glean and learn. It will make you a better cold call seller.

A potpourri of broad and situational advice, from building trust to getting through gatekeepers, how to use scanned articles or handwritten notes, being careful about building trust and not betraying confidences. The devil is in the detail. Don't take the Visa client to lunch and pay with your MasterCard.

Interesting experiences in the sales trenches, breaking barriers and being disarming. Walking in cold on a chief marketing officer and fostering a multimillion dollar sale. How a unique seller commanded a room in the most charming of ways.

Inspirational cold calling stories of sellers who converted soft variables into millions in cash, including famous naming rights deals like Nextel/NASCAR,

Moda for Rose Garden in Portland and Barclays Center in Brooklyn. Additionally, there are stories of how cold callers landed deals for Wise Potato Chips at Citi Field, Aaron Rentals for naming rights to the Talladega racetrack, women-targeted Reynolds Wrap for the Yankees radio broadcasts and many other heartwarming success stories.

Foreword

Dr. Bernard J. Mullin, Chairman and CEO, The Aspire
Sport Marketing Group LLC

There seems to be two types of books that address highly practical topics such as *The Fundamentals of Sports Sponsorship Sales: Developing New Accounts.* I believe that I am unusually well placed to offer my perspective on this landmark work by David Halberstam, having lived in both realms of the typical author.

As a professor of management and sport marketing at the University of Massachusetts for 10 years, I have seen the "Ivory Tower Approach" firsthand. I then followed my academic career by spending the last 30 years as a C-level executive in professional team sports and the entertainment industry (MLB, NBA and NHL) along with operating world-class stadiums and arenas. Additionally, I have served as an athletic director for an NCAA Division I Intercollegiate program and as founder/CEO of the leading outsource revenue enhancement firm globally serving over 150 iconic sports and entertainment properties in 17 different sports in 8 countries.

The first type of book invariably is written by practitioners who are in desperate need of real-world training materials and how-to manuals to educate their own staff and the industry at large. As the primary author of the first ever text on sport marketing, I am well aware of how many areas of this niche are severely devoid of tried and tested strategies and tactics that produce real results and provide real-world examples of the dos and don'ts with accompanying business case results. While many of these manuals and practical guides provide excellent ideas, rarely do they meet the academic rigor to which university professors hold themselves accountable. Therefore, these practical works invariably don't provide the necessary theoretical and philosophical framework (the skeleton) onto which very practical programs and actions can be attached (the muscles and skin) with accompanying practical details on how to implement and execute them. For these reasons, universities rarely recommend these books be exposed to students.

The second type of book is usually written by a university professor and does focus on the theory and philosophy behind the subject matter but with minimal regard to practical application. Normally, these works—while providing a 30,000-foot overview—do not offer "drilldown" tactics, nor do they outline the nuances needed for success. Even when professors have strong consulting backgrounds and industry connections, they generally have neither been in the trenches selling nor have they been in the C-suite, building the strategy. Therefore, these books lack the specificity and experience of the "hand-to-hand" combat and negotiation skills needed to bring large, medium and small deals home. This necessary judgment generally comes only with extensive experience, numerous successes and failures, which so often produce the wisdom expressed in this book. Consequently, the professor-written texts invariably are never purchased nor recommended by practitioners.

By contrast, David Halberstam has operated at every single level of this business. "Halby" started selling sponsorships with small broadcast properties and grew into on-air talent with an NBA Championship club. Always growing, learning, teaching and achieving superior sales results, he rapidly progressed through numerous middle-management positions until he became EVP, Sports of Westwood One, which at that time was the largest sports radio network nationwide. These extensive "life lessons" helped him to know how and when to start small and service the heck out of a marketing partnership/sponsorship account and how to grow it in future years into a major account. To my knowledge no one else in the industry possessing this background has ever taken the time to so clearly outline how this can be done, and to educate young professionals in building and growing the sport marketing partnership/sponsorship business the right way.

David Halberstam's landmark work is clearly this "third kind" of text that combines the best of the two approaches outlined above, thereby avoiding the shortcomings of the insular academic text or the "how to mechanics" workbook which fail to set the context. As an industry pioneer who has continuously reinvented himself throughout his career, he has now written the definitive text that addresses selling sport sponsorships by building true marketing partnerships. In particular, his focus on how to acquire and grow new accounts is unique. In this manner, he has clearly demonstrated the importance of sponsorship in the overall financial equation—whether running a major league or minor league team, the league itself, a Power Five, mid-major or emerging collegiate athletic program or, any sport or entertainment venue or property needing marketing partnerships and corporate support.

In my 30 years, I have hired, trained and mentored thousands of entry-level professionals, first-line, middle and senior executives. I only wish I had this book back then to provide the rigorous training and practical application so many of these colleagues of mine needed.

Clearly this text is the first ever book dedicated solely to sport sponsorship sales that successfully addresses cold calling for new business sales. In today's world, this skill set is vital to any young professional wishing to progress his or her career. In this manner, David has demonstrated just how critical it is to develop *new business*—both on the sponsorship and corporate sides of ticketing and hospitality. There are only so many beer, soft drink, financial services, apparel, wireless and insurance companies willing to spend millions of dollars in sports sponsorship in this world. And just about every sport property is hounding all of the big spenders on a constant basis. Therefore, it is vital to the success of any young professional to learn how to grow the pot beyond the big staples. In recent years, companies like Chobani Yogurt (NCAA), Bose (NFL and U.S. Ski and Snowboard Association) and ANCO Blades (NHL) entered the sports sponsorship space—nationally, not just locally. What would it mean to your career if you were the person to uncover such emerging gems? Well, this book is without doubt your best chance to learn how to do just that!

Halby's book is not just a compendium of his extensive work experience. David is a student of life and has ensured that his text outlines how to develop overall sponsorship inventory by finding new opportunities. Many of his peers' response to new digital media—social network opportunities, podcasts and other forms of online sponsorships—has been to "throw them in as deal sweeteners." Not David. So often new media inventory has not been monetized, and in fact, the fan databases created have been frequently "spammed" by passing them on to sponsors for non-targeted, one-size-fits-all, intrusive advertising campaigns that annoy fans and increase "unsubscribe" rates. Instead, readers of this book are clearly shown how, where and when to use these new opportunities to not only maximize property revenues but also grow fan engagement and entertainment value, along with how to really activate the partnership with maximum benefit to the sponsor and the fan. Whether it is the role of uniform advertising heretofore taboo in the U.S. Major Leagues or cutting-edge digital and social media programs using players to grab the attention of fans, modern corporate partnerships rely on one-on-one communications from the team and/ or its coaches and players who are truly fulfilling corporate partner commitments with the right balance of positive role-modeling and edgy brand image that provides the authenticity to attract millennials.

Having been in the same trenches as David pitching to corporate partners for 30 years, starting with static outfield, courtside or dasher-board signage through the evolution of complex multi-media deals and then massive long-term naming rights deals, I have seen very few people survive, let alone thrive, the way he has. Amazingly, he has never become jaded by seeing some arenas so cluttered with ads that not only are the ads right in your face like a male fan standing at the urinal but also form the target site when these fans inevitably look down. Instead, he maintains the same passion he had as a young professional cutting his teeth in radio ad sales, which is about as tough an apprenticeship in this business as outbound telemarketing to non-sport fans.

As one example of his industry impact, just take a look at the industry leaders David Halberstam has trained and mentored over the years: Brian Lafemina, SVP at the NFL and former SVP at Madison Square Garden; Randy Freer, COO of Fox; Andi Poch, formerly WNBA; and Mike Dresner, formerly of the NBA.

In all of these years in the business, there has been a complete lack of training materials for sport sponsorship sellers. New sellers were invariably thrown to the wolves without being prepared for how tough it is, how sophisticated this business has now become and how to avoid the pitfalls. The book includes snippets of guidance from key corporate partner marketers providing insight on what they really want to see in a presentation, what they consider overbearing, the difference between good and professional persistence by sellers, and when the line is crossed to becoming a stalker. It also covers just how these corporate marketers feel technology has changed the way their company sells. Some of the top decision makers quoted are: Ed Gold of State Farm; Betsy Wilson of UPS; Tim Sullivan of Wendy's; and Michael Robichaud of MasterCard, who collectively handle billions of marketing and advertising dollars annually.

In short, it is hard for me to conceive of a better text that teaches the philosophy behind sports sponsorship sales and servicing coupled with the nuances that make a true corporate partnership. This book is not just for the rookie starting out. It is also for veterans who may never have been taught the right philosophy, the proper context or the real tricks of the trade. This book is also for those people who haven't kept up with new media and those who may have lost their desire and fire to sell. It is an invaluable re-motivator and guide to be kept on the shelf to remind all of us in the industry of what we may have forgotten. Although it might sound cliché, David Halberstam has truly forgotten way more about this niche than most people in the field have ever learned.

Preface

This is a pioneering handbook. It spells out, from start to finish and in frank detail, the step-by-step process of developing new sponsorships, beginning with the conceptual framework of a partnership theme and ending with ringing the celebratory bell after closing a mutually beneficial deal.

"Creative Cost-Cutting: Silence the Voice Mail" was the sobering headline of a *Barron's* story covering the elimination of voicemail at Coca-Cola headquarters in Atlanta and on many employees' landlines at JPMorgan Chase.

At Coke, unanswered phone calls result in a uniform corporate voice message: "You have reached the Coca-Cola Company. The individual you are calling is currently not available. Please call back at a later time or use an alternative method to reach this individual."

The *Barron's* headline should have read, "Stymieing the Salesperson." Heck, to inveterate cold callers, shutting down voicemail is like pulling tools from carpenters. How else do they leave heartfelt messages that fuel returned calls?

But don't despair. Effective cold callers are an irrepressible breed. It takes a seismic earthquake to knock them off-kilter.

When front doors are padlocked, they find side entrances or back windows. Even Gordon Smith, head of JPMorgan's consumer and community banking unit said, "We're all carrying something in our pockets that's going to get texts or email or a phone call."

Resourceful sellers today scour LinkedIn and communicate through social media sites, such as Facebook and Twitter. Whether it's Instagram or Pinterest today or other fresh apps tomorrow, innovative cold callers are hard to stifle. They find ways to reach prospects in a hyperconnected world.

But raw sports sellers are forced to learn the hard way, through trial and error. Before bosses throw them to the wolves with a sobering dictate to land new accounts, there's little formal training. Yes, the revenue opportunities are potentially fertile, but the untrained are ill-prepared for the harsh realities they'll invariably face.

The book addresses solutions to sales' daily obstacles and recognizes uplifting success stories that have enriched salespeople's pockets, swelled sports' coffers and stimulated others to follow in similar career paths.

Managing a group of new business sellers means being part manager and strategist and part psychiatrist and counselor. Both managers and sellers have to be talked off the ledge every now and then. You've heard it often. Success is a journey!

The Fundamentals of Sports Media and Sponsorship Sales: Developing New Accounts is dedicated to the bosses who hired me, the colleagues whose friendships I continue to cherish and those whom I had the opportunity to train.

I was lucky to learn from wonderful talent, beginning with Jim Greenwald who spent some forty years building what is now Katz Media Group, the country's largest broadcast sales representative. Jim used his extraordinary memory to bond with clients and his imaginative vision to build a juggernaut. Ken Swetz ran the Katz Radio division with military precision and determination. Ken was one of the most commanding, decisive and charismatic leaders I ever watched run an organization. Joel Hollander ran Westwood One and later CBS Radio. Joel assessed the field as well as anyone. He was a marvelous scout of talent who was seamlessly disarming and naturally cogent. I had the opportunity to meet people with whom I had agreements for many years and never needed a contract. Their words were their bonds. It's how I will always remember Jack Kaiser, now St.

John's University's athletic director emeritus.

Folks like Randy Freer, now chief operating officer of Fox, and Brian Lafemina, senior vice president of Club Business Development at the NFL, are both brilliant executives whom I happily can say worked for me when they were green sellers. Randy and Brian were thrown the yellow pages and learned the ropes quickly.

There were others whom I had a chance to touch, just too many to mention. Lewis Schreck, Andi Poch, Sandy Diamond, Stu Heifetz, Michael Schreck, Marc Steir, Brandon Berman and Michael Dresner all make me feel proud. John Massoni, a top executive at Van Wagner, and broadcast executives Mike Agovino and Darrin Klayman interned under me, and I'm not at all surprised that they have excelled.

The sports business today couldn't have exploded without sponsorship sales pioneers—people like Art Adler who turned the soft variables of radio play-by-play into a rich source of revenue; John Lazarus who ran ABC Sports in its years of spiraling growth; the Yormark twins, Michael and Brett, and energetic others who hit the streets with briefcases in their hands and hope in their hearts. Their spirits were unconquerable. They got it done when sports marketing was still in its nascent days. There were no guarantees.

I hope that this book gets the attention of corporate fathers. Cold callers need more than tacit support. They need management's guidance, training and patience! It is time and money solidly invested.

Finally, writing is a solitary activity. It takes time away from family and friends. So, I thank my immediate family for understanding, starting with my wife, Donna, and our three young adult children, Manny, Mollie and Jaime. David Hillman, general counsel at Simon & Schuster, and Ken Samelson who edited my first book, *Sports on New York Radio: A Play-by-Play History*, offered constructive advice. The indomitable Joe Bannon of Sagamore

Publishing encouraged me. He felt that there was room for this type of title in sports management classrooms and among embarked practitioners.

Once the manuscript was completed, I connected with Rosemi Mederos who wowed me with her passion and impressed me by her knowledge of the publishing process. She held my hand all the way to the finish line, editing the text and steering the project from beginning to end. From a football equivalent, Rosemi went the extra yard.

Introduction

Unless you're born into a life of entitlement, life starts with a cold call.

America is a wonderful country and has always been the land of opportunity. Our parents and grandparents came to these shores with nothing or little. Many of them thought that the streets were paved with gold but learned otherwise. The streets were only paved with opportunity.

But opportunity provides a chance—a chance to advance and progress.

Still, they learned, and happily so, that, as opposed to the countries they came from, where the citizenry was often oppressed, opportunities in the New World were plentiful. Prospects for growth and productivity were golden.

So our ancestors went to work, some in factories, some on farms and others in retail. Some started businesses, built their sales, socked away savings and made life more comfortable for their families.

Later, the Greatest Generation, as Tom Brokaw aptly called it, endured the Great Depression by helping their parents put meals on their families' tables while still doing their best to enjoy their youthful years. Then, during World War II, they willfully took up arms to defeat oppression and imperialism in foreign lands.

After the war, Baby Boomers cultivated the landscape and strengthened America's might as a world power and as the richest country on the globe.

Through these last 75 years of fabulous growth, extraordinary salesmanship helped produce revenue, the nourishment essential to expand. America has always been a country of motivated, articulate, strategic and gifted sellers.

For those who can sell, are passionate about sports and are unshakably confident, the opportunity to succeed will always abound. Supported by outstanding sellers, the business of sports has leaped off the charts.

In 2014, the sports industry reached an implausible $62 billion. PricewaterhouseCoopers is projecting a robust increase by 2018 to $70.7 billion.

It's the human touch that sells. Yes, driven by new, speedier and more convenient communication devices, technology is overpowering. Technology, though, is an impersonal tool. Human communication is what we fully control and what enables us to succeed.

And, yes, technology companies help sports sponsorships' bottom-line revenue too. For instance, Microsoft came to terms with the NFL in 2014 to become the "official tablet" of the league. The company agreed to pay the NFL a sobering $400 million for five years.

Reflecting on what she calls the 'knowledge economy' and the fact that technology has devoured jobs heretofore done by humans, Jenna Goudreau wrote in *Forbes*, "The jobs that will survive all this change will be those a robot or piece of software cannot do, requiring social skills, eye contact and personal touch." As the country moves further to a service economy, Goudreau sites communication skills as one that will move to the fore.

While technology continually changes the communication protocol, management will always bet on the sales jockey, not the communication device. Because of this, the effective seller and the seller's family will never starve.

Cold callers, most of whom are inexperienced entry-level sellers, do well when, truly in their heart of hearts, they are sufficiently passionate about the sports product they're selling. They just won't tolerate unreturned calls that are sensitively placed in unhurried doses. They're so enthralled about the power of sports, the power of what they represent and their personal career goals that they won't accept excuses for being ignored.

The determination of effective cold callers runs deep. They target those who parry attempts to reach them. They do so with an unbending resolve to connect. It doesn't mean scream, yell or threaten that you'll take your life if they don't get back to you. To get attention, sellers often have to be different and creative, without it being perceived as cunning. In sellers' minds, even the most insensitive prospect has an obligation to communicate, to return a call.

Effective sellers can always apply their skills in a variety of venues. If selling sports sponsorships or sports media doesn't work out, good sellers can always camp out on street corners and sell pencils, so to speak. Selling is a skill with which you can cast a wide net of products, goods and services.

After several unanswered calls to a sales manager at a television company when I tried to break into the business in the late 1970s, I misguidedly called his secretary again and told her that the call was personal. It worked for about 30 seconds. The sales manager got on the phone with me immediately and asked why I was calling. I brazenly told him that it was about a job. Annoyed, he didactically cut me off in midsentence, "You're coy. I would never hire you." The lesson was to be honest and forthright and not to mislead. If not, you might win the battle but will lose the war.

Successful multimillion dollar companies anticipate rough patches and account attrition. They recognize that developing new business is critical. Revenue may be good today, but who knows about tomorrow? It's why even in good times they're digging in the trenches for new accounts. After all, didn't Noah build the ark when it was still sunny?

As historian John Keegan said of World War I, "War came out of a cloudless sky." In business, companies, too, suffer account attrition unpredictably, even when times are healthy. Reliable accounts dry up, just when you don't expect it. New ones have to be found.

When sports seasons approach inexorably, unsold sponsorship and media inventory become melting ice cubes. Management is then forced to discount rates, sending an unwanted message to the marketplace. This generally occurs as a result of soft business among traditional and transactional advertisers. It's during these periodic ebbs that the success of cold callers becomes paramount. With fresh, nontraditional business already in the till, management avoids a maddening and dreaded last-second sales fire drill.

In these tough times or when the headwinds of an economic crunch prevail, cold calling success is a fabulous way to make a name for yourself. It will enable you to grow within the company for which you work. Sales productivity elevates your status, awards you with existing fertile accounts and perhaps, over time, a promotion into management. Our golden 'sales orders' as rookie sellers often define our early careers. It's not the many prospects that say no but rather the ones that say yes that establish your legacy.

But don't fool yourself, cold calling is entering an island of frustration. It's lonely; you're out there on your own. No one really understands your suffering or your frustration. The potential buyer on the other side certainly has no sympathy for the pain that you're going through.

Then again, cold callers enjoy sovereignty and freedom. Every day is truly fresh. You won't be bound to an active territory because the new business landscape is frequently endless. While veteran sellers fight the same tired, granular battles with transactional accounts and awake to the daily grind thinking, "Do I have to deal with that crotchety buyer again?" cold callers' days can be stimulatingly unpredictable. You never know when good things might happen.

Cold calling is proselytizing; negotiating with active accounts is cajoling. Cold calling is indoctrinating; transactional selling is often battling for unrealistic shares of budgets.

If you enjoy fresh relationships, cold calling in the sports space is for you. You'll make some of the best friends and business associates. Many of these relationships will be enduring and might last a career. Unlike dealing with the same old buyer, there's no baggage. In strange ways, it's enlightening. If it's a hardened buyer, you'll often be dealing with incorrigible and myopic attitudes. The new business sellers must have an innate desire to meet new people, learn a little bit about what makes these new contacts tick and, more importantly, what makes their businesses tick. There has to be a gift of curiosity to delve into and learn about the inner working of a target's business.

Quite a few sports business leaders were once rookie sellers who took their early and deep dive into the cold calling trenches. They were given the yellow pages and instructed to go for it. These eventual industry leaders weren't raised in silver spooned homes. They were ordinary aspiring youngsters who had little sense of entitlement. They started with little or nothing and learned quickly what it took to compete and produce in sales.

In 2014, the bible of the industry, *SportsBusiness Journal*, did a little spread on half a dozen sports executives' first sales. Steve Rosner who co-founded 16W Marketing and turned it into a mint before he eventually sold it, got a local New Jersey sporting goods company to shell out $150 for a recreation league he was involved with in high school. Greg Walter, vice president of partnership development at Speedway Motorsports, started his work career in tiny Wilson, North Carolina. "My first sponsorship sale was to a local car dealership, and by anyone's standards the sponsorship wasn't very big, but it was to me!" And Greg obviously never forgot it. Undoubtedly it propelled a successful career.

Cold calling can be broken down into geographical categories. Locally, sports can play off passion. Walter was selling NC State football and basketball on radio in a region where the Wolfpack are on the consciousness of the community. When he walked into a car dealership to sell NC State, the decision maker responded to emotions and Walter effectively converted this soft variable into hard cash.

As imposing as it is to walk in unannounced to a car dealership to sell anything, it's even more difficult to do the same nationally where there's less passion for a favorite team. Moreover, the seller is likely asking for a lot more money.

Nationally, too, it's hard to fathom walking into the lobby of Toyota's corporate headquarters, for example, and requesting an immediate appointment, much less an order on the spot. And today, with security being what it is, it's impossible to even use the restroom without going through a security device. And when you approach Toyota, you'll likely be asking for more than $150. You might be seeking up to a million bucks on your first cold call. It's not the local flower shop down the block whose owner will take $150 out of the cash register and give it to you.

You're not selling raffles either. Decisions on national sponsorship sales are multi-tiered. Many folks will be involved in the discussion and a lot of information will be required. The client's marketing and sales management team will be involved as will a battery of agencies.

To a young new business seller, the process can be daunting and overbearing, if not bewildering. Take comfort, though, in the fact that your job is to open the door, get the hearing, present your property and move the ball down the field. You won't be working alone. Most organizations that sell rich programs to major corporations have teams of experienced colleagues and departments that will serve in excellent support roles. They'll design the presentation, substantiate values, prepare a customized research story and concoct an effective activation program.

Gary Thorne, who started his career as an attorney in New England and moonlighted doing sports in Maine, wanted to get a play-by-play gig in the big leagues in the worst way. He knew the Mets had an opening, so on his own dime, he flew to Houston to baseball's winter meeting in 1984. Thorne cold called the team's GM, Al Harazin, in his room from the hotel lobby. He worked Harazin hard, got hired and eventually moved on to ESPN. It's a good lesson for all. Don't be afraid to do something bold.

Young new sellers aren't the only ones who cold call when need be. Even seasoned executives with a reputation for success do so. And it's not always to get an order.

The esteemed Vin Scully isn't shy either when need be. He's been known to go door-to-door in his neighborhood to raise money for charity. It would be tough to say no to a man with such a mellifluous voice. Yet, there he is, the Voice of the Dodgers, ringing bells and collecting for good causes.

In 2001, Anne Mulcahy became CEO of Xerox. The company was facing a liquidity problem with $18 billion of debt. Mulcahy cold called the icon, Warren Buffett. The Oracle of Omaha took her call, although he anticipated that Mulcahy would ask him to have Berkshire Hathaway invest in her financially strapped company.

Taking a "counseling" approach, Mulcahy was able to get an appointment with the Berkshire Hathaway CEO who suggested that she focus on Xerox' own employees and its customers instead of company investors and bankers. Mulcahy took Buffett's advice by hopping around the country, making changes and restoring the company financially. As a result, she warded off bankruptcy and continued to invest successfully in the future.

While Mulcahy later acknowledged that, yes, she hoped Buffett would invest in Xerox, she did effectively pick Buffett's brain and got sound and lasting advice that saved her company.

You, too, will find that, when you're fortunate to strike a conversation with an executive, the result will not always be an order. Yet the advice that results comes in various forms, how to better package programs for other clients, or sometimes leads and contacts at other companies. Networking at corporate levels invariably pays dividends.

In other words, cold calling emanates from all levels, the high school student selling ads in the print programs at sporting events to the CEO of Xerox.

Studies show that 20% of CEOs started in sales, second only to finance which represents some 30%. Jeffrey Immelt spent 20 years in sales at General Electric before taking over as CEO for Jack Welch.

Younger and less experienced sellers who thrust themselves into new business sales at the start of their careers are often more audacious because they don't know any better. Young sellers are not as jaded, so they do not have the natural bias of veteran sellers who say to themselves, "I've tried that account. Forget it. They'll never buy."

Yet cold calling isn't just for beginners who are wet behind their ears. Seasoned sellers, too, need to develop new business to recharge their batteries and as insurance for losing existing business. Prospecting is a key to success. It keeps veterans young and sharp.

I can recall my own experience. All I wanted to do is basketball play-by-play on radio, and when St. John's University didn't have a station to broadcast its games, I found a small one on Long Island, WGBB. The manager of the station said to me, "I'll run the games and you can announce them, but you'll have to sell sponsorships."

When I asked how to do it, he turned around, shoved his hand into the credenza behind his desk and pulled out the Queens and Nassau yellow pages. He looked at me sternly and said, "Here you go, get started." It was the beginning of my media experience. I got into the trenches. It hardened me. I learned about life and thought twice thereafter before asking my parents for anything. I realized how difficult it is to make a living.

It takes guts, determination, resiliency and belief. It takes a tough stomach and more, which will be addressed in these chapters. Yet the feeling of fulfillment and achievement is indescribable; the emotional high lasts weeks. If you're zealous about sports, your unrestrained enthusiasm will be naturally evident when you're on a sales call. Your excitement won't be fabricated.

When you're successful at it, you'll also make good money, which contributes of course to overall satisfaction. Selling vacuum cleaners is one thing. I've never done it because I'm not passionate about it. Yet if you live and inhale sports and have the other qualifications that we'll review, go for it.

There has to be a bone-deep desire to succeed. Because heck, there will be enough roadblocks to deter the most hardy of souls. Business development, a euphemism for cold calling, is one of those things that can be frightening.

Negotiating transactional accounts that are already on the table, such as renewals or agency requests for proposals (RFPs) is critical. But there's always that pressure of getting the lion's share of the allotted budget or the rate increase management demands. When you get the order, it's like being born on third base and coming home to score.

Starting from scratch and building revenue without a real road map is invigorating. No one called in a lead and no one said there's money on the table. So when you close a piece of business that's brand new, that you initiated and that you nurtured on your own, it's yours! You hit a home run. You weren't born on third base.

The feeling is magical. If it's your first order, you'll feel like it's falling in love for the first time. Nothing beats the accomplishment for building your own self-confidence. You don't want the feeling of that magical high to ever go away.

If cold calling is in your blood, it's the self-actualization of Maslow's theory of hierarchy. There will always be a need to make another call and close another new piece of business. It will be embodied in your makeup, a craving you'll never be able to shed. The cold caller knows there's always another one out there. Human nature dictates that we're never ever satisfied. We're always hungry for more.

Another enjoyment of cold calling is the level of people with whom you'll deal. Ideas are sold at the top. Concepts have to be endorsed at the decision-making level.

Cold calling is both science and art. The science involves call volume and research. Like it or not, there's an outbound numeric imperative, no matter the entity you're selling. If you're to succeed, probing for accounts requires a heavy volume of account calls. Conversely, a limited outbound volume results in a lower percentage of closed business. Preparatory research, narrowing down prospects from 'potential' to 'less likely,' is a science that helps tighten the process. Finally, there's a fundamental need to strategize scientifically, a cogent angle to present to a potential customer. It requires statistical and qualitative substantiation to help prospects project effective returns on their sponsorship investments.

The art is style: how you interface with prospects, the confidence you build, your interpersonal skills, how you endure the vagaries and emotions of sales, and the personal creativity you apply to the daily mission.

The number of calls requires great self-discipline, staying focused, no distractions, no straying from the mission and not succumbing to your stream of consciousness by drifting into any personal online pursuits. Your day should be steadfast, exclusively reaching prospects, following up with those you've already broached and making in-face presentations.

Be introspective. It's healthy. When your mind begins to wander, remember why you're there, your lifelong passion for sports and how hard it was to land your job. Work with blinders, minimize disruptions, shut off your personal cell phone. To grow your career, you'll need to perfect your overall sales skills. It begins with prospecting.

What I will attempt to do is take you through the rudiments of what's required and expected. You'll thus know if you're cut out for sports media and sponsorship sales. If so, where do you start? How do you identify targets? How, when and where do you contact potential customers? What do you say in a letter, in an email, in a conversation and what do you try to accomplish in a presentation? How do you use social media?

How do you overcome obstacles? How do you get through gatekeepers? They come in various forms today: human administrative assistants, caller IDs, email firewalls and voicemail. How do you deal with objections? Cold callers, by the very nature of the job, will be reaching for people incessantly. How do you stay organized? Organization is probably more critical than you deem.

How do you deal with rejection or depression? What tricks are there? And, lastly, there are chapters on anecdotal experiences, tips from leaders and uplifting stories of impressive cold call successes.

While the sports business landscape continues to grow, it is getting more fragmented. In the 1970s, the industry was a shell of what it is today. Leagues and teams didn't have sales staffs working turfs every day, trying to drum up sponsorships. If they did, there were very few. Sponsorships were limited.

Baseball teams broadcast all games on radio and a chunk of the games on television but never all. For that matter, when Walter O'Malley moved the Dodgers from Brooklyn to Los Angeles, he swore off a repeat of his perceived mistake in Brooklyn, where he put all home games on television. During their first few years in Southern California, the Dodgers only televised the 11 games played in San Francisco each year. That was it.

There was no paid tier, cable or even a true national over-the-air network package until 1965. So local advertisers had just four choices: the radio broadcasts, the limited telecasts, the few available signs at the ballpark and print programs sold at games. The preponderance of sports advertising was sold by the radio and television stations carrying the games. These media sellers did well financially because broadcast companies paid their people well. Remember, this is before cable and even the growth of FM radio. Sellers had it good!

It was well before the Internet and mobile communications brought a frontier of craziness at the start of the millennium.

Teams in the 1970s had a handful of staff in the ticketing department, not the army of sellers today who telemarket season packages to anyone with a landline or cell phone. The ticketing staff was then made up of order takers, functionaries. They often had additional responsibilities, too, like working ticket windows on game day.

Many of the sports sponsorship categories today were not even in business then. There were no cellular phones, Intels or Apples. In the early 1970s, entities like Southwest Airlines and FedEx were embryos struggling to survive.

Of today's biggest sports sponsors, GEICO was a sleepy little company in the 1970s and Subway was limited to 16 'submarine' shops in Connecticut in 1974. Home Depot wasn't founded until 1978, and it wouldn't become the behemoth it is today for a score of years.

In the early 1970s, the New York Yankees, despite their unmatched legacy, struggled to find sponsors. The colorful Phil Rizzuto, who started broadcasting Yankees' games in 1957, read announcements on game telecasts asking viewers for sponsor leads. The team even had challenges finding a local radio station to carry all their games. When they finally did, it was WMCA, a weaker New York signal that didn't cover much of suburbia. The Yanks had to pay for the block of radio time and couldn't raise enough revenue to cover expenses. WMCA didn't even carry all late night games from California because it insisted on running a political talk show at that hour. Can you imagine that happening today?

It was roughly then, 1973, that George Steinbrenner paid a mere $8.7 million for the team.

Steinbrenner commissioned Arthur Adler to sell sponsorships. A charismatic radio and advertising executive, Adler ravenously scoured the marketplace. Over the next dozen or so years, he built the radio broadcasts into a multimillion dollar giant. The play-by-play was sponsored wall to wall. Adler had the knack, the vision, the salesmanship and the hustle. He was truly one of the progenitors of sports marketing, building demand at a time when activity was light to nonexistent.

In time, the world erupted and the sports space exploded. New products came into being, sparked by technology and the creative American spirit. There was the advent of cable and network programming. By 2015, *Forbes* valued the Yankees at $3.2 billion, some 368 times the amount Steinbrenner paid in 1973.

Rights fees, once measured in millions of dollars, swelled into the billions. NBC is paying over $7 billion for the Olympics in a deal that extends through the 2032 games. Fox, CBS and NBC will be paying close to $10 billion each to the NFL by virtue of their most recent nine-year deals.

With it came greater expenditures by rights-holders and the accompanying revenue demands to cover costs. In addition to collecting huge paydays for broadcast carriage, teams and leagues sell intellectual rights, shields, experiential opportunities, luxury suites and courtside seats.

There is a fundamental need to sell tickets. So by-products were born. Stub Hub was one. Aspire Group was formed. It serves as successful outsourcers for both pro teams and major colleges, not staffed to aggressively market their ticket inventory.

And with it came more and more jobs. Unlike back in the day, when media companies sold most of the sports advertising, teams were getting heavily in the act.

Knocking on doors can be quite humbling. Yet the sales consulting organization Miller Heiman released an interesting statistic. It asked sellers why they do what they do and some 43% said they love interacting with people. The number represents sellers overall, in sports or otherwise. I would imagine that those who call on trash hauling companies or meatpackers are not as pumped about their jobs as those engaged in sports.

It doesn't take creativity, anticipation or much convincing to pick up the phone or act upon an email to accept an unsolicited order. It does, though, require vision and incisiveness to anticipate a prospect's future needs and pursue it. The leaders of the sports industry will also tell you that it's hard to hang onto good sellers, especially those who can develop new business.

In sales, there are those who suggest that 'target' and 'prospect' are semantically different. A target is an account that you've never talked to that turns into a prospect once it is engaged in a more serious discussion or one that at least heard your pitch. For the purposes of this publication, these designations 'prospect' and 'target' are used interchangeably.

Before throwing your hat into the ring, ask yourself whether this is what you want to do. If sales are up your alley and you're passionate about sports, go for it!

If you can do it, you'll always make a good living; you'll grow and you'll reach the promised land.

Chapter 1

Qualifications Required to Succeed as a Sports Seller

Doctors can't be squeamish, bridge workers can't be afraid of heights and basketball point guards can't orchestrate a floor game without astute court vision. Lacking any of these representative qualifications is a prescription for failure.

The trinity of qualifications for cold callers is a hungry stomach, an intuitive nose and an organized day. By not measuring up to these requirements, new business sellers are vulnerable to an ungodly fall.

A Hungry Stomach

In the days of World Team Tennis, the New York Sets were owned by Sol Berg, a wealthy commodities dealer. Sol spent most of his time around the team, Billie Jean King, Virginia Wade and Fred Stolle. He made his money working a couple of hours a day behind closed doors, immersed in phone conversations with commodities brokers all over the world. Fortunes were at stake in a single transaction. Sol won more than he lost. Sol won big. As we traveled the country, I once asked Sol what it takes to make it big in commodities. He looked me sternly in the eye and said, "a stomach," one to deal with the huge daily risks.

To proceed in the sports world, sales prospectors need iron stomachs but not for the same risk factors that Sol Berg faced every day.

Be emotionally prepared:

- The pit in cold callers' stomachs should growl with hunger every day. Hunger can't be taught or nurtured. You're either born hungry or you're not. You're either fully consumed by a visceral, bone-deep desire to succeed or you're not. 'Content' is a dirty word in sales. It's usually the incipience of losing interest in selling.

- As you wage everyday sales battles, you'll trudge through unfriendly and unresponsive roads burdened by bumps and pitfalls. Developing new business is a lifelong obstacle course. It's strewn with emotional barriers and callous apathy on the other side of the desk. Your good senses will be challenged quickly, regularly and furiously.

- Your sanity will be tested almost every day. The gutters of sales roads are littered with victims and quitters, beginners who embarked and just couldn't endure the strains. At some point, they had enough and swallowed a bullet.

- To strive and thrive, there has to be an unbreakable determination to overcome all corrupting thoughts. You have to build a mental firewall, stopping pessimism from overpowering you. The prize at the end of the road is worth it: money, more money, pride, a corporate promotion and new job opportunities.

- You'll have to be impervious to setbacks. Always remember that it's just a setback. It's not a disaster. In prospecting, tomorrow is always another day. There's always another prospect. Determination requires confidence. Never crater. Focus on the end goal. It starts with getting the appointment, the opportunity to present, and it culminates with the order.

- Cold calling is also about self-restraint. You'll find yourself paralyzed by the legacy of prospects who dig themselves into their impenetrable corporate fortresses. Remember: no animals, no circus and no ballgame. No targets, no job and no money.

- Don't do anything you'll regret. Your equanimity will be challenged regularly, and you'll want to lose it often. The dismissive treatment you'll suffer is almost imponderable. The laconic indifference you'll fight through every day is painful.

- While you'll be working feverishly to loosen the punishing grips of a gatekeeper, your patience will wear thin—all while your stomach is hungry and angry. So, when an administrative assistant puts you off or, worse, ignores you, take a deep breath. The stomach is saying lace into the administrative assistant. The brain, though, has to assuage the tongue's temptations. Be tough. Employ self-discipline. Don't do anything rash or you might end up unemployed.

- Cold calling is not for the faint of heart. It's a daunting job. You'll be given a blank canvas and asked to turn it into hard cash. You'll be afraid. Most people would be. Yet, if you can handle it, you'll be one of a special breed. You'll be an elite member of sales' Navy SEALs. In the words of former baseball manager Tony La Russa, "When in doubt and when in fear, be aggressive." The things that scare you the most are the most worthwhile.

The stomach reinforces the fortitude both to fight the antagonists and to neutralize mental dyspepsia. I can't tell you how many sellers keep Tums in their backpacks. Just scrap and claw. Be headstrong. If you're good, you'll prosper.

Developing an Intuitive Nose

In baseball parlance, cold callers bat under the Mendoza line. Heck, even the best of them average way under the Mendoza line. Cold calling is harder than hitting a big league fastball, even if your name is Ted Williams.

Prospecting might be clinically fractured by design. An IBM performance study showed that only 3% of traditional cold calls are effective. Importantly, though, the study shows that a seller's lack of understanding of a prospect's needs contributes to the dismal success number.

While Noah Syken, IBM's advertising head, is not associated with the IBM performance study, he tells of his frustrations fielding calls from sellers, "Younger, less seasoned people who have no understanding of my business...only theirs. To this day, people still want to talk to me about helping me sell more 'computers'...when we sold our PC division YEARS ago."

Understanding a prospect's business is critical. Ask David Lim, former Amtrak CMO. He cites his moments of frustrations, "when the seller doesn't understand the basics of 'need satisfying selling' and thinks he/she should jam their proposition through by talking fast and over me."

While some 67% of recipients respond when a seller reaches out via LinkedIn, it is important to note that top-level decision makers, those generally committing to expensive sports sponsorships, are harder to reach via social media sites. In other words, there are no easy answers and no shortcuts. Yes, the Mendoza line—batting .200—looks pretty good, doesn't it?

How do you overcome a daunting number like 3%? First and foremost, target selectively. It improves the success ratio.

In the beginning, young sellers go through a lot of trial and error, usually tons more failure than success. Even when your research is thorough, you're a beginner and inexperienced. You're likely to get a runaround. Even after making contact through unending persistence, the person might not be the precise decision maker who has complete responsibility for determining whether or not to buy what you're selling. You might get someone in a company's home office only to learn that you should reach the target's representative in your local market.

Often, a prospect will refer you to others within the company. If the person you reached is one of several decision makers, you might be told that a conference call is required involving a gaggle of marketers. Then, after weeks, you're able to make a group presentation on the phone and asked to follow up on next steps. By the time you do, one of the decision makers moved to another department and everything is placed on hold.

Recently, a young seller pursued popchips, a sound target for a national sports talk show. The on-air host happened to love the product, making an endorsement a fit made in heaven. The seller made a presentation to a trio of inclined marketers at the company who, shortly afterward, amidst a change in marketing strategies, were reassigned. The callow seller had a plausible target but fell victim to the vicissitudes of the decision-making process. It is one of the many early lessons young sellers learn.

A nose of where to go is empirical. You'll develop your first list of diverse leads based on personal and unscientific experiences and conclusions. Attacking the list will give you, over time, a better feel of what generally works and what doesn't, where you've gotten traction and where you've had the door slammed on you, which industries and accounts are more likely to reap results and which won't.

For starters:

- Train your nose for prospecting. Observe the assorted industries that interface with sports, locally, regionally and nationally.

- You'll often find leads through brands you've sampled personally, advertising that you yourself have seen, sponsors you're aware of that have partnered with other sports entities, products that you've witnessed used by others, new services you've read about and those that are otherwise in your consciousness.

- Because epiphanies occur in the strangest of places and at the oddest of hours, keep a pen or your smartphone handy. A lead might hit you when you're half asleep. If you convince yourself that you'll remember the lead when you get up in the morning, you'll be very disappointed. You'll likely forget.

- It is imperative to have more familiarity with the target's past marketing history, a better understanding of the inner workings of the company you're prospecting and the way decision makers perceive and evaluate sports properties.

- Sports sellers' noses of where to go are strengthened by their gift of curiosity, an eagerness to learn about companies' personnel and how they appraise value propositions. There has to be an innate desire to understand prospects' business goals and learn their marketing history.

- You'll learn mimic selling. You might witness a small scale, successful promotional undertaking by a community retailer in a neighborhood school. You'll think it can be successfully mirrored on a grander scale through a bigger business. You'll work eclectically. Your mind will always race. You will think of ideas, companies and products, 24 hours a day. You'll be consumed endlessly with leads and prospects.

- You will differentiate the obvious targets from those that aren't as obvious. If, for example, you are selling sponsorships for an Atlanta sports entity, you might know of staple hometown sponsors like Delta, UPS and Coca-Cola. Yet, have you considered O'Reilly Auto Parts? If it was to expand its territory and open new stores in Atlanta, wouldn't it be a prospect? If you keep your ear to the ground, you'll know that O'Reilly has sponsored sports elsewhere and is a fitting target for an Atlanta-based sports property.

- If you were a Miami seller in the fall of 2014, you would have been aware of Tech Bash, an experiential event at Marlins Park. There were 120 vendors, from Intel to Dell and from Samsung to Lenovo.

Intuition tells you that many of these accounts are targets for sports properties in South Florida. Each of these vendors likely had local representatives at Marlins Park. How difficult would it be to begin dialogue with these natural targets!

- By keeping your finger on the pulse, you'll know that, in Buffalo, Cabot Cheese sponsors the Sabres. Why not? Cabot is headquartered in Western New York. What are the local companies in your area?

- If you knew that state governmental offices in several states have budgets for anti-smoking campaigns and have used them to buy sports broadcasts, it might dawn on you to cold call the related office in your state to broach local sports. It's an inkling that comes with some detective work, experience and knowledge.

In time, you'll get better at ferreting out prospects. You'll get sharper. You'll have a simpler time identifying prospects. You'll understand which targets have a history of having budgets that support your product or project. It's only a matter of time. You'll feel it. It's visceral. One way to accelerate the pace is by devouring information. You'll have to grow a thirst for overall business knowledge, more than just sports.

The nose is about intuition and intuition is the vapor of experience. The nose is the road map to cold calling success.

The Vow to Stay Organized

The third requirement is organization and discipline. Because it's a fluid business with hundreds and hundreds of potential leads, it's critical to keep active and copious notes.

It's so central to sales success that there's an entire chapter herein dedicated to it. If your effort isn't efficiently organized, if leads are not written down or stored in your notes app, they will be forgotten. Many fertile leads and valuable ideas will be lost. Organization can be taught, inculcated and perfected. Discipline takes focus. It's inspired greatly by the robust rewards of following the game plan.

The organization chapter later in the text granularly details these everyday requirements sellers must maintain to excel.

Breaking Down Basic Expectations

It's the negotiated, transactional and renewal business that is paramount to properties and sports media companies because of the huge dollars from sponsors representing staple industries like beer, auto, financial and telecommunications. These sponsors are on management's radar constantly. Heaven forbid a television network's share of an advertiser's media marketplace budget shrinks or a league loses an existing multimillion dollar sponsor.

It's why the negotiating business is life on an emotional fault line. As such, one nice advantage of prospecting for a sports property is that there's a moderated level of expectation. You're expected to work hard and smart, yet your bosses won't realistically expect an order every day. You're also often unburdened from the residue of baggage from the day before because there are new accounts to pitch every day.

For those who choose to chase new business full-time, consider these points:

- You'll want to be disarming. A cold caller is a seller, not a telemarketer. You won't be reading repetitive scripts. You'll believe in yourself and in a shared dream, working symbiotically with colleagues on your team to achieve greatness. You'll think, plan and strategize collectively. You'll also celebrate and agonize together.

- Have a natural eagerness to propose gripping and customized concepts to marketing teams at higher echelons. Cold calling is not, for instance, the linear negotiations that day-to-day sports media reps engage in all week with buyers at ad agencies whose goals are to buy rating points inexpensively.

- Research targets' channels of distribution, their sales histories and their successes. Then work on the conceptual framework of a driving corporate partnership that is mutually beneficial. Propose plans and develop authenticated data to support your presentations. Think like marketing teams and problem solvers.

- Sponsorships are evaluated on ROI (return on investment). How do you justify a sizeable investment when you're selling hobnobbing and sizzle? You'll have to inculcate advantages that are oftentimes intangible and difficult to quantify. You'll always be challenged for an answer.

- Learn the clear differences between presenting to sponsors that market to other businesses and those that market to consumers and some that do both.

- Develop the depth of knowledge of your own sports property and the assets that correspond strategically with prospects' goals. Try to get into the head of the marketing directors and think the same way they do. Examine their past promotional successes. Also, what have the prospects' competitors done that have worked or not worked? Learn from their marketing successes and failures.

- Be prepared for stimulating meetings and ponderous meetings. If you're lucky, you'll have more meetings than Gamblers Anonymous—with advertising agencies, sports marketers and clients. It means there's more business in the pipeline.

- Be a voracious reader. Start with the business pages and identify companies and industries. Read the industry trades and pursue those your entity can help.

- A cold caller needs patience, which is not a good seller's strong suit. The timeframe, the gestation to close new pieces of business, is galling. Your management too must be supportive and aggressive and encourage an energized climate. For this reason, try to avoid working for companies that have a history of flaccid leadership and blithe neglect when it comes to new business.

- Set projections for yourself. Beyond a financial quota, there's a goal, whether self-imposed or prescribed by your bosses, of the number of new sales calls a day, how many letters, how many email messages, how many phone calls and how much interaction through social media sites. Ultimately, as you become more successful, there will be more face calls. As those multiply, you'll know that you've made progress and will probably be closing business.

- The road to success is often tormenting. You'll be part self-psychologist, part glad-hander and part teacher.

- Selling will harden you because of incessant rejection and unreturned calls. Albert Einstein said, "In the middle of difficulty lies opportunity."

  As difficult as it is to cope with numbing experiences regularly, every one will strengthen your character. They toughen you. It almost changes your view of life, for good or bad. So, to maintain your sanity and to allow you to survive the nastiness of the workday, compartmentalize your mind. Store the cold calling experience somewhere in a lobe apart from the rest of your life.

- Cold callers must lead a balanced life to escape the tribulations of the business day. Enjoy the camaraderie of friendship and the conviviality of family. Engage in physically and intellectually stimulating hobbies. By doing so, you'll laugh off the ugly cold calling encounters.

  As you grow, you'll also ask yourself where you want this job to lead. Do you want to be promoted to a "list" or "street seller?" Do you want to grow to management? Do you want to use this experience to get into another business? Even as a rookie prospector, it's healthy and essential to be cognizant of your sales career and what you'll pursue next.

- You'll need initiative, discipline, dogged follow-through and determination to seal the deal. If you're young, you'll need the look of success to strike an impression that you're precocious. Clients can read you from the moment you cross the transom. A diaphanous smile is infectious. A taut and terse smile is disingenuous. The prospect will take note. Have success written all over you. Give the appearance of being upwardly mobile.

- You'll want to get up every morning and head to work with alacrity, ready to attack every opportunity. In the office and when you're out on calls, be obsessed. Don't get smug and haughty after your first couple of orders. It will bite you on the behind down the road.

- Targets aren't generally the embodiment of goodness and kindness. They frown upon reps, whom they don't know, reaching out to broach something they deem superfluous. They'll view cold calls as "interruptive marketing," and it's most likely the reason they choose to ignore them. Marketers will tell you that, in today's fast-paced world, they simply don't have the time to take unscheduled phone calls and attend extraneous meetings.

- It's easier said than done. Enthusiasm will sometimes be tempered by reality. You will always need some strong fight in you to survive tough stretches. It's okay to have a few days when you're working out of muted conviction and mercinary pragmatism, a moderated belief in the product and a simple desire to put the meals on your table. As difficult as it is, maintain a single-minded determination and unshakable commitment.

- Your prospect shouldn't sense any personal issues you might have. When you're making your pitch, brim with enthusiasm. The pioneer and popular baseball announcer Red Barber always called games under the mantra of 'leave your problems at home.' The audience, he said, doesn't care.

- You're like a Broadway actor who's doing the same show for the 50th time. The audience doesn't know it's your 50th performance. You have to make the audience feel like it's your first. Sound fresh.

In summary, in addition to having the DNA that embodies a strong stomach, a nose for where to go and an organized disposition, you're likely to succeed should you have

Halby's 57 Characteristics for Sales Success:

1. Love selling unconditionally, no matter the emotional roller coaster and nausea you'll experience. Unlike riding a roller coaster in an amusement park, you'll likely finish ahead of where you started.

2. Appreciate the internal recognition of coming up with the big hit.

3. Motivate yourself through a fear to fail. In other words, you're competitive.

4. Ask good questions of all—yourself, clients and agencies.

5. Play nicely with your colleagues by being a decent team player. You'll need the help of your sales teammates to succeed. Cold calling is an emotionally eviscerating task. Don't undertake it alone.

6. Fact find eagerly. Decipher the pertinent from the non-pertinent.

7. Lock yourself comfortably into a cold calling mindset, not allowing external influences to get in your way and infiltrate your resolve.

8. Think positively and expect success. Ignore the ambient negativity.

9. Remain somewhat thick-skinned. You need some sensitivity so that prospects won't be unnecessarily abrasive.

10. Stay firm and not wishy-washy when talking with clients.

11. Endure pressure comfortably because pressure is insidious and it mounts.

12. Cut the emotion out of the process and employ a scholarly detachment to better assess the discourse with a prospect.

13. Command respect internally and externally.

14. Crave the freedom to essentially function in a mental sales setting on your own.

15. Don't need hands-on supervision.

16. Eager to learn.

17. Good at engaging around people, although it doesn't mean you have to close down every bar in town every night.

18. Enjoy meeting new people and making new friends and have a natural curiosity to learn what makes companies and their decision makers tick.

19. Thrive around people who have responsibility for big budgets.

20. Exude a no-lose attitude.

21. Follow strategy consistently to reach objectives.

22. Good at setting goals and able to map a plan to get there.

23. Comfortable interfacing with technology and can effectively convert the software of a smartphone to connect with a prospect.

24. Look respectful.

25. Smile infectiously.

26. Demonstrate sophistication by being equally comfortable talking with corporate executives in the corner office, inexperienced administrative assistants or mechanics under the hood.

27. Business generally interests you.

28. Remember personal traits of clients and prospects. In other words, you have a solid memory.

29. Work at an energized pace, pitch and tone.

30. Execute good follow-up.

31. Persuade comfortably.

32. Possess a sales gumption.

33. Share your enthusiasm contagiously.

34. Interpret the nuances of dialogue.

35. Analyze, absorb and apply new information easily.

36. Golf (many commitments are made on the golf course).

37. Pumped by starting your day with a fresh canvas.

38. Motivated by making money.

39. Bold enough to ask prospects for big money.

40. Comfortable speaking publicly.

41. Build a determined mindset and indomitable attitude.

42. Fast on the learning curve.

43. Command a room.

44. Quick on your feet.

45. Reach corporate level executives where you can convince marketers on the merits of a broad-based multiplatform program.

46. Read people well.

47. Resilient, particularly after a series of sales setbacks.

48. Somewhat creative.

49. Speak articulately and are able to present confidently.

50. Stimulated to come up with resourceful proposals to present to prospects.

51. Enjoy a temperamental makeup.

52. Solve problems.

53. Poised and passionate. Your confidence swells when you bring new accounts into an industry you love.

54. Accept risk. Sellers are paid largely by commission.

55. Pleasantly persistent.

56. Stay current. Keep up with trends covering sponsorship and sports media.

57. Facile with industry buzz words and nomenclature. You'll sound savvy. For instance, there are phrases today that weren't used just a few years ago, such as "package deliverables" and "halo."

Generally, cold calling is a three-pronged attack. There's an appeal before the first human vocal interaction. It's a petition that comes in a variety of forms: letters, email, voicemail and social media. Then there's the first formal discussion, generally on the phone about core capabilities and concept, followed by a detailed and customized presentation.

Remember, it's not a 'new' bona fide piece of business if it came in over the transom or the account arrived as a call-in that you happened to pick up. That's not a cold call. New business is one that you develop from scratch.

Before you pursue a job, make sure you have it in you. You'll have to cover a lot of ground, work smartly and penetrate a hard-to-reach buying hierarchy. The sales challenge is also getting more difficult by the day. Some sports media buying is executed programmatically and in rapid fire. Only the best-in-class sellers will succeed. Be prepared.

The historian, Paul Johnson, described George Bush's commitment in Iraq, "It's his resolution, pertinacity and steadfast consistency." No matter your politics—and I don't know about Bush and Iraq—if you take the same firm attitude in cold calling, you'll succeed glitteringly.

Chapter 2

Getting a Job in
Sports Media and Sponsorships

On SiriusXM, music legend Smokey Robinson said, "Everyone is blessed with a dream. Some people discard it. Some people never realize it. Some let it carry them through life."

If selling sports media and sponsorships is in you, go for it.

At First

Be prepared. It's hard getting sports jobs even in good times. When times are challenging and everyone is out there looking, it can be impossible. In 2009, during the heart of the Great Recession, the Phoenix Coyotes of the NHL had 180 resumes in just four hours after posting a job.

While the industry has exploded since those economic headwinds and entry-level positions are more readily available, newcomers working for teams generally begin in the ticket sellers' bullpen where they're paid minimally, endure anguish and earn a rewarding baptism by fire. Organizations that sell both tickets and corporate sponsorships will take their best ticket sellers and ramp 'em up to canvass for new sponsors.

So, for candidates with little to no experience, ticket sales are the point of entry. While it isn't the factory sweatshop of the depression era, you'll be issued quotas on both the number of outbound calls you must make and the number of tickets you are expected to sell. Not easy. In fact, some teams keep tabs of telephone calls electronically and monitor the number of phone calls each seller makes.

You'll be selling full season packages, game packs, hospitality suites, luxury boxes and maybe even facility rentals that customers use for entertainment, like birthdays and office parties. Virtually all the work is done in an open space room where sellers are figuratively sitting on top of one another. Everyone can hear their neighbors' conversations, the number of hang-ups, the visceral appeals, the humility endured and the vocal rite of passage that sellers go through to grow to the next level.

At places like Aspire Group, headed up by Dr. Bernie Mullin, formerly the CEO of the Atlanta Hawks and Thrashers and head of team services for the NBA, the environment is spirited and upbeat. Aspire is a leading outsourcer of ticket sales, primarily assisting colleges to fill seats for both basketball and football. Every time a seller in Aspire's jam-packed backroom gets an order, the bell rings and the whole office breaks out in applause.

Folks who excel at selling tickets, hospitality and the like enhance their credentials sufficiently to be considered for an entry-level sponsorship sales job.

Differentiating Employers by Mission

Where should you look?

Study the entity before pursuing employment there. Always ask yourself how important sales are in the mission of the organization. How do they recognize successful sellers? What kind of training program do they have?

When a company is revenue driven, you're more likely to grow when you're a successful seller. Broadcast stations and their national sales representatives, teams, leagues, cable and television networks are about profit. Sellers climb the ranks, from account executives to managers to vice presidents and above.

It's about the organization's mission. If you work for a nonprofit, you can be the next P. T. Barnum, but it's unlikely that you'll climb the ladder to the top of the administrative charts. The goal of a nonprofit institution of higher learning is to educate, whether it's the next wave of chemists or economists. While fund raising and building institutional endowments are essential, educators are promoted to the top, not sellers. Athletic directors rarely become their school's provost. They often retire or are forced to retire as just that: athletic directors. At an educational institution, sports revenue is an enclave, not an essential part of the broader body. That's not to say it's not where you want to be. Just understand the setup and limitations going in.

Developing new business is sales' hardest challenge. The good corporations recognize the inherent difficulty, the unending gestation and high cost per sale that it takes to replace lost business. As such, committed sales organizations strongly value new business and provide the training and resources cold callers need to succeed.

Because of how difficult it is to replace lost business, sales management often grudgingly acquiesces to incumbent advertisers' compromising demands so that it can maintain renewals. Whether it's agreeing to more tickets, another on-court promotion, more media or even price concessions, sports properties understand that replacing current sponsors is an unsettling and worrisome process.

How deep is the organization committed to sales? If you go to work for the Dallas Mavericks, you'll know who they are. Team owner Mark Cuban writes in his *How to Win at the Sport of Business*, "Sales cure all. If executives won't go on sales calls, run away. They are empire builders and will pollute your company."

In summary, make sure that the employer you're targeting rewards and promotes its good sellers, appreciates the difficulty of cultivating new sponsorships and has training programs in place for its cold callers.

When you start the job-seeking process in sports, your resume and cover letter should brim with passion for the customized position.

In your initial email, think creatively. By using the word *resume* in the subject line, your email might potentially land in the junk file.

Sports Broadcasting

If you're hoping to work for a regional sports cable network, selling a particular team, for example, study the product. Know it like the back of your hand. When you're pitching the job, make sure you know its sponsor list by heart. It's generally on the website or on the broadcasts. Draw up a list of sponsor benefits and sales features. Rattle them off to yourself. Memorize them.

When you are interviewed, have ideas that you can share on attracting more advertisers. Think as though you were already working there. If the ideas you present are eye-popping, the interviewer will feel compelled to give you serious consideration.

Practice your spiel. Articulate it out loud in front of a mirror. As such, when you talk about your potential role on the interview, you'll express your thoughts impressively.

Don't tell the potential employer that you'll take any entry-level sales job. Be precise; show some anticipatory wisdom by demonstrating how you would do the job. Show a prepared schedule of the first month or two and how you envision spending your time. Be ahead of the curve. Fire a preemptive strike. Show the boss that you're different.

If you really want to knock the interviewer's socks off, come into the interview with a list of accounts that you plan to pursue and how many you think you can close in the first six months. Detail it granularly, listing whom you'll call account by account and the angle you will use. In other words, you want the employer to feel that you'll be starting ahead of schedule and ahead of other applicants even though you are less experienced.

Interestingly, for many years, the heads of the sports divisions at television networks weren't reared in sales. They generally traced their experience to production, programming or law. The iconic Roone Arledge at ABC, who brought the NFL to prime time television on Monday nights, Dick Ebersol at NBC, Sean McManus at

CBS and Tony Petitti, also at CBS and later MLB Network, were never street sellers.

Times might be changing. When Mark Lazarus succeeded Ebersol at NBC, he became the first ever over-the-air network sports head to trace his roots through sales. On the cable side, David Levy at Turner has years of advertising sales experience. John Skipper brought advertising sales experience with him to Bristol's top position when he was appointed president of ESPN in 2012.

DirecTV, a number of years ago, hired a special group of new business pursuers to hit up small businesses, those that could benefit from its addressable advertising business.

Radio stations committed to sports—those in New York and Boston, for instance, with large commitments to baseball and football—have dedicated play-by-play sales staffs. These staffs are somewhat independent of the mainstream sellers who peddle non play-by-play programming.

Interviews

During interviews, be warm, expressive, quick on your feet and tout the fitting experiences of your youth. At the start of your career, when it's about getting in the door, don't be afraid to freely express why you would love to land the job you're pitching and how far you would go to succeed. Be firm, look into an interviewer's eyes responsibly and make your case somewhat beseechingly. Let the interviewer feel the fire in your desire.

While running the sports division at Katz Media in the mid 1980s, I had an opening for an inexperienced seller to break into sports broadcasting. Lewis Schreck was referred to me. He walked into my office energized, brimming with enthusiasm, articulating his credentials clearly, and demonstrating knowledge about the job for which he was being interviewed. He was fresh out of Boston University and burdened by student loans. From the guest chair on the other side of my desk, Lewis raised the sole of one of his shoes to show me that a hole had worn through it. "I want to sell for Katz, make some money and fix this pair of shoes." He got the job.

Lewis was eager and talented. In short order, he embarked upon a successful career in sports sales and sports station management. When you're pitching a job, understand the nuances of what the company you're pitching does, its challenges and opportunities.

Whatever sales experience you have, flaunt it during the interview. If you sold magazines, raised money for charities or were in any way entrepreneurial, don't be shy. Share it. Tell the story of Warren Buffett selling chewing gum, golf balls and magazines as a youngster. If you had some hands-on experience in your days in college, play it up. In college, there's a chance to sell ad time for the school radio station, the newspaper or serve as a campus rep for various national companies. If you did, it might give you an edge.

Never leave the impression that you're just a sports nut who can talk stats. Many beginners have a solid liberal arts education and well-rounded interests. They can talk politics, business, history, pop culture and the arts. Not all interviewers and sponsors want to talk batting averages all the time. Show the interviewer that you're diverse.

Knowledge is powerful on interviews. When you demonstrate lofty qualifications, interviewers will feel comfortable having you meet their bosses because the good impression you give makes them look good too.

If possible, dig for information on what competitors think of the employer you're pursuing. The competitors themselves might share good intelligence. The cumulative effect of the contacts you make and the intelligence you absorb will pay off handsomely. Bounce ideas off and seek advice from seasoned professionals who might have taken a liking to you, whether it's a professor, an astute alumnus or others. Use them for counseling and sounding boards during the job-seeking process.

Convince the interviewer that you're swift, that you're flexible and that you learn new systems speedily.

Give examples. Good sellers have to interpret what buyers are saying. Show that you quickly read dialogue and interpret its nuances.

Yes, you're young and have limited experience. Still, dress conservatively for interviews and talk a mature game but not in a blustery tone. Talk about your skill for office camaraderie, demonstrate that you're a team player and review related accomplishments.

Yes, follow up with your interviewer but don't be overbearing. Use handwritten notes. Send it snail mail. Do things with a twist. Stand out. Have a unique missive arrive from an impressive endorser. Think of everything you have to do to close the interviewer.

Using Technology in the Job-Seeking Process

Use technology to your advantage. Share a story on social media about a sports partnership that might have caught your eye or blog about sponsorship sales and related developments.

There are many people eager to get into sports. Be creative in the interviewing process. In 2009, 23-year-old Jamie Varon did something that was eye-catching.

Dying to get a gig with Twitter, she showed up at the company's headquarters and left the recruiter a bag of cookies. After she still didn't get an interview or a call back, she set up *twittershouldhireme.com*. It included her resume, accomplishments and recommendations. Jamie then kept a blog on her efforts to be hired by Twitter. She ended up getting a lunch meeting. In this littered world of communication, it's all about being noticed. Be bold and do so in good taste.

LinkedIn is arguably the most valuable currency in business networking. You'll want to cash in on common geography and reach out to school colleagues and others with similar interests. Engage regularly. Recruiters scour social media sites for candidates. Have impressive recommendations in your profile and spell out precise accomplishments.

Compose a narrative that's to the point, that's you and that's not verbose.

In the fluid world of social media, LinkedIn allows users to publish posts in personal profiles, albeit with commercial limitation. Recruiters, sales managers and human resource directors might spot an insightful and trenchant post, germane to a position they're looking to fill. Keep the post short, sweet and to the point. Don't be critical or controversial. One person's treasure is another's trash.

With LinkedIn, it's quality not quantity. When making a connection request, customize it. Why do you want to connect? Let the invitee know a little bit about you. As you grow your career, you'll likely be more selective about the extent of your LinkedIn community. You might be judged by the quality of your community. Yet as you launch your career, expanding your world of contacts judiciously will be a help.

Third Parties

By now, you likely know about TeamWork Online. The company is Cleveland based, and it was founded in 1999. Its website says it "is an online sports and live events job match-making engine that connects 2.2 million applicants with the right jobs and 750+ employers with the right candidates, 93% of the time in the last year." In other words, they're big and a centralized site to peruse and through which to pursue jobs in the world of sports.

Buffy Filippell founded TeamWork in 1987. When it opened its doors, TeamWork's mission was to recruit middle to senior level sports executives for teams, leagues, sports associations, governing bodies, sports marketing agencies and arenas. One of Buffy's early recruits was Tim Leiweke who most recently was president of MLSE Properties which owns the Toronto Raptors and Maple Leafs. In the period since, TeamWork has grown in lockstep with the enormous development of the sports industry in general. During the technical boom of the 1990s, Filippell expanded her business creating TeamWork Online. By 2014, the organization had placed 75,000 jobs.

Ticket sellers' salaries remain almost stagnant. Yet the opportunity to sell premium tickets, those with pricier commitments, gives sellers the opportunity to make some more dough. "Ticket sellers still represent our greatest request for job placements but sponsorship sales is the hottest," Filippell said with certainty in early 2015.

The TeamWork boss says, "There's been a run on finding good sponsorship salespeople. IMG and Learfield, the major college rights holders, started picking off the good sellers from NBA clubs and other teams. When the country's economy stabilized after the recession, the demand to find good sponsorship sellers picked up enormously."

Filippell elaborated, "There's been a dichotomy in income potential. Before the recession in 2008, some of these sponsorship sellers were making $500,000 a year. When business dried up, teams began outsourcing some sales assignments to sports marketing agencies. Now leagues and teams are beefing up their staffs again. Years ago, teams would have one or two sponsorship sellers; now there are six or seven and they're looking to expand."

Bring a Plunger to Your Interview

My wife, Donna, is a member of the faculty at the University of Miami medical school. She is active in decisions covering admission to both the residents' program and the medical school. Donna tells a story worth noting in these pages because it's applicable to a candidate of any pursuit, particularly sales.

Recently, Donna received a letter of recommendation, endorsing a candidate who had applied to the medical school. It was written by an undergraduate professor who by absolute coincidence witnessed this candidate in a mutually anonymous setting and episode moments before they ever met.

The professor walked into the men's room one day and was greeted by a peaceful commotion involving the candidate, a third gentleman and a stuffed and unusable toilet. As it turned out, this fidgety third gentleman was about to scurry out of the bathroom's lone stall to search for a workable toilet on another floor.

With alacrity, the candidate, a stranger in the building at the time who hadn't yet met the professor, stopped the man and genuinely offered to quickly fix the toilet. He reached for a nearby plunger, took his jacket off and proceeded to speedily repair the toilet. Impressive! There was truly nothing in it for the candidate other than being helpful.

After witnessing this incident, the professor proceeded back to his office. Minutes later, the professor answered a knock on his door. It was the student with whom he had an appointment. Surprise! It also happened to be the same take-charge young man he had just observed in the men's room. The candidate had an appointment to visit the professor but didn't know what he looked like, and the professor didn't know what the candidate looked like until his office door opened.

The incident left a lasting impression on the professor. Years later, after getting to know the student professionally, the professor wrote the medical school an inspiring letter of recommendation on his behalf highlighting among other things the 'toilet story' and his giving nature.

The moral of the story is to bring a plunger to your interview!

In sports sponsorship and media, cold calling is not only the soul and fiber of effective selling but also the life-blood to success. The good cold callers consider their jobs war. Because it's impossible to sanitize war, the good ones bring the tenacity of a missionary to work every day.

Once You've Embarked

After you do accept an entry-level job, whether it's ticket sales or corporate sponsorships, you'll know it's time to leave after you've concluded by introspection that you're vastly underpaid, you've ceased to learn further on the job or you've not been justly promoted. At that point, pick yourself up and move on. You'll find something better.

Cold calling is an unending journey. The borders are endless!

Tips for new sellers
getting into the sports sales business

It's that time of year. A fresh crop of college graduates, many full of vim, vigor and unbridled enthusiasm, begin their pursuit of careers in the business world of sports.

Graduates who chase jobs in sports sales and are fortunate enough to land them will likely begin at the bottom rung. They'll be given the proverbial Yellow Pages and told to make a million sales calls a day.

The effective sellers will be duly recognized by management, will make a good living and will be in demand throughout their careers.

But let's not foster any false illusions. Developing new business is a herculean challenge that only the strong survive.

So what is required of a cold caller, particularly those selling broadcast advertising or team sponsorships?

1. Confidence – A belief that you can open up new doors and can convert soft conceptual variables into hard cash. It requires a bone-deep nerve which if you nurture will serve you well throughout your career. Selling is an art. It's not a science.

2. Inflaming Emotions – Believe in the power of the product you're selling, the history and tradition of the institution you're representing. Have the obsession. Have the drive.

3. Brim with enthusiasm for every presentation, every day. Like a Broadway actor, your 100th pitch should be performed with the same eagerness and excitement as your first. Your audience shouldn't sense it's your 100th time! You have to be emotionally invested in the mission.

4. You're charged with selling ideas! Sell with the heart. Sell with the stomach. Appeal to a sense of civic pride and the unequaled spirit of sports. Other programs and events like news on television are often full of calamities that advertisers want to avoid. You're selling something truly special.

5. Fresh Relationships – There's something very refreshing about cold calling every day. You never know whom you will get to know or the people you'll meet. There's something exciting and enlightening about the unknown.

6. The fulfillment is lasting! When you get the order after canvassing from scratch, it's a legitimate homerun! You didn't start on second-base like times when you're following up on a lead you're given. The feeling is unmatched.

7. Coping with rejection – There will be many failures for every hit. Be bold, tough-skinned and impervious to unreturned calls and unanswered emails. Life is about expectations. Don't expect a returned call or a reply to an email. If so, there won't be thwarted expectations. Don't allow setbacks to temper your enthusiasm. Keep moving.

8. Volume – It is a numbers game – You'll have to make a ton of calls every single day. Remain focused and spend your time efficiently. You'll need a handle on how many calls it takes to close a piece of business. If it takes 20 calls to get one sponsor or advertiser and you're hoping to close five, you'll need to make 100 calls. There are no shortcuts. There are no excuses not to make tons of calls. In the words of my first boss, "Excuses serve those who make them."

9. Scout your prospects – Prospect by prospect, find out who are the real decision makers. Don't pitch some discouraging underling who has no power to give you the order. Start at the top. CEOs and marketing VPs appreciate the value of sports.

10. Put yourself in a prospect's shoes. Be creative. Years ago, Hebrew National's slogan was, "We answer to a higher authority," meaning observance of kosher restrictions. The slogan suggests that Hebrew National attempts to appeal broadly, to kosher and non-kosher alike. So the seller of St. John's basketball in densely populated New York concocted the idea that Hebrew National, a kosher dog, would stand out sponsoring a traditional Catholic school. It worked. Hebrew National did it.

11. Keep your eyes open. When you drive around town, mark down new businesses and prospects that you come across. Use your smartphone to record leads. Train your mind and eyes to do so. Go to the local drug store, department store or supermarket and scout the aisles. Check out the products. See if there's a local distributor of these products that you can pitch.

12. Reach out in measured intervals. Just as a coach conservatively allocates his timeouts, you do the same. Plan ahead of time how you'll expend the communication assets at your disposal; a typed letter (yes, snail mail in 2016 can occasionally work too), a handwritten note, a phone call, an email, tickets,

invitations to a sponsors' function, a letter from an announcer or from one of the coaches to the prospect.

When you pitch a new piece of business, map out your communication resources. It's a long process. Always leave something in the hip pocket. You can only interact with prospects in measured intervals. So be strategic, tactical and pleasantly persistent!

At commencement exercises this May, the award-winning chef and entrepreneur Jose Andres Puerta preached to departing George Washington University students on the value of three Ps: passion, purpose and possibility.

This article was written by David Halberstam and first appeared in *SportsBusiness Journal* on June 16, 2014.

Chapter 3

Organizational Systems
That Sports Sellers Must Follow

Yes, this might be the most boring chapter of the book, but it addresses one of the most important requirements to succeed in cold call selling and, in many ways, life overall.

If you're to excel, it's mandatory to lead your day in an absolutely organized and constructive fashion. In the rat-race world of sales, it's critical to maintain an efficient daily schedule, an orderly structure and a daily journal of phone calls and other sales interaction.

Frankly, if you're not organized, your sales career might be short lived. Unlike the bone-deep desire to sell and succeed, an inborn quality that cannot be taught, you can absolutely learn organizational skills. It's never too late. They can be easily taught, practiced and nurtured. It's not painful and not a root canal. It doesn't take the brains of a surgeon to devise a system nor does it mean that you follow the thoughtless routine of a simpleton. It requires only one thing: discipline.

Cold calling is fluid. It entails moving pieces. The organizational structure and system you follow serves as your daily bible, as a central source that pulls all the pieces together for you at all times. It allows you to keep tabs on phone calls, written communication, pitches and information due, pending accounts and leads. It will help you regularly assess your progress, where your likely prospects are situated, where your time is well served, where you have a shot to succeed and where you're getting frustrated. It will help you focus on whom to phone, when to do it and which accounts are scheduled for callback to check on the status of a pitch.

Committing to good organizational practices early in your career will pay healthy dividends throughout your selling and business life. Staying on top of activity in a tidy fashion boosts personal confidence. It's also mentally liberating to have paperwork in order, pitches completed and the next day's to-do list finished. Systemizing records, prioritizing account calls and cataloging data are all functionally therapeutic and soothing. It gives you a clearer perspective and sharpens your viewpoint emotionally and physically, figuratively and literally. It puts you, the seller, in control!

Because cold call success, whether in virgin territory or not, is largely a numbers game, it's not only imperative to identify the best targets but also critical to maintain organized files, notes and records. You can set up your own convenient organizational system to suit your idiosyncratic needs and technological system of choice. But don't be frightened or deterred. It's not all that challenging.

I use Microsoft's Outlook, so I'll demonstrate how I do it. You'll then see what's needed and you can set up your own system as you please.

Between a datebook, a laptop and a smartphone, you're in business.

Times are changing but the telephone is still so dominant. It's still the prevalent means by which clients and sellers interact by human voice. It's the way most cold calls are initiated, although they're often preceded by written communication.

Because you hope to reach out to many people, detailed telephone recordkeeping is imperative. Email retains its own copies that you review religiously all day. It might be worth color categorizing your sent email so that you can easily find cold call entreaties by subject. If you sell more than one property, you could consider labeling each a different color. You might designate different colors for internal email or prospects by geography and industry. Develop a system and stick to it.

Face-to-face visits are committed to an electronic calendar and meeting notes are kept, so you're unlikely to forget to follow up expediently with accounts you've actually seen in person.

The telephone is an inanimate object. Often our minds are elsewhere when we dial or we're otherwise distracted. Messages are routinely left in an eye blink, often hardly reaching one's consciousness. So let's tackle it first.

Logging Calls

Before you begin, be prepared to log every phone call you'll make in your career. Sounds daunting? Not so; you'll benefit greatly from adhering to the process. I've required it of every seller I've ever hired, folks who've since excelled brilliantly through their careers.

Years ago, sales executive Vince Daraio kept meticulous records of his telephone activity. Every single day, he started a new page in his 8" x 11" notebook and logged all the calls he placed and received. The notebook was part of his desk's fabric, sacredly placed next to his phone. It looked something like Figure 3.1, albeit handwritten. Vince was a seasoned seller. He had an active list and spent little time chasing accounts blindly.

Nonetheless, there were buyers with whom he did business who would also not return calls. When Daraio started out, he might have made many more new account calls every day. As such, there would be many, many more names with LMs (left message) next to them on his list. Daraio amassed page after page, notebook after notebook in a sales career of neat recordkeeping.

Figure 3.1. Sample of Vince Daraio's phone log

Harry Jones	LM*	OMD Shipping-College
Bill Keeler	(LM)	Wings of Man-Wants audience research M 25-54
John Perry	OK	Parsha- Playoffs-no money-call back in October
Bruce Donner	(OK)	Sweets –hoops – send pitch
Joe McKenzie	LM	Tasty Inc – playoffs
Bill Rosenbaum	LM	Fast Cars-playoffs
Harry Katz	LM	Sports Addictions – playoffs
Paul Mahoney	LM	Laptops for Sale-Golf
Barry Stiller	LM	Mugs and Caps- Derby (his VM says he's out till 3/10)
Ivan Winner	LM	WWWI-football "official waste provider"

*Legend:

    LM-Left a message
    (LM)-Left me a message
    OK-I connected
    (OK)-Caller called me and connected

The notebook served as an indispensible tool. It enabled Vince to look back at a daily log to capture a snapshot of his day at the desk. It helped him establish:

1. whom he called;
2. whether or not he connected with the individuals he dialed; and
3. what required course of action he had to take after the telephone conversation.

Vince thus used his telephone logs to see who owed him return calls and how many messages he placed to the party he was trying to reach. It also enabled him to glance at his phone logs every day to gauge his own productivity. On this mock sheet, Vince would note that he owes Sweets a hoops pitch.

While the phone log is primarily a vehicle for the seller's own use, it also comes in handy internally. When corporate management is seeking information from a seller about a particular account, a group of accounts or volume of calls, the seller has verifiable information readily available.

How many calls will it take to get an appointment? How many appointments result in closed business? Having some sense of the numbers helps sellers measure their own productivity. How many more appointments will I need? How many calls will I need to make?

Daraio started keeping his phone logs long before electronic voicemail. Yes, the advent of ever-present voicemail wasn't until the 1980s. The gatekeepers back then were human administrative assistants who answered phones and took handwritten "While You Were Out" messages on pink pads. Clients' desks were flooded with these pink slips.

In those fun days, the pink slips were full of misspellings, incorrect telephone numbers and other misinformation transcribed from phone to paper. These were also pre-cell phone days. Sellers would rush back to their offices, hoping to get "While you Were Out" messages from prospects they were trying to reach or those who already have pitches. More often than not, the messages, if any, were not from prospects.

In some ways, it was easier back then to be more creative and charming. You could coax secretaries, as they were then called, to put prospects on the telephone. In other ways, it was more difficult because, when sellers placed their fifth or sixth call into a prospect, what more could they say? How much of a nuisance could they be? And by then, secretaries were probably no longer passing their messages to their irritated bosses. In fact, the assistants might hear your voice and tune out.

The message slips were sterile. Voicemail is more entertaining. It affords sellers the opportunity to inflect passion, personality, humor or a beseeching tone.

The days of Daraio's handwritten phone logs are obsolete. Today, with laptops and iPads, the organizational opportunity is a cinch. Instead of having to dig through pages upon pages of daily information to find a particular note that you might have committed to writing, it can all be inputted digitally. Finding a note, a phone number, a name or the contents of a conversation is as easy as pie.

How? In Microsoft Outlook, there's a notes section to log phone calls. At the beginning of each week, use the first available note as a tab by indenting and listing the dates of the week. Then open a new note for each phone call that you place. Outlook will automatically stamp the date and time the call is placed.

List the person that you're attempting to reach and the phone number. It should include the company, the subject of the phone call and whether or not you connected (per legend above). It should be followed by details, observations and course of action.

A note will look much like the one in Figure 3.2. Each note will accommodate as much information as you type. By Friday night at the end of every week, you'll have a summary of all your weekly phone calls. You'll see whom you called, whether or not you connected, who called you and whether or not you spoke. At the end of the week, leave a space by opening a new note, skipping a line and marking xx. There will now be a space between the weeks. On Monday morning, you'll be ready to start a fresh week.

There are many advantages to logging calls on a computer. To begin with, notes can be copied and pasted so that, on second call attempts, information from the first attempt is simply transcribed by copying the first note and pasting it onto the second. This might include the name, telephone number, the company, some buzz words to trigger ideas you might want to use in the conversation and other useful verbal tools for effective interaction. The notes component in Outlook features many helpful tricks. (I've kept the options fairly simple, sufficient for the purposes of logging phone calls.)

For more details and options on Outlook, consult the *Microsoft Outlook Bible* or other related helpful manuals.

It might also be a good idea to grade telephone calls with one, two or three stars, depending on how encouraging a conversation you had.

Figure 3.2. A general note on the Bank of Halby client

Craig Arnold, ok, 704-386-8135, Bank of Halby
Reviewed Olympic sponsorship potential,
Craig says his budgets are shot but might look at something small
if there's a promotional component. Review with our marketing team.

5/1/2008 10:34AM

One resourceful highlight of logging calls in notes is the ability to isolate all your conversations or attempted conversations with one account or one person. Type in the name of the account or person in 'find' on the top of the page, and it will search all the times you've reached out to this person, the exchanges you've engaged in and the notes you made during each attempt. In Figure 3.3, there's a list of all calls to Lowe's. By opening each note, the content of the conversation is visible and readily available. The beauty of the system also allows all notes to the prospect to open at one time, allowing you to view the whole history at once.

Figure 3.3. List of all calls to Lowe's

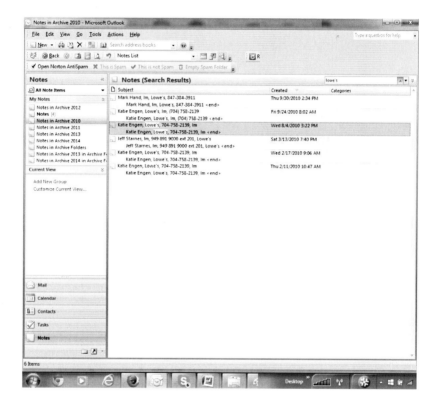

When you want to view a list of all your calls, you can do so by checking off 'list' in the View tab. It would look like this in Figure 3.4.

Figure 3.4. List of all calls opened at once and viewed at one glance

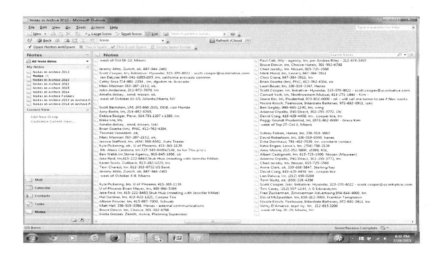

How Your Computer Should Appear Every Day

When you sit down at your desk each morning, you'll want to have at least three Outlook resources at your disposal. You'll want to see it in one convenient and consolidated glance. They are: Notes for the phone calls as illustrated, Inbox for mail and Contacts so that phone numbers and email addresses are handy. See Figure 3.5.

Figure 3.5. Outlook Inbox, Notes and Contacts at one glance

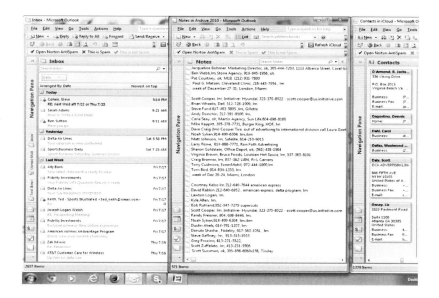

To do so, open Outlook. If it's programmed to open Inbox, right-click Notes in your navigation pane and hit 'Open in New Window.' Then do the same for Contacts. At this point, all three are open. To view all at once, right-click the toolbar at the bottom of the screen and hit 'Show side by side.'

You can tweak it, as you get comfortable with the system, to customize the screen to your liking.

Either way, you're ready to go to work, ready to dial and smile. Logging calls is imperative and the laptop is a seller's best friend.

Datebook

This is fairly self-explanatory. While the calendar component of Outlook is best used for appointments, the traditional non-digital weekly diary is a good tool for a weekly to-do list. If an account suggests that you check back in six weeks, advance your calendar to the prescribed date and mark down the name and number of the client due a call. It's also the chief source for ticklers, follow-ups, birthday greetings and other predetermined specified commands. Yes, you can use your electronic calendar for follow-up reminders too.

Yet, if you're a smartphone addict, keep notes in the Notes app and sync it with iCloud.

If you're selling seasonal sports or media, the best time to strike is when a particular program is enjoying great visibility. In other words, when you're selling baseball, you're best suited to initiate sponsor developmental efforts during the World Series. And the NFL is best sold in January when the league enjoys unmatched hype. Have all these account assignments marked accordingly in your datebook. You should always be ready.

While we do indeed live in a digital world, a datebook is still handy to many for general planning, jotting down chores and notes of all sorts. In Figure 3.6, you will note that I have habitually used pencil for my datebook so that it's not sloppy from redaction. Plus, who wants ink running down the page?

Figure 3.6. Page from Halby's datebook

MARCH 2015

S	M	T	W	T	F	S
1	2	3	4	5	6	7
8	9	10	11	12	13	14
15	16	17	18	19	20	21
22	23	24	25	26	27	28
29	30	31				

APRIL 2015

13 MONDAY   103/262

Check in with Stub Hub
Call Bill Morningstar
@ Victor Garcia at Burger King

tax on extension

MLB Hall of Fame idea

package review with Chris Kane at Zimmerman

14 TUESDAY   104/261

book Colorado trip - late May

Sal Sino
Ryan Eddy at MLB

pacing on billing due

start article on Vin Scully

check in with Tony Pace @ Subway

15 WEDNESDAY   105/260

Account thoughts:

Valvoline
Wells Fargo
Golf Smith

NSU - post season review!

Contacts/CardScan

As you get appointments and meet potential customers and other business associates, you'll begin to collect many business cards. If you just stack them and put them away, it will be of little help.

Scanning business cards is convenient. While different companies make these scanners, one that's popular is CardScan. It will keep a visual of all your cards as well as catalog names, titles, companies, numbers and other data. Most importantly, it transfers all vital information to Contacts in Outlook. You can then stack the business cards in a cabinet somewhere, and if, heaven forbid, your computer crashes and there's no backup, you'll have hard-copies. Some ad agencies and advertisers don't even print cards anymore. We live in a world that's more and more environmentally conscious. Virtual business cards (vCards) today are popular for sharing contact information electronically by email and instant messaging. You can also add vCards to your website.

Make sure to keep little tidbits of information on clients you're chasing or those with whom you're doing business—where the client went to school, kids' names, birthdays and more. Showing a potential customer you care will get you a long way. If a prospect went to Notre Dame, for example, and you're scheduled to meet, brush up on the Irish before the call. You can then strike an innocuous chord at the start of a conversation and ease into the business discussion. Today, targets are busier than ever. There's less chitchat before digging into the sales presentation.

Don't try to be too cute. A number of years ago, Bradley's basketball team advanced a couple rounds into the NCAA Tournament. After its second win, I sent an email to Ken Cohen, an Exxon executive who's an alumnus. I said something like, "Way to go Bears!" He sent me back an email immediately, "Thanks. It's the Bradley Braves not Bears."

Under contacts, too, you might want to keep basic account information; marketing goals, decision-making calendar, marketing history, hot buttons, evaluation criteria, planning cycles and other pertinent information. It will come in handy during subsequent dialogue.

Having information at hand, allows you to do more of what you do best and what you enjoy most: selling.

Synchronizing to Smartphones

Synchronizing your smartphone and computer software is seamless in today's world. Updates on one populate on the other almost instantly. You'll have your calendar, contacts, notes and reminders synchronized on three devices—computer, smartphone and tablet. We live in a beautiful world, at least technologically.

Appointments

Bring a spiral notebook, your tablet or your smartphone to take copious notes. If you take notes manually, transcribe information afterward to your computer. Do so as soon as possible when the results of the meeting are still fresh.

Handy-Dandy Spiral Notebook

You only have one reputation. Prospects who might have met you for the first time will judge you strictly on how you follow up with requested collateral and research. No matter how inconsequential or trivial the request, deliver it immediately.

If, in passing at the meeting, you blurted something like, "Oh, I saw an article of interest to you in *Forbes* this week. I'll send it to you." Mark it down at the meeting and send it immediately upon your return to the office. It's why at a meeting you must commit to writing down everything you promised to do, no matter how trivial, and everything that the prospect promised to send you.

When prospects see that you are organized and buttoned up, you're building their trust. Once you do so, you're fostering a relationship and will eventually get an order.

Time Efficiency/Discipline

Active accounts and repeat business are the revenue mainstreams of any sports and sports media sales organization. Cold calling is necessary because these new customers might become recurring business in the years ahead.

The cost per sale of cold calling, though, is prohibitively expensive. If the gestation is shortened even an iota, it helps efficiency and lowers the expense related to generating fresh business. At the end of the day, staying resourcefully organized saves time, contributes to the bottom line and enhances margins.

Have your product and presentation materials readily available. You don't want to get a prospect on the horn and have a question posed to which you don't have the answer. You then begin palpably ruffling through papers, and the prospect senses your tentative reply. It's unnecessary.

There are just so many hours in the workday. You'll want to remain optimally productive, as much as humanly possible. Be mindful of the time you spend selling and the time you're digging through information for leads and more.

The more time that you're pitching new business, the more money you'll make for yourself and your company. Use every last minute efficiently. Don't sit around schmoozing about superfluous subjects with your cohorts. It reduces critical time that you can spend making sales calls. Yes, we all need a break. The stress and frustration of working new business all day, trying to connect with unresponsive and frosty prospects, take a toll. Without a break, you'll begin talking to yourself and hiding in the bathroom. Nonetheless, avoid wasting time by engaging in small talk with other sellers, assistants and friends on the phone. It just raises the cost per sale and it will achieve little, other than the ire of your bosses. It takes great focus and determination. Self-restraint makes us stronger, and in sales, it will make you more successful. Time is money.

"There are time masters and time robbers," trainers and executive coaches will say. There's productive internal socializing, the kind that's inspiring and brainstorming, and there's unproductive internal socializing, the kind that leads nowhere other than being dispiriting and discouraging.

There was an alarming study recently published by Microsoft that revealed sellers spend only 22% of their time selling. At that horrid pace, a cold caller might close something in time for the 2050 Super Bowl.

Set up a rough schedule every day and adhere to it. The day entails cold calling new accounts, researching and identifying targets, writing presentations, following up and outside appointments. Once you're embarked, an allocation of time might look something like this:

Time Allocation

Seize the day!

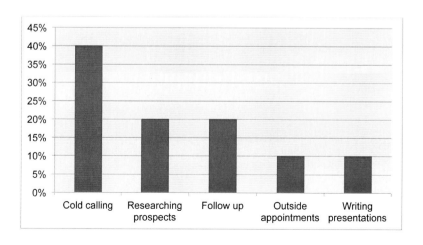

This doesn't mean that you can't change this or you should hold yourself to this exact allocation every day but this will help provide direction and serve as a road map.

Let me suggest one rule that is healthy and helpful no matter the circumstances. Always end the day positively. If you've had a rejection or a series of unsuccessful calls, try to wrap things up positively. At best, it's getting a new appointment, and at worst, it's leaving a stimulating message for a well-targeted new advertiser.

Rules of the Road

At some point, once you're established or sometimes if you are only in the process of building your sales capital, your management will have you spend time on the road. For those young and new at it, the travel experience might seem novel and glamorous even if it's Buffalo in January. Those who have spent too many years doing it are dubbed 'road warriors.' Road life is difficult. Adapting to the demands of the road is difficult enough. There's the most difficult challenge: setting up appointments. What should you do when you arrive and the person with whom you have an appointment bails? Never lose it. It will do you no good in the long run. Be patient. Remember the customer isn't always right, but the customer does always make the decision. Once in a while, the one who stood you up has a sense of guilt and will give you a more generous hearing the next time around. If the decision maker begs off and has an underling see you, don't bristle. See this person if you're not given a choice to reschedule. Treat the fill-in royally, maybe the experience will be positive. Perhaps useful information will emerge that will be helpful down the road. (This eventuality is addressed in greater detail in the presentation chapter.)

Travel

I always tried to make my appointments well in advance to save on expenses. Doing so enables you to book your trips earlier and generally take advantage of cheaper airfares. Print out your instructions, get the ten-day weather forecast, travel lightly—a light raincoat, heavy sweater, workout stuff. Try not to check in any baggage.

Today we can make the waiting area near an airport gate our office. All we need is a smartphone and we're off and running. With a laptop or iPad, you're in even better shape. Reconfirm your appointments. If you get stiffed, try to reschedule while you're in town. If you're good at what you do, don't worry about having to go back a second or third time. The company will pay. Remind your boss that you don't make any money sitting around the office.

Don't look at evaluating each trip for efficiency. Productivity is based on the aggregate. If it's a morning call, bring a cup of coffee or the morning paper for the prospect you're visiting. Something that will make you standout is always helpful. Travel with one airline; you'll get more benefits, upgrades and more. Map out directions. Save yourself agony on the road. If you're not confident that your smartphone will reliably provide immediate and accurate directions through an app of your preference, car rental companies will make GPS devices available for a daily charge.

Don't drink on the road. It impairs your thinking and slows you down. Work out every day, whatever your routine, running, weights or cycling. If you can't get out because of inclement weather or limited time, run the stairwell of the hotel.

If possible, schedule the first flight every morning. There are generally fewer delays. The nights are best spent in your hotel room working on your laptop. Review email, catch up on pitches and update your pending list. Very importantly, get a good night's sleep. You want to be well rested when you get up to fight the wolves the next morning.

Funny thing about traveling, when I started going on the road as a young seller in the late 1970s, airplanes, particularly in first class, were filled with executives. Now when I'm in first class I sit near technology or blue-collar workers who are upgraded because they are frequent flyers. They sit in shorts and T-shirts. Some have bold tattoos. The business executives have moved on to private planes. It's a changing world.

Assessing Your Cold Calling Progress

Before you call it a day, it's good to consult and update your Excel spreadsheet, which provides a quick snapshot of business that you're chasing. It would look something like Figure 3.7, except a lot longer if you have many pending accounts.

Figure 3.7. Sample of ongoing business Excel spreadsheet

Account	Status	Outlook	Next Step
FoodKing	Waiting for direction	If budget is approved—could be an A	If I don't hear back in a week, I'll cajole Mike Kapp
Suits and Shirts	Pitched revision	Interested	Conference call with Barbara's boss
The Text Gang	I'm optimistic	Good	Given them until 1/15
Hotel for Sleep	Awaiting more feedback	Clouded	Call Harriet H on 1/18
Sweet Cake	Preliminary	Too early to grade	Circle back early February
Save A Bundle	Awaiting sales numbers	Not rosy	Call Kevin Smart in mid January
Yummy Steakhouse	Waiting on Bill Sullivan	Cautiously optimistic	Need to see Sullivan
Max's Houses	Mike has reviewed	Awaiting the big dog's signature	If we don't get order by 1/15, I'll get nervous
Scoop it Up	Rick has seen first draft	Joan is next	Readdress on 2/1

The beauty of this scorecard is the ability to share it with management.

If your management doesn't make you do this, there's also a little exercise that you can perform that will not only help you assess your projected productivity but also give your bosses a handle on how you're progressing. Take all the accounts that you have pitched that are legitimately pending. Grade each one from A to C. A's are those you feel fairly comfortable will materialize. These accounts generally demonstrate a productive track record, whether historically or through one of their current executives in a past role elsewhere. Somehow, there's a relationship and you've been given some implicit assurances through dialogue that an order is forthcoming. Simply put, you're feeling active buying signals.

B's are those that are asking good questions and, in your assessment, are a step or two away from moving to an A. C's are prospects that have seen a pitch, say they are considering the proposal and have shown some legitimate interest. These C's could potentially jump to A's but are not entirely predictable. A's, B's and C's are graded at 80%, 50% and 10%, respectively. Figure 3.8 depicts this make-believe spreadsheet.

Figure 3.8. Sales projections (should be updated every two or three days)

Account	Category*	Package Price Submitted	Projected Billing
Yummy Steakhouse	A	$ 100,000	$ 80,000
Office Supplies	A	50,000	40,000
Driving Car	A	75,000	60,000
Strong Forklifts	B	50,000	25,000
Johnny's Tires	B	60,000	30,000
Halby's Mufflers	B	75,000	37,500
Suits and Ties	C	100,000	10,000
Yummy Hot Dogs	C	80,000	8,000
Technology and Friends	C	90,000	9,000
Toro	C	150,000	15,000
TOTAL			**$314,500**

*As are weighted at 80%, Bs at 50% and Cs at 10%.

For each account you pitch, you might want to add additional columns indicating those that go through a multi-tiered decision-making process. You want to make sure that you and your sales colleagues cover all levels of the buying process. Often, on the national front, they're in different parts of the country. In some instances, in the case of ad agencies, there are layers within layers; planning, account teams and buyers. Figure 3.9 can serve as an overview or punch list. Keep tabs to make sure all layers are pitched.

Figure 3.9. Internal decision-making team coverage by account

Account	Client Contact	Regional client	Ad Agency	Sports Mktg Agency
Halby's Mufflers				
Jaime's Mustard				
Donna's Salads				

An office sales manager with three sellers can project dollars based on the pending accounts as depicted in Figure 3.10.

In my days with the Miami Heat, I would walk into Managing General Partner Lewis Schaffel's office, and I would notice through the billow of his cigar smoke that every piece of paper was in perfect order. I once remarked to him how organized he was. His throw away comment was, "You can get disorganized in ten minutes." Yes, you have to stay on it or, in Lewis' case, have a good assistant who does it for you. A couple of misplaced files, notes or documents and one unlogged phone call can throw you off and set you back.

Figure 3.10. Very simple manager's spreadsheet

	Account	Grade	Pending Amount	Projected $	Closure Date
Pending Accounts			Mock-Abbreviated Sales Manager Tool-*New Business*		
Seller # 1					
	Burger King	A	200,000	180,000	30-Mar
	Southwest Airlines	C	300,000	30,000	14-Mar
	IBM	B	175,000	87,500	1-Apr
	CDW	C	190,000	19,000	30-Mar
	Honda	B	275,000	137,500	25-Mar
Seller # 2					
	Progressive	B	500,000	250,000	2-Apr
	Sports Authority	A	300,000	270,000	1-Apr
	Barbasol	B	225,000	112,500	25-Mar
	Delta Airlines	C	325,000	32,500	28-Mar
Seller # 3					
	UPS	A	400,000	360,000	10-Mar
	Amtrak	C	190,000	19,000	15-Mar
	Fidelity	C	230,000	23,000	20-Mar
	Meineke	C	275,000	27,500	1-Apr
Total			$3,585,000	$1,548,500	

Customer Relationship Management

Ah, the beauty of technology. Today, customer relationship management (CRM) serves as the hub of all sales activity, information and templates.

Up until a few years ago, organized sellers developed their own individual systems to keep track of all the new business that they alone were chasing. It served as a personal road map. What's pending and what are next steps, notes on the last interaction and new targets on the horizon?

As the business world evolved from analog to digital, it became considerably easier to maintain a formatted team scoreboard of pending activities. One consolidated document listed all account activity across all team sellers.

CRM acts as a clearing house for managers and sellers. It is updated regularly by each seller so that the overall sales performance is readily visible to management at a moment's notice on one spreadsheet. It also further improves efficiency and sales productivity by the seamless exchange of internal information departmentally.

In time, outside sources brought a degree of sophistication to the reporting game. One such company, Pittsburgh-based Matrix, blends this complexity with granular detail. Its CRM system articulates data by advertiser, property, network, industry category and more. While Matrix specializes in broadcasting and has sports heavy Westwood One as a client, the report brings the detail of an NBA box score. Microsoft is also in the CRM business serving businesses that are both large and small. It customizes its software, company by company to fit size and needs.

CRM capabilities are expanding whereby leagues can share team-by-team activity with all their members. In other words, CRMs can now also consolidate account data for an entire league, team by team, and make it available to each franchise.

Professional leagues like the NFL share sponsor information across their landscape of teams to cross-generate leads for each franchise. So, if the Chicago Bears have a list of all the sponsors of the Dallas Cowboys, their own aggressive sales staff will be served up some healthy leads. If the Cowboys get advertising dollars from Carrabba's Italian Grill restaurants and the budget is generated through the Carrabba's Dallas office, the Bears know that the casual restaurant chain has a predisposition to sports. As such, if the Bears can convince the Carrabba's Chicago regional manager of the merits of their sponsorship, they might successfully foster a partnership. The NFL-wide document of all accounts, team by team, provides a diffusion of information that all teams can use to convert leads into orders. The data is also fresh and fluid. So, in late spring, each team knows what its sister teams have on the books.

CRMs are also programmed to link social media doings account by account and recent representative online news clippings. Talk about having everything at your fingertips. Goodness!

As Microsoft, a purveyor of CRM software and more, points out in its handy ebook, *Always Be Closing: The ABCs of Sales in the Modern Era*, linking social media to a CRM enables sellers to "gain a more holistic customer view by instantly seeing a social networking profile for each contact." And as you prepare for your first interaction or interfacing with the prospect, you will be able to "utilize interests and discussion threads for more relevant conversations."

So, when you're driving around town and come up with a lead, you'll be able to go online, perhaps even using your mobile device, access your company CRM and see whether the lead has ever bought anything from your company or, for that matter, has ever been pitched. If you're working for a team that's part of a league that has a collaborative and consolidated CRM, you'll see whether the lead has done business with other member teams.

If there hasn't been any dialogue with the lead, you yourself might be able to stake a claim to pitch the account. You can then request, via a CRM request, to your sales manager to be assigned to unsolicited accounts you've identified. Sales managers can approve these requests effortlessly.

A CRM is a one-stop shopping resource for sales data, account assignments, pending activity and projections. It covers a confluence of activity inclusive of an entire staff. It's an indispensible tool to orchestrate and organize a sales effort that runs the gamut from account renewals to chasing new business.

CRMs are used by ticket offices too, to keep tabs on suite renewals, corporate hospitality sales and group and season ticket sales.

There are CRMs for managing a broad sales effort, and there's a CRM for servicing. In other words, CRMs can be formatted for use by the promotional or marketing team to service existing clients and fulfill contractual commitments to them. If sponsors or ticket holders are due a schedule of hospitality dates, visits to the field, scoreboard and public address announcements, trips to road games and a variety of goodies, CRMs help manage and schedule these obligations.

Some CRMs even allow customers to post comments and service ratings, no matter if they're good or bad. Management can then peruse the CRM to gauge customer satisfaction. So CRMs have a major social media component to them, albeit client comments are not available to the general public.

Depending on the customization of information, the CRM role in summary is:

- account information, contact and history;

- account status;

- calendar references for follow up and other time sensitive activity required;

- links to correspondence related to each account and to telephone logs on said accounts;

- related research and presentation information by account;

- social media information and press coverage by account;

- internal intelligence;

- contact information for mass-marketing blasts when the opportunities call for them; and

- cross-selling opportunities with other departments within the entity for which you sell, including digital, broadcast, signage and hospitality.

For those selling nationally, there are informational tools—generally requiring a paid subscription—to which many media, leagues, broadcasters and teams subscribe. They provide contact information account by account, sponsor by sponsor. There are telephone numbers and email addresses. They also provide some general history of the nature of the account's spending pattern, target demographics, yearly budgets, geography of distribution, media mix and more. AdDataExpress is the source that comes to mind first. Another company that engages and is worth considering is Green Beacon, http://www.greenbeacon.com/GreenBeaconWebsite/docs/default-source/resources/Datasheet_-_Sports_CRM_-_July2013.pdf?sfvrsn=4 In the growing field, you might also want to view the site of http://www.koresoftware.com/products/kore-prosports-crm-modules/kore-prosports-sponsorship/

For instance, if AdDataExpress suggests that Dunkin' Donuts is expanding in the Midwest and will be seeking experiential activity, you have a lead if you have the goods in the region to sell. You will then want to draft a quick, enthusiastic email offering up a package that meets Dunkin's criteria, namely sampling and organic media.

Likely to be crafted soon is a CRM (see Figure 3.11) that can serve schools that are members of smaller college leagues. For instance, there's a mock illustration of Division II's Sunshine State Conference in Florida. It provides sponsors by member schools and where decisions are made. Again, if Crown Plaza sponsors Florida Tech, Rollins might take a stab at the account.

Figure 3.11. Sharing information among members of an athletic conference

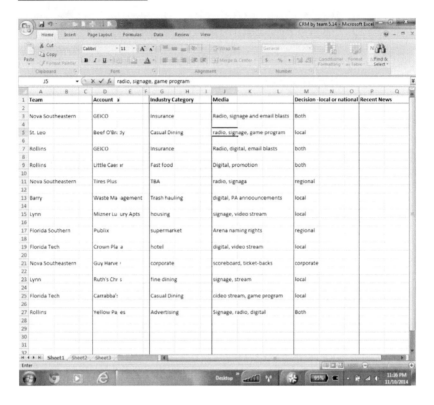

Social Media

In decades past, polished sellers targeted their leads through analog means. They sent articles by fax, generic data in snail mail and urgent documents by overnight mail. They also planted themselves on industry boards, got placed on conference panels and otherwise discreetly doled out advice and counseling. As such, they burnished their own image as smart, forward thinking and, most importantly, caring. These talented sales executives employed their didactic and preachy skills insidiously, swaying their targets insouciantly.

In other words, before the advent of the millennium and instant communication, best-in-class sellers worked conventional means to demonstrate their wares. They did so adroitly, nonchalantly and delicately, gaining reputations for being 'industry experts.' As late as the 1990s, sellers were taught to take consultative approaches. Buyers embraced sellers' perspectives and expertise and would then buy as 'counseled.' It was said that buyers don't like buying from sellers. They felt most comfortable buying from experts.

As much as things change, they really do stay the same. For all the dominance and relevance of social media today, technology is an instrument, an implacable juggernaut, but still just an instrument. If a seller's goal in using social media can be summed up in a few words, it's about informing and helping. Sellers' messages, posts and content are accepted as educational, although tendentiously so. Salespeople appearing on social media are like most team play-by-play announcers who report the game. They do so with a biased eye.

On social media, personality and knowledge sell. If you follow its globally accepted code of behavior, it's taboo to use social media as a platform for hard selling. Like the helpful generic information sent by old school sellers in generations past, content on social media has to appear to users, at least ostensibly, as selfless.

Sellers use LinkedIn, Facebook and Twitter to discretely enhance their images and the products, goods and services they're peddling. Buyers feel more comfortable doing business with those sellers who are saliently visible on social media. It is becoming such a critical qualification that human resources executives often assess candidates' social media skills and presence before they're hired. If candidates' existence on social media is scant, it might not help them land jobs.

As Kendra Lee, author of *Selling Against the Goal*, says, "Sales reps need to inspire trust!" Social media affords sports sellers to build their trust by accelerating the informational process and by broadening their influence and audience. In today's ubiquitously connected world, social media gives sellers the opportunity to establish themselves as 'go-to sources' in an unassuming and understated fashion.

Because of everything that's available today with a few key clicks online, buyers are 57% through buying cycles before they reach out to sellers and 70% for complex purchases. On the sports side, decisions to pursue conceptual sponsorship strategies are made long before clients reach out to teams, leagues and rights-holders for proposals. So, by keeping their fingers on the digital and social pulse and by monitoring social media threads of all sorts, sellers will recognize a constellation of buying signals so that they'll know when to reach out, how and with what resource to strike.

Planning, preparing, traveling, and servicing eat a lot of sellers' precious time every day. It's why effective use of every minute is so critical. A Sales Benchmark study indicates that 79% of sellers achieving quota use social media while only 15% of those who don't use social media achieve quota.

As such, effective CRMs are rich in content and make social intelligence accessible, account by account. They'll help sellers cut down significantly on preparation time. So, the 22% of the day that salespeople generally use to actually sell might actually increase because the preparatory time digging for corporate and contact reconnaissance can be pared. Companies have social media specialists to organize these critical functions. They cull and curate to help sellers build an armory of account and contact information.

Barbara Giamanco, president of Social Centered Selling and co-author of *The New Handshake: Sales Meets Social Media* summarizes the power of today's social media sites as follows:

- A referral network is one of the most powerful ways to increase sales opportunities.

- Give your sales team social insights on their leads, contacts and accounts.

- Provide reps with content and tools that make it easy for them to be productive on social media.

- Make social connections on LinkedIn and Twitter a key part of the process workflow for top accounts.

In Figure 3.12, selected executives, representing major advertisers and marketers suggest how they prefer sellers best reach out to them.

Figure 3.12. Communication preferences for advertising and marketing executives

Tom Peyton HONDA	Email is preferred. If it's really a substantial property (i.e., Naming rights for new Football Stadium in LA), send a professional presentation FedEx or snail mail. Believe it or not, I receive very little "real" mail, as a result, it stands out when received.
Anonymous AUTO-RELATED MARKETER	I respond or react to email opportunities rather than phone or snail mail.
John MacDonald ENTERPRISE	Email communication that is succinct and to the point.

Figure 3.12. *Continued*

Drew Iddings HERSHEY'S	When approached by sellers, my first preference is to receive an introduction from a trusted common contact.
Noah Syken IBM	Email for sure.
Rex Conklin HOME DEPOT	Email. In general, I prefer seller to go through my agency partners, which is where I would typically redirect for evaluation. We also have a sponsorship proposal portal.
David Lim AMTRAK	Email because I have control over when I want to open it, read it or delete it efficiently. If the subject line and email piques my interest, the body copy should get to the point quickly and clearly identify how to contact the person via email or phone. Telephone solicitations are disruptive. Like email, snail mail allowed me to decide to open the letter and act on the solicitation or not.
Julie Lyle HHGREGG	Email is probably best because I travel a lot, I am constantly in meetings and I get so many phone calls and voicemail messages every day.
Stephen Quinn WAL-MART	I prefer that they have a robust presence available somewhere online so I can pull it to me. I cannot recall a single call over the past thirty years that ever made a meaningful difference to my business. You have something to sell and you think it's great, but you don't know my customer or my business. Therefore your cold call is of negative value to me because, as I'm engaging with you, I am not working on the issues that my company is paying me to solve. However, once I have sorted out the problems in my business and what my customers want, I am happy to find you and call you to do some business. I try to have someone delete as many emails as possible that contain a sender I don't know.
Phil Wang WELLS FARGO	Initially, email. If it's worthwhile, then a meeting can be set up.
Ed Gold STATE FARM	First, there is the sponsorship proposal website we utilize. Then, I am open to calls, emails and regular mail. But if you email, DO NOT send 5+MB files. Learn to make them smaller. Do not clog up my email system.
Betsy Wilson UPS	I prefer e-mail – it gives me a chance to review information or proposals on my own time.

Figure 3.12. *Continued*

Paul Hodges REGIONS BANK	Email. Get to the point. Show me that you know something about our business and marketing strategy, and show me how you can add value.
Mark Eckert EDWARD JONES	Email is the preferred form of communication.
Tim Sullivan WENDY'S	Initially, via email. Follow up with phone call once/if I express interest in learning more.
Brad Barnett NATIONWIDE	Most brands have Sports Marketing agency representation. Cold calls and emails are rarely effective and often times are pushed to agencies to respond on behalf of the client. I prefer sellers do their homework on not only our business and brand strategy but also who the agency is and work through them. If the idea is big enough, it will get to the client. I once had a seller say, "I don't know what it is, but we should be doing something together." Nine times out ten that's not true, I say no significantly more than I say yes...sellers should do the homework and work through the proper channels.
Michael Robichaud MASTERCARD	In general, the only sellers I work with are ones that I already know and have a relationship. MasterCard gets thousands of proposals a year, so there is no way I can review them all. I also have a very good handle on the types of partnerships we'll consider. We'll look at an NFL or MLB team in one or our key U.S. markets, but not NBA or NHL. This isn't because one is better than the other; it has to do with our overall strategy and what our competitors do. American Express, for example, is an NBA partner. Given, we have a clearly defined partnership strategy, we know and approach those partners pro actively that we want to work with. We don't sit around waiting for the ideas to come to us.
Ellie Malloy JOHN HANCOCK	I prefer email. I don't often read snail mail because they're general part of mass mailings. If it is customized, I would pay more attention to it.
Jack Hollis TOYOTA	Email is still a great way to communicate; it's the most respectful of our time when receiving a pitch. To help you find the contact most suited to your proposal, I recommend using tools such as LinkedIn.

Chapter 4

How to Identify Prospects

Micky Arison made tons of money building Carnival Cruise Lines, a company started by his father, Ted. But Micky, the owner of the Miami Heat, a franchise that *Forbes* values at more than $1 billion, says that the toughest business he's ever tackled is sports.

It certainly holds true for sports sponsorship sales.

The majority of cold callers in the United States sell consumer staples or business necessities. They reach out to companies that have budgets for essential products like office equipment, light bulbs, coffee services, health insurance or pension plans. These cold callers employ the imperatives of basic salesmanship: to chip away at existing orders placed with competitors. They do so by touting the qualitative elements and pricing merits of their products versus those of their competitors.

Office equipment sellers, for instance, can identify buyers at target companies who spend their budgets with the competition. These buyers, those negotiating pricing and placing orders, have metrics in place to juxtapose one product against another. The sales challenge is linear and programmed.

Most companies don't advertise at all and fewer have budgets to buy full-fledged sponsorships. Businesses generally don't consider sports sponsorships critical to their needs. So, from a seller's perspective, the challenge is developmental. There's no prescribed starting point and no road map to the finish line. As such, cold calling sports sponsorships is a Herculean task.

Sports sellers fight to get audiences with decision makers, then present them a conceptual framework and push hard to have the dollars approved. It takes time and the patience of a saint to shepherd the process through its lengthy gestation. The sales cycle seems punishingly unending.

Prospectors' minds always race, their eyes always explore and their ears never rest. Yes, the cacophony of advertising on radio, television, newspapers and websites produces occasional leads. But cold callers find it virtually impossible to enjoy programming for its entertainment and informational merit because it is sprinkled with advertising placed by unreachable and disinterested prospects, painful reminders of ongoing failed pursuits.

Cold call sellers try to find needles in haystacks. Once they do get hearings with targets, they must cogently sell through the abstract and intangible values of sponsorships, virtues that these prospects have often not officially experienced and have no know-how evaluating.

Welcome to the sports sponsorship world!

It was said that, if Lou Carnesecca, who coached St. John's to the Final Four, would have an hour to live, he would choose to spend it at practice. Coaches hone their players' skills on the practice floor. It's where game plans are practiced and opponents' strengths and weaknesses are dissected. It's where coaches rehearse endgame situations and get ready to overcome shortcomings.

Identifying prospects and preparing the appropriate strategy to present to them should largely be pondered on the practice floor too. It should generally come at off-hours when you're not rushed and when you can dig, scrap and muse. It is often fun and stimulating, especially when you develop promising lists of prospects.

When you're suddenly struck by the epiphany of a particularly strong lead, one you're especially confident about, it's an uplifting moment. You'll feel good and will want to pursue it immediately. But never rush into contacting a lead without research, a game plan and anticipating the dialogue.

Leads are the nourishment of cold call sellers, but if pursued without thought, you will be unprepared, run into pitfalls and be terribly disappointed. Picking up the phone blindly without being ready is suicidal.

Just as doctors get complete patient histories before prescribing medications, you too must do the same before throwing yourself against precious leads. Study the target's chart. Be completely ready. Don't kill the opportunity.

First things first, how do you identify targets?

Leads are produced in a variety of ways. They're gleaned from competition, whether sports or otherwise. They're based on educated hunches, reconnaissance and intuition, and they're pursued through persistence, creativity, cogency and aggressiveness. Like a military campaign, there will be tons of fronts.

When you're at the drawing board, assigned the task of preparing an initial list of prospects for a designated team, broadcast or property, organize your thoughts.

First, understand the depth, strengths and shortcomings of the entity you're selling, the geography of the property's reach and the accounts and decision makers therein. Think creatively. Do your homework!

Let's break these out.

Understanding and Assessing Strengths of the Property That You're Selling

- What are the components of the package you're selling?

- What exposure will it afford the prospect?

- What are the media components? Is it multi-platform or is it limited?

- What are the hospitality, promotional and activation elements?

- What kind of personality participation can a client expect? Because implicit endorsements are of great value, particularly today in an age of commoditized media, how do you position your offering? Have you talked with these personalities to see which products they use? Is there a staid company whose image can be emboldened by a lively personality?

- What is the price tag? Are there packages that are flexibly priced?

- Are ratings and attendance strong?

- Is the environment at the event considered upbeat? Is it viewed as a desired event to attend? Is it an event to see and be seen?

- Is there substantiation for delivery of package components? Is the research strong?

- What is the stature and popularity of the entity in its geographic reach?

- Does the entity get a lot of coverage in traditional and new media?

- What social media elements can you include?

- What is the age, educational and income demographic of attendees, viewership or listenership?

- Will a coach, top administrator or broadcaster assist in the process, meet the prospect or engage with clients' customers?

- Do visible and popular personalities affiliated with the property have top-line connections at major corporations?

- What are the objections you expect to hear from prospects?

- What is the seasonality?

- What is the willingness of your entity to integrate clients organically in program or event fabric?

- Is it a local college sports package that you're pitching? To what extent is the team or event embraced by the community? What's the enthusiasm for it like? Can a sponsor do experiential marketing there? What are the entry-level points to do so? Can clients reach the school's alumni?

- If it's an Olympic or ancillary sport, what's the relationship like with vendors who supply equipment for the sport? What entitlement opportunities would a client have? How does the particular sport or event do against various age cells and educational levels? Which companies internationally support each of these sports?

- How do you position your product so that the prospect can cut through the clutter? How will the marketer stand out? Which other sports entities in the marketplace afford prospects similar opportunities to break through the clutter cleverly and organically?

- What is the competition of the entity for which you work doing? What are their competitive gaps, their strengths and weaknesses?

- How do these competitors develop sponsor tie-ins? Is the media coverage of your sports entity structured with few enough restrictions to blend church and state, making team and advertiser interchangeable? For instance, the NFL restricts sponsor tie-ins on the network telecasts. Most other sports governing bodies don't.

- Can you weave a charity into a proposed sponsorship, the so-called cause-marketing? Do you have the ability to invite a potential customer to the playing field?

- How are you underscoring the fact that sports sponsorships don't have the aura of non-sports programming that's replete with controversy, atrocities and scandals?

Once you've painted a broad picture of your property's strengths and shortcomings, ask yourself, Which companies within the entity's sphere of activity are likely candidates? Which prospects are civic minded? Which are traditional sports sponsors and which companies might want to sample products at events?

Understand the profile of the prospect. Characterize its relationship with its customers. How can your property assist the prospect? What does the marketer value? Identify a problem that a prospect is tackling. How can your package be a part of the solution? No one is giving you charity. Sponsorships must pay off. You'll have to sell through an ROI.

Securing commitments to sports sponsorship requires companies to have an appreciation for both the emotion of sports and the benefits of osmosis by association. You'll generally sense whether prospects are inclined or disinclined almost immediately. If it takes a lot of proselytizing to convince a target of the benefits of sports, you're best moving on. If the roar of the crowd doesn't get the prospect's toes to tingle and there's no recourse of appealing to a decision-making colleague with heightened sports passions, you're unlikely to develop traction.

In true sponsorship settings, companies must be prepared to activate programs beyond the simple payment for intellectual rights to marks of leagues and teams. To buy the ability to use logos, official sponsors must usually commit to spend a specific number of dollars with the league's media partners. And, depending upon related stipulations, they will also have to undertake promotional and charitable activities.

You'll do best when you find fans at corporations who believe in the dream that sports invoke. Reach out to those who are prepared to put their necks out because they're confident that sports bring unique qualities. Gimlet-eyed 'buyers' are usually overly sensitive to the myopia of numerical efficiencies and are harder to convince of these qualities. They're generally following tightly defined goals that sports won't always meet.

Homework

- In the sports space, there's nothing as basic as monitoring your competition. The NHL knows which companies sponsor the NBA. CBS has a deep list of NBC's sports sponsors. It's all pretty basic.

- Usually, sponsors of one local team are good targets for another and national sponsors of one are also valid prospects for another. There are, of course, nuances. Golf is considered more upscale than indoor soccer and hockey might be viewed as more regional than football.

- If you're selling the University of South Carolina, have a list of Clemson sponsors. If you sell Georgia, have the list of sponsors of Georgia Tech. I'm often amazed at how few people do this. The Yankees on radio are sponsored by McGladrey, a major accounting firm. I'll bet that few sellers have pursued the firm or gone after McGladrey's competitors. It's Sports Sales 101 and many fail. Fortunately, most sports properties have a menu of pricing to suit spenders that runs the gamut of available budgets, large and small. Have you tried local accounting firms?

- If you're selling local sponsorships, have you pitched law firms or the state arbitration board to sponsor the referees' names? Sounds corny. It's done, and the dollars are just as green!

- In media, radio advertisers for general talk shows might be targets for sports talk shows. But not all sports talk advertisers are targets for play-by-play. Talk is generally used for direct response, cashing in on implicit endorsements of popular hosts. Talk advertisers generally expect immediate results, a command to action. Play-by-play has historically appealed to brand-building sponsors. Play-by-play is less of a command to action medium than general sports talk!

- Broadcasters might also keep tabs on underwriters of noncommercial radio and public television programs. These companies often partake in public broadcasting because they're civic minded. The same companies might view their sports properties as quasi-governmental and want to foster a relationship with them.

- Some organizations have a system where the responsibility to monitor competition is shared. But if you're an aggressive seller, do it yourself. Leads trigger other leads. If Bose is on the competition wouldn't you think of going after Tivoli or other competitors?

- There might have been a prospect that engaged in the negotiating process with your entity awhile ago but then turned down the proposal. The property for which you work might have dead-letter files. Perhaps the prospect's budget grew since. It then tweaked its marketing goal and is now prepared to talk again. You never know!

- As you drive around town and spot company names, always mark them down or, in the interest of driving safely, use voice memos on your smartphone. Always keep your eyes and ears open.

- If you call the prospect and are told that a sponsorship might be too rich for its blood but it would like to buy a season box, be a good team player. Turn over the lead to the ticket sellers. The ticket seller might reciprocate your thoughtfulness one day when a corporate ticket purchaser wants to upgrade from tickets into a small sponsorship. There's nothing like teamwork!

- The devil is in the detail. If you're selling a medium that skews older, you might want to scout older targets. Cadillac, for instance, will have little interest in sponsoring Xtreme Sports which attracts younger fans. Yet golf is right in its wheelhouse. Stephen Quinn, CMO of Wal-Mart, shares what he deems a poorly placed cold call. "Sellers: 'In attracting today's teens, Xtreme Sports is highly engaging.'

Me: 'I'm not trying to attract teens.' Sellers: 'Well, Xtreme Sports are growing in popularity with all age demographics.' Me: 'OK....'"

- The three Rs. Read, read, read! It starts with the business pages of the local daily. Read the trades every week. If it's a regional property, the local business journal is essential. You will also want to peruse the business sections of the local newspapers, the *Wall Street Journal* and *Barron's*.

- Knowledge is powerful. A company is inanimate; human beings have heartbeats. Appeal to people's emotions and passions. You might learn about prospects' hot buttons. Years ago, a seller read that a decision maker was very active with the Arthritis Foundation. The seller then proposed a program to the executive that bonded the company, team and charity through an on-field performance and a donation to the Arthritis Foundation.

- If there's an article about a state government campaign or an undertaking by a state union, get on it. Tons of dollars are earmarked to advertising for anti-smoking campaigns and seat belt use. The Plumbers Union, an industry group, invests in sports sponsorships.

- Are there are any nonprofits that can benefit? Schools and charities often advertise. Cold callers too easily dismiss them as prospects. Mark Neville of the San Diego Bowl didn't. He creatively sold the naming rights to the old Holiday Bowl to National University.

- You might have seen a vanity sign at Yankee Stadium promoting Syracuse University as New York's college sports team just miles from the St. John's campus.

- *Fortune* magazine ran an ad placed by PCIA, the Wireless Infrastructure Association, a trade group representing companies that make up the wireless telecommunications industry. As wireless technology continues to evolve from its telephone communication and GPS roots, PCIA touted V2V, shorthand for vehicle to vehicle communication. The ad suggested that V2V has the potential to reduce the likelihood of almost 80% of vehicle crashes where there is 'impairment.'

Good sellers would see this ad and ask themselves which companies manufacture these safety devices. They would look into other tentacles of wireless technology that are good fits for sports. It might be as simple as a phone call to PCIA to learn more about its membership and to get a list of affiliated companies and their missions.

Garmin, for instance, once focused its marketing campaigns on its handy portable GPS devices. But now that auto manufacturers universally embed GPS systems inside new vehicles, Garmin pushes its wearable technology, 'activity trackers and watches for every lifestyle.' Knowledge spawns ideas and leads!

- Sports partnerships might be fostered to boost employee morale. Memphis-based International Paper sponsors the Grizzlies in a measure of goodwill as a community citizen. Frequently, partnerships are undertaken as quid pro quos. Financial institutions that manage college endowments will commit to sponsorships although the visibility they get from them does little to generate outside business.

  It is said that NBC spent billions on Olympics rights over the years not so much because the telecasts were a company profit-center, but rather as an entry opportunity for then parent General Electric to do business in many international destinations, including China in 2008.

- Talk to counterparts around the country. If Jack in the Box, as an example, sponsors UCLA, there's either an outlet or a similar fast food company in your area—Hardee's, perhaps—that you can pitch.

- Keep an eye on marketers executing brand extensions. For instance, in 2014, Chobani Inc. made a significant tactical commitment to IMG College to support its yogurt brand extension, brand twists like Chobani Kids and Chobani Indulgent. It likely would have looked at the NFL but Dannon already owned the category. IMG did a good job closing this sponsor.

- If your sponsorship program is working for a local insurance agency eager to reach a middle-aged businessperson, you might target investment firms, banks or financial consultants with similar customer profiles. You can prove that the investment worked for an insurer and that its customer profile is similar.

- Go to the local drugstore, department store or supermarket and scout the aisles. Check out products that you feel would be helped by sports' saliency. Nationally, take a stab at the products sold at chains like Wal-Mart, Home Depot or CVS. Locally, see if there's a distributor of these products that you can pitch. Try to obtain spending reports for the marketplace brand by brand for TV, print and radio.

- Selling college? Have you scoured the campus to establish the companies that market their products on campus?

- Your college alumni office should supply you with a list of its graduates and their corporate positions. This was a license to steal for years, but Sarbanes-Oxley and Dodd–Frank have thrown a wrench into the process. Companies and executives are not as comfortable making these commitments today.

  For example, Subway in the 2000s made a concerted effort to identify with sports of all sorts. It was all good news for radio and television networks.

Subway's marketing head, Tony Pace, a savvy buyer of the space, is a Notre Dame alumnus and die-hard Irish fan. For this very reason, he shied away from sponsoring the Irish broadcasts. He went out of his way to avoid proprietary activity.

- Try to diversify your leads among many industries and estimate the number of phone calls you'll have to make to solidify actionable leads. Be disciplined.

- If you're not up against an exclusivity problem, have you gone after all competitors of incumbent accounts? You'll be surprised how often sellers don't do so.

- Work the hospitality suites. Talk to season ticket holders, especially those who are well endowed. Find targets that are consciously willing to go through the sales process. Again, be sure that these targets qualify monetarily. Of course, get your bosses' approval to do so too. Hospitality and suites are often sold by your ticket-selling colleagues next door, so you don't want to traipse through them without permission.

There are no secrets in sports media. Lists of sponsors are readily available. As time evolves, mutually shared CRMs among leagues, conferences, regional cable systems, properties and multi-rights holders will serve you as a helpful guide. If you're a stand-alone property or rights holder, it's always beneficial to stay in touch, connect and network with counterparts across the country.

During the Great Recession, there might have been a noticeable slowdown of sales, but marketing executives—whether out of the goodness of their hearts or because they had more time on their hands—were more willing to take meetings with sellers.

Finding the right party for the program you're selling is often like espionage, chasing someone through a maze of mirrors. It goes without saying: as you scout prospects, find out who are the real decision makers. Don't pitch some discouraging underling with no power to give you the order.

If you're struggling to find the right decision maker's name and you're getting a runaround, one avenue of assistance is the public affairs department. Some public relations officers are quite helpful. They'll provide corporate information, like rudiments, mission and goals. If you work them, they'll give you the decision-making hierarchy and the top gun's administrative assistant. They're usually pretty good about sharing phone numbers and email addresses.

Social media can serve as a source. If there's little information on the decision maker's name or contact information, you might seek help from someone closely connected. In other words, there might be an "assistant to the CMO" or "promotions manager." You can request guidance from these 'related' employees on how to best reach the decision maker.

Be prepared if you're selling signage at a stadium. You might think it's the best thing since sliced bread. Truth told, the visibility for a brand is wonderful, but if the brand is already well known and has a high-recognition rating, what will it accomplish? What is the value to a well-known brand to have a sign with just its name, logo and slogan on it?

Yes, it's the power of association, and companies do it anyhow! But popular brands seek to promote competitive gaps or unmatched features. For example, Volvo regularly promotes its safety features; from automatic braking to a slew of other protective and defensive components. Volvo needs to showcase these benefits in its marketing. A sign alone won't do the trick.

While, yes, sponsors appreciate the value of identifying with a local institution, it's your perceived value versus theirs, that discounts the value of a stagnant sign for its limited messaging. It's this 'value gap' that you'll have to address if you want to get the order. Spell out how you'll fill these gaps and tackle the deficiencies.

Think of the value gap; before you make a presentation, position your value versus a prospect's perceived value. Have the answers.

Geography

- Teams today provide their sellers, particularly those peddling tickets, with analytics to tighten direction on leads. Sometimes these wealthy ticket subscribers own businesses that don't advertise to consumers and, as such, are not sponsor targets. Yet many of these ticket or suite holders are well connected in the community and can provide sponsor leads. Cultivate their support for beneficial introductions.

- Businesses that are about to expand into your area are targets. They'll look to make a big splash. You can convince them that, by buying sports, they're buying a piece of the rock, a piece of City Hall. Locally, the chamber of commerce has a list of local businesses and their sizes.

- When your list of prospects is completed, the top of the list should begin with businesses in your community that market toward consumers, have the financial wherewithal to enter into sponsorships and partnerships and the customer target that matches the fans of the property you sell.

- Which companies have historically done sports? What motivated the buy? Was there a particular sponsorship component that was especially appealing?

- Another unusual course is calling some top venture capitalists. They're supporting products that need visibility and, as such, have dollars allocated to support the businesses that are targets of the packages you're selling. Befriend these venture capitalists. Some will take your call. If nothing more, it's all part of networking. These VCs will put you in touch with the right brand people.

- Which categories do similar sponsorships in other markets? For instance, AAA sponsors sports in some markets. These programs are locally funded and driven. Call your counterpart to find out why and what motivates the decision maker. Draw parallels and work the corresponding AAA chapter in your market. There are tons of such leads from car dealer associations to bottlers to co-op retailers to local non-profits. Local management is often given the flexibility and budget to foster sports partnerships. And they'll help you because they themselves benefit the most from sponsorships.

- If it's a major national account and local decisions are made at corporate headquarters, go after the local managers anyhow. They can steer you to the decision maker and put in a good word. For example, Heinz developed a theme around the Red Zone in the NFL. When the ball is inside the 20-yard line, Heinz gets a plug. The theme can be extended locally to college franchises but would require a push by the Heinz distributor or head of sales in the region to get approved. There are other similar products.

Tabs on Movements

- Sometimes, something as simple as the appointment of a first-time marketing director is a bright sign of potential spending. The very fact that a new director was put in place is a sign that there might be an increase in budget and a change of strategy. Send the new marketing director a welcome note. It might be appreciated.

- A decade or so ago, before it aggressively embraced sports sponsorships, Kia didn't have the financial resources or the conceptual appetite to consider big packages. When we learned that there was a new marketing sheriff in town, we moved forward.

  Instead of the rigmarole of channeling our effort through underlings, we reached out directly to the new marketing head for an appointment. He granted us a meeting and we were off to the races. He liked our NFL media program and asked us to sit tight. Weeks later, the agency reached out to us and began to negotiate a program. (Kia later gave the NBA a big commitment and dumped the NFL. Nothing lasts forever.) Keep track of personnel changes. For good or for bad, a new broom means a new sweep. Sometimes it's to your benefit and sometimes it's not. It's part of the vicissitudes of the sponsorship business.

- When a company appoints a sports marketing agency for the first time, it's a bull's-eye target. It'll be buying soon!

- There are some basics. If an executive with a history of indulging in sports moved from one company to another, it has 'target' written all over it. Keep tabs of movements throughout industries. Check the people listings in the trades. Oftentimes, if there's an ad agency change, it might create an opportunity. Some agencies are predisposed to certain media that enhance chances of something developing.

  The proof is in the pudding. When Steve Heyer, the architect of the mammoth Coke sponsorship of NCAA Sports, left for Starwood, the process to sign up the hotel group began almost immediately.

  Steve Odland did a tremendous job at AutoZone. He came there with roots in retailing and brand management. Running a grocery chain in New York State, he effectively used radio. When he arrived at AutoZone, he dictated to the marketing department that it use network radio. He was very hands on. He had very specific goals which he monitored carefully and regularly. The program was a phenomenal success. Sales soared and the stock price did too.

  When word surfaced that he was moving to South Florida to head up Office Depot, it was only a matter of time before his new employer would engage in radio. The sellers, on it and aware of it, earned a few healthy commission checks.

- Sometimes, the marriage section of the local newspaper might give you a good reason to check in with a prospect. In the *New York Times*, I noted where the Burger King client tied the knot. I immediately sent him a congratulatory email. He appreciated it.

- Technology today provides a godsend of intelligence and reconnaissance. LinkedIn is a veritable online tome of people info, contacts, common colleagues, connections, fellow alumni, executives' outside interests and more. LinkedIn is all about widening your circle of acquaintances and enriching your opportunity to reach out to decision makers with referrals.

   "We encourage our sellers to meet businesspeople in the community at functions of all sorts and use these networking contacts when reaching out to prospects," Chris Beyer, longtime Los Angeles Clippers' sales manager says. "Referencing an earlier interaction warms up the first formal sales greeting."

   But be careful. Sponsors are sensitive to throwing names around. Tim Sullivan, vice president at Wendy's, suggests that sellers can go over the line when, "acting like they know me to get me to take a call. Acting like we are buddies when we don't even know each other."

- Facebook is invaluable, whether it's corporate sites, consumer comments, posts or photos. Before visiting with a prospect, you might be fortunate to get a look at a photo of the person you're meeting with and his or her associated hobbies, favorite movies or family information.

- Twitter, too, is an indispensable currency of communication. There's incessant tweeting of all sorts

365/24/7. The challenge is to find executives who tweet about their companies. Once you find the people who do so and who can help you, follow the person on Twitter.

- Today, of course, it's all about social media. And absolutely, join groups, participate on discussion boards. Research profiles, corporately and personally. It will help you tighten your direction. Sales have certainly changed since the technological antebellum.

What is the most effective way to exploit the web for leads, find profiles of decision makers and search for common acquaintances and colleagues to offer introductions on your behalf? Sam Richter addresses this issue in his aptly titled, *Take the Cold Out of Cold Calling*. It's a generic cold calling book, not one on the sports industry alone. In organized fashion, Richter helps navigate sellers through productive and salient websites to find information that warms up cold calls.

Richter goes through the ins and outs of helpful websites with great detail, from prominent sites to obscure ones, from google.com to publiclibraries.com and from reachable.com to warmselling.com. The author navigates readers through social media sites like Twitter to help you squeeze every last bit of available helpful information.

Among other pertinent tips, Richter suggests checking out the USGA website, ghin.com, to see if the prospect you're chasing is a member of the organization and whether representative scores are posted. If your target is a gifted golfer, raise the topic to your benefit during your interaction.

Derivative Ideas and Eclectic Leads

Rich Karlgaard pointed out in *Forbes* in 2013 that Bill Walsh, the accomplished coach of the San Francisco 49ers, chose quarterback Joe Montana because, among other reasons, he was an all-state basketball point guard perfectly suited to run the now famous West Coast offense. Walsh actually concocted the West Coast concept by watching a high school basketball game. "How was a team inbounding the ball able to beat a full court press? Picks, rolls, short passes, training your eyes to see multiple receivers."

The sales lesson from Walsh is to be unafraid to take a different course. Look beyond traditional sports advertisers and related industries to chase leads. Go against the grain.

For instance, signage on the floor in the NBA and at college basketball games was really an outgrowth of an international practice. That's right. America, the birthplace of marketing, mimicked the European advertising architecture and brought arena signage to heightened sports revenue levels on these shores. Don't be too proud to imitate. Never stop observing how things are done elsewhere, in other marketing spaces.

Coach Walsh said, "More than creating, innovation involves anticipating. It is having a broad base of knowledge on your subject and an ability to see where the game is going."

In 2014, in an extension of Walsh's 'anticipation and innovation,' IMG, the largest seller of college sports inventory, used its stadia state-of-the-art video boards to get an order from a movie producer to run trailers promoting a film release. It was a first for the marketing industry to do so in a stadium.

In television's early years, game shows embedded vehicles in the fabric of programming as giveaways to contestant winners. Early on, programs were named for their sponsors, like *The Texaco Hour*. As network television grew into a dominant monolithic framework, the practice ended. Advertisers' names were no longer parts of program titles.

In recent years though, with hundreds of cable channels and the need of each to compete in a littered marketplace, the practice has come back strongly. On network television, sponsors are organically a part of play-by-play whether it's Toyota in *NBC's Sunday Night Football* or Dan Patrick swinging Callaway clubs on his television show. It's another example of innovation, digging into bags of old tricks now forgotten.

In other words, think differently. Leads come from anywhere. Let your mind flow. Fertile thoughts will sometimes hit you when you're going to sleep. Keep your smartphone or notepad handy near your bed so you can mark leads down before you forget. I can't tell you how many leads I lost falling asleep through the years. Write them down immediately.

Michael Lewis, the author of *Moneyball* pointed out in a *New York Times* magazine feature that Shane Battier made the Houston Rockets a better team when he was in the lineup, albeit he was somewhat more deliberate and not as fleet afoot as other gifted NBA players. He successfully studied his matchups on game film and mentally noted an opponent's weak suit.

By forcing an opponent to the left baseline and not letting him get to the right, Battier generally held down an opponent. His man was much better physically, but he used his determination and smarts to sufficiently survive in the competitive NBA world.

So, just because you might be selling a smaller sports program against a big behemoth, say Harvard football against the Patriots in New England, there's opportunity. There's always an angle. Study the Harvard audience, the qualitative profile, the alumni, the companies that the school supports through its multibillion-dollar endowment and the osmosis of being identified with this citadel of higher learning. Watch the traffic coming in and out of the campus. Find out where they shop. Harvard football might not enjoy the broad-based mainstream support that the Patriots enjoy, yet it and other institutions bring a lot to the party.

When asked how he led hockey in scoring so many years, Wayne Gretzky said, "I skate to where the puck is going not to where it has been." A good prospector has a sense, an instinct of where to go, where the puck hasn't been.

What are the growing industries that can benefit from sports sponsorships?

What is the next big industry to dive into sports? In 2014, DraftKings, a fantasy site, made a big commitment to sports. Which sites compete with DraftKings? Identify other companies you can target that share DraftKings' marketing strategies.

One answer might be FanDuel. Eilers Research estimated that it spends $20 million a year on television advertising. Is it working? Eilers thinks so. It estimates that it paid $68 per customer acquisition and made $100 off each customer in the first year.

Innovation is not invention, as we learned from Coach Walsh. Innovating can be finding existing marketing budgets earmarked elsewhere and having them converted to sports. It's an extension of what already exists.

To this end, when you study big company prospects, there are all sorts of pools of moneys. At an automotive company, there's the mainstream budget to support the sale of newly launched vehicles. These dollars, while the largest of the budgets, are generally fairly well earmarked once vehicles are in the showroom. There are other advertising silos too. There's regional money, which might sometimes be cobbled to be spent nationally. If you're selling a national program, reach out to the person who controls budgets for all regions. There are also campaigns on behalf of pre-owned, parts and services, finance and other automotive profit centers. It all goes back to digging to see what's available.

Desultory Observations

- Teams are now putting together midrange hospitality packages. In other words, there's now less of a chasm between the courtside seats and the nosebleeds. In football, it might be at the 40-yard line instead of the 50. It might not be the suite with all food and service amenities and limousine trips. Yet, it might provide other accesses that the rank and file doesn't get.

Small businesses might look at packages that provide this experience. This significantly expands the gamut of sponsorships that can be sold and the range of prospects that can be identified. It enables sellers to appeal to emotions without having to go to major public companies that can afford top-level packages but might not consider them because of recent governmental regulation. A mid-ground package gives a sponsor some "status," even without the white-glove services.

- If you're unsure whether a company is a target, don't let a little doubt dissuade you. Go after the account anyhow. How bad would you feel if it ends up as sponsors of a competitor?

- Remember that your mission when selling sports media is to position the property you're selling for its intrinsic and inherent sports values, not just as a vehicle within a diverse media package of both sports and non-sports programming. You're selling sports sponsorships not parcels of media or flighted advertising.

- Talk with your talent and coaches. They're often tied into the community and connected at high levels. They can help uncover leads through businesspeople they know personally.

- Before reaching out to talk with a prospect that buys the competition or something similar to what you're selling, make sure you understand why and what. In media, for example, selling radio to an advertiser that doesn't generally buy the medium but was nonetheless heard on a competitor, you might be told it was part of a cross-platform deal, and "we didn't pay for it." OK. If so, what's your angle? Telling them that you're calling because you heard them on the competition alone isn't compelling enough. You'll need a plan. Maybe your property is beefing up its multi-platform programs, and you'll have a permeating idea that will be enticing.

- It is a numbers game, and you'll have to compile an unending list of prospects if you're to succeed. There are tons of resources. Online today, the opportunities are endless. Gone are the days of having to stock offices with thick advertising directories. The info is on the web. You can subscribe to Hoovers, the Red Book or Advertising Database. There are places to get local directories and national listings, market shares, top 50 of this or top 50 of that. Don't let a stone go unturned.

- At times, once a prospect is in place, it's healthy to begin at the very top of the buying hierarchy. CEOs and marketing VPs want things done right away. They're impatient. They're less calculating. They're more prepared to act on impulse than to sit and deliberate. They like sports and they like to hobnob. They often focus less on budgets. They'll find a way. They also like beating the competition to something exciting. They're bigger picture in thinking than the number crunchers are. They've risen through sales and like big ideas.

  If you work the process properly, you'll generally start with a letter or email to the chief decision maker. In a cogent and customized letter, personalized accordingly, the gatekeeper will make sure that the executive sees it. If it's well constructed, it might be sent with some positive notes to the correct underling. When you follow up, the gatekeeper will likely provide positive direction.

First order of business is identifying prospects, and then it's how to reach out to them and how to nail down an appointment. Reading voraciously and interacting regularly with businesses and prospects will sharpen your ability to sniff out leads. It will also strengthen your intuition. It's precisely why you can never dig, network or learn enough.

A lead might be passed along internally at the water cooler or by the company receptionist who innocently tells you about an inquiry that came into the front desk. Jump on it, of course, but remember that, by definition, closing these leads won't give you the 'hitting the home run' sensation that begins with pursuing an account from scratch.

Lewis Schreck, vice president of the Washington Redskins Radio Network, gets romantic about cold calling: "I love the 'Sherlock Holmes-ing' that goes with cold calling. I am an explorer by nature. I love going into the car with my wife and exploring back roads. The spirit of exploration is alive and well in digging up information while cold calling. You never know what is around the next bend."

Chapter 5

Preparing to Contact New Prospects

How difficult is it to reach clients? Ask Steve Robinson, CMO of Chick-fil-A. "We take a long-term strategic approach to sponsorships. Everyone we have ever done, we initiated the conversation." In other words, Chick-fil-A isn't waiting for the phone to ring from cold-callers.

Jack Hollis, Toyota Group's vice president of marketing says, "I would recommend that cold callers resist the request for an in-person meeting during initial contact." So you know what you're up against.

Before you reach out to the prospects you've identified, be prepared and effectively armed. Make believe you're preparing a 'case study' for your final exam in business school. Sophisticated prospects want to feel that they're interacting with an educated seller and, if young, one who's precocious. Prospects love to talk about their companies' goods and services, especially when they're comfortable that the sales representative is genuinely interested, prepared and well versed. It's imperative to do so to build trust and respect.

According to Brian Lafemina, the NFL's senior vice president, Club Business Development, "It used to be enough to be an expert on what your product was and how it could help a client achieve their advertising or marketing goals. To be successful today, sales executives need to understand their prospect's business as well know their own. They need to understand their client's *business goals* not just their *marketing goals*—and they need to find a way to help their client achieve those goals through the sponsorship. Teams are uniquely suited to do this, but it takes a new mindset where you are not just selling your intellectual property rights, but instead are truly integrating the two brands in an authentic way."

Customized approaches that are well thought out will likely get you a hearing. Boilerplate or scripted approaches won't work.

Prospects' websites are a good start to educate yourself about the prospect. These tendentious websites won't often elaborate on controversial issues, but you'll learn about core goals, management, goods and services. If you Google the company by name and add the words issues, challenges, complaints, competitors or a ton of other search words, you'll likely download unbiased assessments.

How's the economy overall? Does it dictate spending by consumer, sponsor and advertiser? Years ago, Milt Maltz, chairman of Cleveland-based broadcaster Malrite Communications walked into an elevator and asked one of his managers what the unemployment rate was in Cleveland. When the manager didn't have the correct answer, Maltz gave him a look that could kill. Be on your toes when around management. You might get on an elevator one day and be asked to name a handful of advertisers that are on the competition but not on your property. Sponsors and advertisers partner with one entity but not another for a variety of reasons. But it's a basic imperative to instantly know the bigger ones not in your camp, so to speak.

Examples of Prospect Preparation

Sink your teeth into current issues. Be more than ready, be drilled.

UPS
Before a discussion with UPS, for example, study the challenges the company faces. According to a September 2014 article in the *Wall Street Journal*, UPS is the biggest player in the ecommerce space. It represents 21% of UPS' total revenue. In 2013, it represented $11 billion in revenue.

But due to competition, price squeezing and incestuous shipping by the likes of Amazon, UPS now ships 42% of ecommerce packages, down from 55% in 1999.

So UPS is challenged to slow its declining ecommerce share because the business sector is growing exponentially. In 2014, ecommerce represented almost 6% of all U.S. retail sales, up from 3.6% in 2009.

The company was continuing to research ways to cut costs out of its ecommerce shipping operations. At the same time, it was changing its rate structure, basing costs on size of the ground shipment, not on weight alone.

Diversion to cost savings impacts sponsorships and advertising budgets. It also might allow a sports marketer to summon a creative bond to support UPS' overall efforts.

Prepare proposals that address needs, problems and opportunities. When you talk to UPS, you'll sound knowledgeable and caring. Your host won't tune you out.

At the same time, by investigating UPS, you'll have learned that UPS is also competing against upstarts. For instance, in Washington, D.C., Uber Technologies is experimenting with same-day delivery of some 100 various items, including batteries, shaving gel and gum. If you read the UPS article and you're selling a Redskins, Nats, Caps or Wizard package, you would have another lead: Uber.

Additionally, in UPS' headquarter city, Atlanta, Kanga is doing local shipping in a rather novel way. Its goal is to generate a groundswell of activity among Atlantans. It's a business concept based on an indigenous idea. Kanga's website says it is looking for a "crowd of people who want to make extra money driving around town," local people delivering goods. Kanga sounds like a lead to sellers of Atlanta sports packages.

Hyundai

It's a 10-minute drill to peruse online sources to get the latest sales data and product performance, model by model, brand by brand and company by company.

Be sensitive to slumping sales when calling a prospect. In the summer of 2014, Hyundai recalled 883,000 Sonatas due to a gear shifter problem. Sonata sales slumped badly, and as a result, marketing chief Steve Shannon left the company.

In Shannon's three-year tenure, he beefed up Hyundai's on-the-ground marketing, including college campus activation. Shannon's departure might open up the opportunity to present new ideas. Communicate with those at the agencies that service the account. Folks there can keep you in the loop on potential changes in Hyundai's marketing.

If you knew Shannon, it's an opportunity to stay in touch with him. He'll land again, and he will remember those who reached out during his interregnum. There are ways to do so. His administrative assistant might have his new email address. You might even address a personal note to him, mail it to his former admin and ask gently for it to be sent to his forwarding address. If by doing so, you're hitting a dead end, you can attempt to reach out to Steve through his LinkedIn account. Don't wait until Steve lands. Check in to show you're thinking about him.

By engaging in a prospect's business, taking a deep dive into understanding what makes the target's industry tick, you'll feel a lot more comfortable, confident and interested when you do connect. You'll then engage with alacrity. Your enthusiasm will light up the room. You'll capture the necessary emotion. You can't sanitize cold calling. It's war. Yet knowledge of the prospect's business warms up a cold call. Well armed is well prepared. Failure to prepare is preparation for failure.

If you're pitching a car advertiser, engage in discussions covering per-unit transactions, incentive spending, month-to-month comps and sales productivity per classification, luxury versus mainstream and SUVs versus compacts. The same reason that you're in sports is the same reason the client is behind the desk in the car business. There's a passion. Just as you might be able to rattle off basketball stats, learn to spew car stats. Show some passion for prospects' products.

Microsoft
If you have the special opportunity to talk with Microsoft, you will want to be cognizant of recent marketing changes under CMO Chris Capossela.

In 2014, Capossela talked about going from product-specific ads to undertaking a broader consumer campaign. You will want to know about the company's NFL sponsorship and its results, anecdotally and numerically, and the performance of its retail stores. You will want to have knowledge of the integration of Nokia, which Microsoft purchased. How does it plan to show off its cloud service using Nokia? Are Microsoft's recent results likely to establish Windows as the premier smartphone?

You can consider setting up Google Alerts on companies, industries and executives. The news will be delivered right to your digital doorstep—that is, your inbox or RSS feed. These updates can be categorized, changed or removed at any time. These pieces of pertinent news will help steer your follow-up strategy, prospect by prospect.

In your proposal, you'll include a program compatible with the storytelling mission that Capossela has embraced. As he says, the goal is to tell "cohesive stories that are not simply related to a single product." You don't have to prepare for a doctoral dissertation, but know the basics well. Like a play-by-play announcer, know the roster, the human interest stories and the strategies. Sound erudite!

Think about whom you're going to dial and what you're going to say. Start with an astute comment that's sufficiently disarming to segue into a rhythmic and intelligent business exchange.

Credit card companies

The credit card category is flooded with activity. Before you delve into a pitch to the spenders in this category, you'll want to be familiar with operational and marketing nuances. You'll also want to draw parallels on how these companies spend their sports sponsorship dollars.

American Express is different from the other major cards. Unlike the other biggies, MasterCard and Visa, Amex issues most of the cards on its own, not partner banks, and targets upper-class working professionals. It is an official NBA sponsor.

When reaching out to Discover Card, you'll want to have a full grasp of MasterCard's partnership with Major League Baseball and Visa's sponsorship of the NFL. Discover isn't a player of the magnitude of the latter two, but there's still much to be observed. Visa does almost 50% more revenue than its archrival MasterCard and has issued some 40% more credit cards (in 2014, 250 million vs. MasterCard's 178 million). Still, the two make hefty sports commitments.

There's little difference between owning a Visa or MasterCard because policies regarding interest rates and rules of the rewards program are made by the issuing banks. Yet consumer decisions are based largely on emblem or shield preferences of the two cards. So cachet means a lot.

Know what credit card sponsorship heads are saying. For instance, Michael Robichaud at MasterCard will tell you, "We'll look at an NFL or MLB team in one or our key U.S. markets, but not NBA or NHL. This isn't because one is better than the other, it has to do with our overall strategy and what our competitors do. AMEX, for example, is an NBA partner."

Discover is a different breed. It issues a significant percentage of its cards through its own financial institution, Discover Bank. It also offers a cash-back feature. Because Discover is not as widely accepted as the other major cards, the cash back benefit is critical. Discover is an official NHL sponsor in the United States.

In 2014, Discover offered 1% cash-back when Citigroup stepped up its game. Its new Citi card offered double cash back. That's 2% versus Discover's 1%! The Citi move presented Discover with a steep challenge.

You'll need to dig deep to present marketing ideas to Discover. It does get glittering five-star ratings for its student credit cards, which might conjure up creative thoughts. But before you juggle ideas on promoting credit cards for students, you'll have to find out what, if any, marketing budget Discover has to promote its student features. The point here is that there are many factors to consider before picking up the phone and reaching out to a prospect.

If you open your conversation with a positive development that you found in your research, it sets a healthy tone. It shows the client that you did your homework. Naturally, if all you can find is grim news, talk sports or about something innocuous.

Home Depot

When you are planning a pitch to Home Depot, it might be good to know that it accommodates non-do-it-yourselfers too. The retail giant has service agreements with local installers and contractors. When Home Depot sells garage doors, it has a team of distribution partners market by market who work the field to service customers. It's an additional financial opportunity for Home Depot as well as a service convenience for the customer. How do you plan to promote this customer benefit into the package you're preparing?

GEICO and Progressive

Direct-to-consumer marketers like Progressive or GEICO are less likely to need goodies. There aren't any middle channels, brokers or distributors. Then again, Procter & Gamble, which works through distributors and retailers, can use hospitality.

FedEx

Even in the depth of a crisis, there was a way to open a conversation on a pleasant note. When the country's economy plummeted and corporate America announced broad layoffs in late 2008, FedEx opted instead for companywide salary cuts. The press lauded the move for being somewhat democratic. One columnist said that it was a model that other companies should follow because across-the-board pay cuts were more manageable, would cause fewer defaults of mortgages and would sustain price-easing across the board.

You'll learn the hard way after mistakes. Years ago, I called a sugar company in shotgun style. It's easy to get trapped. While the marketing director was a gentleman, he politely undressed me for being unprepared for the call. The sugar industry had been hurting for years. Coke no longer uses sugar for its natural sweetener, diet sodas represent a larger share of the soft drink market and women spend less time baking. I looked somewhat foolish but learned a valuable lesson.

Knowledge Is Power!

- Know, know, know and you'll grow, grow, grow.

- Know the history of accounts beyond their marketing strategies.

- Is it a company that counts on a multi-level channel of distribution? Does it use distributors, wholesalers or jobbers? Is it a business-to-business account? Does it market directly to consumers?

- Is there a history of business partnerships between the prospect and sports properties at all, or are they virgins in the sports sponsorship space?

- Understand market shares, regional biases, recent developments, product planning, features and more.

- Are there personnel at the client who've experienced the benefits of sports and can serve as protagonists for sports in general and your entity in particular?

- What is the company's media strategy? Is the company's advertising visible year-round, or is it flighted so that it's in lockstep with product seasonality?

- How are they doing versus their competitors?

- Are there competitors of the prospect that engage successfully sponsoring other sports entities? Draw parallels and glean from the details of the prospect's competitor's execution and activity. It will help you structure a conceptual framework to trigger interest.

- Get some sales data on the company and the industry as a whole. How's the industry doing this year versus last year, versus five years ago?

- What are the industry's challenges?

- Sellers are problem solvers. What are the prospect's problems? It's also important to anticipate prospects' needs. What are the psychographics of the prospect's targeted group? If you can't get the information online or through social media, Google the prospect's competitors. Have helpful and creative suggestions, particularly in metastasizing economic times.

- Research the prospect's consumer reviews.

- Is the target's advertising themed around branding, price point attractions or other commands to action?

- Understand the buying hierarchy and find out who makes the final sponsorship and media decisions.

- What is the target's demographic? How does that demographic fit the wheelhouse of your product's strengths? Demographics will include targets against age cell, gender, income levels, geography and educational levels.

- Customize your preparation. If you're chasing Ace Hardware, you might want to ascertain its customer profile. Is the customer a do-it-yourselfer? If so, do you have any related qualitative profiles on attendees or broadcast consumption of the entity you're pitching? Demonstrating compatibility will strengthen your story.

- What is the company's spending calendar, its media and marketing planning cycle?

- What is the target's selling feature? What is its niche versus its competition?

- Are there product performance issues? What are its reviews like online?

- What is the financial health of the company?
- If it's a national company, are there regional biases?

Food for Thought

Be fully prepared to present and defend the capabilities of the sponsorship or sports media entity you're selling.

Your mind should be a repository of product and competitive information. Integrate information about the product that you're selling and that of your competitors. Intermingle the two. Know it like the back of your hand. Product features, yours and theirs. We're living in a fluid world. Be familiar with changes, yours and theirs. Be prepared to overcome all objections. Have a co-seller test you. Role-play. It's imperative to have data and knowledge at your fingertips.

Think about it. When you shop online and are unable to have a question answered about an item you're considering, you'll move on. Either you'll pass altogether or move on to a competitor's site. Better yet, how frustrating is it to walk into a retailer and ask questions of a sales representative who's ill-equipped to answer them?

When you finally get a potential prospect on the phone, you want to sound confident. Beyond rudimentary knowledge of the company you're pitching, you certainly don't want to be embarrassed by being unable to answer elementary questions about core competencies of the product or service you're selling. It's one thing to buy time when asked a customized question about a promotional execution and it's quite another not to be glib about fundamentals: history of your entity, successes, features and pricing. Knowledge builds the necessary confidence on both ends of the discussion. You'll speak smoothly, smartly, enthusiastically and persuasively.

Don't view internal staff meetings as a burden. Learn from them. You will better understand the capabilities of your entity in its entirety, from finance to promotion and from public relations to ticket sales. It will strengthen your verbal ammunition and build the necessary intelligence you'll need to help you build trust with prospective clients. Ask questions at these meetings. Don't be shy. A greater depth of understanding of what you can and can't do will make you a better problem solver with prospects.

Watch and pick up what your competition does. It might be a competitor running a promotion on the floor or an on-air feature on a telecast. If you've seen something fertile, talk to your own management to see whether it's something your entity will consider. If so, prepare to take the idea to a prospect.

Being fully indulged will enable you to answer basic questions fluently, no matter whether the answer is gratifying to the questioner. When your reply is firm, you'll more likely be considered an expert.

When first-time sports prospects begin their initial investigations as to whether or not to invest in sponsorships, they usually meet with a multitude of vendors. If you answer their questions authoritatively, prospects are more likely to lean on you for more advice and data than on your competitor. As such, if they are to buy sports, you'll likely be first to feel the constellating wave of buying signals. The head start will put you in the driver's seat!

- If media is part of the mix, be a voracious student of your programming space and your medium's reach. Know the geography and ratings like the back of your hand. Are there on-air personalities who are dynamic? If so, what are they prepared to do on behalf of a potential sponsor? Do any of the personalities have connections to products that might want to partake in the program? Who are your play-by-play announcer teams?

- Are you selling a regional cable network? What are the pluses and minuses when juxtaposed against its competition? What is the distribution against those of the competitors?

- If you're selling the NFL Network, for example, know the vertical sports media cold. So, when you're asked by a prospect who sells advertising for the NBA Television Network, Turner should roll off the top of your tongue. There are no excuses for not knowing this. In preparation, role-play by indulging in a question-and-answer session with a colleague at the office. Suggest to your manager to engage you in a pop quiz.

- When a prospect poses a question to a television network seller selling NFL play-by-play as to whether the Red Zone can be included as part of an entitlement package, you'll have to say no. The same question of the network radio or team sales rep would be yes. Nationally, the NFL contract allows it on radio, not on television. There's a lot of rudimentary information that's imperative to know.

- When you're with the target, you might be asked to list your sponsors. Don't say, "Let me look it up." The names should spew from your mouth at a moment's notice. Be prepared to list half a dozen or so of current clients. Start with the big names! Go through a diverse list, technology, communication companies, airlines, cars, financials, insurance, home improvement and beers.

- Is there a unique story that you can present versus your competition? For instance, the NBA talked about placing corporate logos on uniforms. Most other major sports won't permit it. What can you do that your competitor can't?

- On the broadcast side, what organic embedding is a sponsor permitted to do in a play-by-play broadcast? Where is the line drawn?

- If you're planning to pitch retailer hhgregg, you should be ready to answer whether your team will allow an app where fans earn prizes by playing games with one another at stadiums and arenas; hhgregg does this successfully with the Indianapolis Colts.

- If you're selling for a team or a league, what are the capabilities that accompany the ownership of the use of the shield? What can and can't be done digitally, online and via mobile? What are the experiential rights stadium by stadium?

- If you're working for a sports agency attempting to get a sponsor for a particular athlete, know the endorsement deals that similar personalities have.

- If you're working for a local college, know the limitations. Can sponsors get alumni lists? Can they do email blasts to alumni? Can they showcase a vehicle on campus?

- Understand the culture and environment of the property you're selling. At Notre Dame and Augusta, there's just so much corporate engagement that will be permitted. For years, the Masters has limited its broadcast rights holder, CBS, to run a bare-bones number of commercial minutes per hour. Notre Dame has no salient commercial signage in its historic stadium.

- At Michigan, Athletic Director Dave Brandon was eventually fired for, among other reasons, over-embedding commercial sponsorship in the fabric of sacrosanct football and stadium activities. As *Sports Illustrated* pointed out, "Fans of one of the nation's most hallowed football programs are already loyal to the bone. Michigan supporters were insulted by a promotion to give away two tickets to the Minnesota game with the purchase of two bottles of Coke." Know your entity.

Let a Picture Grab a Prospect's Attention

A seller of one of the New York pro winter teams got a prospect's attention creatively. He reached out to a Caribbean tourist agency and sent an artist's rendition of a glass truck in which the temperature was spiked to 80 degrees and decked out to look like a beach: white sand, bright sunshine and beach umbrellas. Inside the glass truck and visible to thousands on their way to games on cold nights were hosts and hostesses dressed tantalizingly in bathing suits and bikinis. If a picture tells a thousand words and an idea can sell a concept, this was it.

He attached the picture to an email and got an appointment.

If you're wondering, the idea did get traction. It did not, though, result in an order. Not yet.

Social Media

Corporate marketing is not what it was even 10 years ago. In our second decade of the millennium, digital's dominance is permeating our lives.

The emergence of social media is also having a profound impact on sports sponsorships because it makes it much easier for brands and rights holders to engage with fans.

In 2010, David Edelman's *Harvard Business Review* article, "Branding in the Digital Age," captured the essence of consumers' behavioral changes in today's instantly connected world.

His first assumption is that consumers bond with brands through channels that are not under the aegis of their corporate fathers. Edelman referenced research titled the "Consumer Decision Journey," which appeared in the McKinsey Report.

In simpler times, when consumers narrowed down choices and then made their final decision, the process was dubbed a "marketing funnel." Today, the "Consumer Decision Journey" is, as the description suggests, a more thorough process. It's made up of four stages—*consider, evaluate, buy* and *bond*—followed by three stages: *enjoy, advocate* and *bond*.

Social media is the ideal place to influence the journey, before, during and after the purchase. In a 2012 article in *Marketing Profs*, Roger Katz writes, "The Consumer Decision Journey has evolved into a Social Loyalty Loop with vast touchpoints. Brands are building social campaign experiences that spread from one brand loyalist to her friends and create a powerful social loyalty loop that, when done effectively, continues to cultivate brand loyalists."

As such, marketing has been completely rethought and the numbers tell the story. An Ohio University study conducted by Dr. Michael Pfahl, assistant professor, sports administration suggested that 85% of sports marketers in 2012 increased their social and digital sports budgets, 38% increased their television spend and some 47% said they were decreasing their print budget.

Kia's 2014 deal with the NBA is a microcosm of a new world sports marketing order.

In addition to traditional media, signage and other staples, Kia's NBA sponsorship is focused on a stepped up digital piece, one that creates a "Top Play" promotion that will live on nba.com. Fans will vote on top plays through the course of the year and at the end of the season, the play with the most number of votes will be selected as the "Kia Top Play of the Year."

Contributor Alicia Jessop on forbes.com details more of the digital components. "Kia's sponsorship involves allowing fans to dictate the direction of a highlight-based commercial. To further this process, Kia's partnership attains a social media element, as the NBA will post clips of the commercial on Twitter and Vine for fans to watch. The posts receiving the greatest number of retweets and loops earn a spot in the final cut. The implementation of these new social media and digital components into its partnership with Kia demonstrates the NBA's willingness to use creativity in meeting its sponsors' needs."

In other words, it's another day. Today, when you walk into a prospect hoping to sell intellectual rights, you better have all dots connected to a social media anchor and the tentacles that they grow.

Dr. Pfahl, the assistant professor, sums up the unbending need to address social media ahead of time, "When you are looking for a sponsorship client, you have to do your research on them. When you walk into a meeting with them, you want to know about them and get a feel for their goals and objectives. You want everything to be customizable for your clients. This all is the boring old part of sports sponsorship sales. The exciting new part, though, is if you use digital platforms and craft a strategy that looks at all of the fans as one community, then you can break the fans into subgroups and work the sponsor through digital means to provide different types of content. When you do this, you are creating value for the sponsor."

Social media is now also being implemented at ground zero, whether it's hhgregg through interactive games at Indianapolis Colts' home games, juicy programs at venues of other professional sports teams or executions at college football games. The University of Wisconsin enables Badgers' fans who use the #Badgers hashtag to see their photos on the stadium video board and on hundreds of televisions at Camp Randall Stadium. The photos come from Twitter, Facebook and Instagram. It not only entertains and engages the fan base but also serves as a revenue stream.

Learfield Sports, which owns the marketing rights to Wisconsin football, sold a catchy sponsorship to Wisconsin Iron Workers Local 383. Using a poll that tracks votes on social media, the Ironman of the Game is identified on the scoreboard and television screens throughout the stadium. At Michigan State, using #SpartansStudentSelfie, students arriving early are encouraged to send photos. Verizon sponsors the display on the video board.

In 2014, Ashley Shapiro of the Philadelphia 76ers effectively used LinkedIn to identify prospects, build contacts and network in the marketplace. As reported in a feature in *SportsBusiness Journal* in 2014, Ashley seemed to have the sales process down to a science.

While she didn't blatantly pitch the 76ers via LinkedIn itself, she studied profiles on the site for potential partner targets, then customized pitches to those whose interests and backgrounds presented potentially good matches. It enabled her to sell hospitality and corporate programs to those she found on LinkedIn whose common geography was conducive. LinkedIn profiles provide a wealth of information that triggers engaging thoughts. They often profile personal interests, alma maters, career paths and objectives. As Ashley said, it makes the cold call a "warmer lead."

How has technology changed communication with sellers in the last decade? Marketers respond in Figure 5.1.

Figure 5.1. Technological changes in communication with sellers

Jack Hollis TOYOTA	Email is still a great way to communicate; it's the most respectful of our time when receiving a pitch. To help you find the contact most suited to your proposal, I recommend using tools such as LinkedIn.
Anonymous AUTO-RELATED MARKETER	In some cases, it has made it more difficult on the sellers. You just need to use technology to your advantage and make me want to engage with you.
John MacDonald ENTERPRISE	Technology has changed execution and implementation. Nothing can change the need for a long-term relationship and an understanding of the goals to be achieved.
Drew Iddings HERSHEY'S	Technology has exponentially increased the quantity and decreased the quality of solicitations that I receive because it's easier for sellers to: 1) find my contact information, and 2) send me generic cut-and-paste email messages.
Noah Syken IBM	Less client hosting, fewer events, more email. Younger, less seasoned people who have no understanding of MY business...only theirs. To this day, people still want to talk to me about helping me sell more "computers"...when we sold our PC division YEARS ago.
Rex Conklin HOME DEPOT	The ease of communication results in a lot of scatter-approach proposals that lack strategic thought and relevance.
David Lim AMTRAK	Direct mail has declined and email solicitations have increased. The speed and expected speed of communication is much faster. Not responding because you are out of the office on travel is no longer acceptable. Communication via mobile phones is the norm today even if one is in the office. Fax copies have been replaced by PDF files, which are much more compelling and persuasive.

Figure 5.1. *Continued*

Julie Lyle HHGREGG	Everyone is distracted and sellers must be adept—as we ALL have to be—at honing your message and articulating it quickly and in a concise but compelling manner.
Stephen Quinn WAL-MART	It's made it much more intrusive, cluttered, irritating and irrelevant.
Phil Wang WELLS FARGO	More accessibility and thus more people trying to get my attention. Too many inquiries on a daily basis.
Ed Gold STATE FARM	We set up a site for proposal submission. We wish everyone would follow the rules.
Betsy Wilson UPS	I think it has improved it. So many people provide links to videos that really bring properties to life – that's a great tactic to tell your story. But the video needs to be short – 90 seconds is perfect.
Paul Hodges REGIONS BANK	Yes. It has increased the number of proposals I receive exponentially.
Mark Eckert EDWARD JONES	Email increases the velocity, efficiency and effectiveness by which sellers can get their products/services introduced to more (and hopefully better qualified) buyers, and buyers can receive, filter, review and respond to relevant inquiries.
Tim Sullivan WENDY'S	Using email to pre-screen most ideas.
Brad Barnett NATIONWIDE	For both sellers and clients it's opened up more methods of contact and communication (e.g., sellers can reach me via phone, email, LinkedIn, in-office, etc.), which can sometimes be challenging. On the positive side, it's provided sellers more opportunities to visually demonstrate what they can do for a client and in return allow clients to better understand more quickly.
Tom Peyton HONDA	It's easier and less costly to send email. It's why we receive hundreds a day.
Michael Robichaud MASTERCARD	Maybe in some of the video and presentations, but not from a cold sell.
Ellie Malloy JOHN HANCOCK	First, in the past seven years, I've been getting more email and fewer phone calls. I'm careful about answering the phone much because it's painful to explain the same thing over and over to sellers calling with similar proposals. Second, while we've been adopting more social media as part of our programs, vendors' proposals still emphasize traditional media and values. Social media too often is presented as an addendum rather than embedding it in the meat of the package.

When you first contemplate interacting with a decision maker, carefully map out your sales communication resources. Just as coaches conservatively allocate their timeouts, you should do the same. You have a litany of assets at your disposal to use as you see best fit to reach out to a prospect. But don't use them all at once or too quickly. Closing a new piece of business is a long process. You'll be pouring your heart out and investing psychologically, so always keep a ploy or two in your bag of tricks.

This is likely what your bag of tricks looks like:

General contact

- Brief introductory phone call, reason you're reaching out and a request to meet
- Similarly, using email or formal letter
- Fixed number of follow-up calls to establish initial dialogue
- Core competency presentation
- Customized presentation
- Social media posts
- Letter from coach and/or talent
- Invitations to sponsor functions
- Handwritten notes
- Letters of endorsements by key clients
- Occasional pertinent articles
- Tickets
- Goodies, trinkets and autographed balls
- Texts
- Additional phone calls and email
- Mock visuals (e.g., photo of corporate name on scoreboard with message *Millions of Gator fans are cheering for ADT to sign on as a University of Florida sponsor*)

Tactical moves

- Solicit others in the buying hierarchy, those directly engaged and others on the periphery who have influence to get you an order.

- Seek support from prospects' colleagues in sales.

- Work regional management when and where applicable.

- Delicately go to ad director's boss.

- Send prospects press guides, stats and other insider info.

- At some point during the process, it's always helpful to invite the prospect to your backyard. Have the decision maker tour the facility and sniff the success. They'll never forget the experience. If this doesn't do it emotionally, little will. It generates imaginations of a win-win partnership.

It takes strong will to get in the door and an iron stomach to close the piece of business. As basketball Hall of Famer Pat Riley says, "Always have your next play ready." Don't be unprepared. As you launch an effort against a new account, be 10 steps ahead.

The Process

So now that you have identified hundreds of leads, what do you do?

Your short-term first step goal is to get the meeting. You'll be halfway to a meeting when you're able to schedule a phone call. Years ago, the process started on the phone. If the prospect didn't pick up, the administrative assistant did. You would make your brief case for an appointment and were occasionally able to identify a date to make a presentation right then and there.

Not that long ago, offices were a hub of vocal activity. Walk into an agency or client and there was a stirring distillation of verbal activity, part cacophony and part chorus, part polemic and part congenial. There was energy. There was life. Those who were writing on a yellow pad then or sending abrupt memos were said to be hiding behind a pen.

Today, it is a new code of communication. Clients are impervious to the strident rings of their phones. Caller identification is a killer, and even administrative assistants pick up their calls only selectively.

Offices today have the silenced stillness of morgues. Executives' voices have been quieted by texts, email and tablets. Having the ability to turn a word is now a lost art. Grammar has turned into a rule of the past, even by lawyers; seemingly the only ones in an office to still use formal stationery. So be it.

We've all embraced technology, and, yes, there's so much of it to love.

First things first, when your message can be limited to just a few sentences, send an email. If there's more meat to the body of your request, send a letter via standard first class mail. Don't overnight it or send it as an email attachment, whether a Word document or a scanned copy.

If there's no immediate response, give it a few days, then forward the first email to the same person, innocently referencing the original missive below it, "You might not have received my first email. I would be grateful if you would reply!"

If you're representing a mighty brand, like the NFL as opposed to some Little League team, you might want to word the first follow-up accordingly, "We (instead of I) would appreciate it if you would reply." The prospect might feel compelled to respond to an enormous institution like the NFL lest his television set might inexplicably implode on game day.

Cold calling is that much more difficult when you reach out without providing any warning. Letters prepare targets or their offices that you will call. So when you do call, a number of things will often happen. One, optimally, the target will have read your letter and agree to see you. Two, the target will have read your letter and ask a colleague or the right party to meet with you. Three, the target responds no. Most importantly, you are more likely to get the target on the horn because you've spelled out what you're trying to achieve.

If nothing more, differentiate yourself and the product you're representing from the rest of the pack. Letters still make mail delivery people bowlegged, and they still catch the attention of prospects more than any other preliminary means of communication.

"Be sure that prospects' names are spelled correctly and that titles are precise," says ESPN Radio's senior executive, Michael Connolly. There's no substitute for a well-written letter that succinctly and intelligently captures the point and your request. It should be properly personalized, respectfully addressed, and grammatically flawless. You might want to spice the letter with an exotic word to gain the prospect's attention.

The great benefit of a letter is it tells the prospect you've given your effort thought, you're to the point, you have an interesting idea and you went through the trouble of sending it. The other advantage is it will sit on the prospect's desk at a time when it's less likely to be buried under piles. Technology has taken care of excesses of paper. Did you ever notice how many fewer file drawers there are in offices today? Additionally, the prospect can send the letter to the right party internally for follow up. In other words, you're less likely to be completely ignored.

There are options today on how to first contact a client. Should it be a snail mail letter, by phone or by email? A recent study by the Pew Research Center suggests adult workers deem these means of communication, interaction and information resources as very important:

61%   email
54%   Internet
35%   landline
24%   mobile or smartphone
4%   social media

If you're sending an email, it should be three pronged:

1. Who you are and the company you represent. There's no need to open the email by stating, "I'm John Peterson, an account executive with the Miami

Dolphins." That was fine on show-and-tell day in the fourth grade. Open simply, "I represent the Miami Dolphins." Your name and title are below the body of the text at the bottom of the email.

2. Why you would like to meet. It should be covered in an economy of words, no long pitches, just two or three brief sentences, teasing your customized idea. If it's a presentation of your organization's general capabilities, a lightning rod description of the entity's reach, growth and success.

3. What you're trying to accomplish. You want to get on the target's calendar.

If an administrative assistant schedules the client's calendar, be sure to alert the prospect that you will be requesting a meeting through these channels. Always end the email cordially; "I will take the liberty to call your office to pencil in a date and will be mindful of your busy schedule." (See copies of letters below.)

In an email, make sure that your grammar is impeccable. Don't be sloppy just because it's an email. Targets don't know you. You're being judged on the text of a brief introductory note. Be respectful too. Put your best foot forward and review the text of the email numerous times before hitting the send button.

In initiating client contact, there are a number of gambits to consider before you take your stroke off the first tee. You might want to couch the email to fit this approach. How are you positioning yourself to the prospect, especially an executive in a lofty role?

- Do you want to start dialogue on developing a partnership? It's bold and getting right to the point.

- Are you seeking the client's counseling? It's a little less aggressive and somewhat more disarming.

- Do you want some time to have questions answered? It's a little vague, but prospects won't feel pressure addressing marketing plans they authored.

- Do you want the prospects' spin on their corporate goals and objectives to help you prepare a customized presentation? This hints to prospects that they're brilliant and that you can't succeed in the sponsorship business unless you get their take.

No matter how you determine to position the initial email, sprinkle in driving words that set you apart from the herd (e.g., "Our reach is pervasive"; "Our fans are ubiquitous"; "Our team has an unmatched heritage"; "We want to establish a symbiotic partnership"). Don't use rich words pompously, but throw in one or two to be different and memorable.

Instead of 'persuading' a target, which is inward in approach, focus on the strong and glittering results that will benefit the client.

You can give prospects gentle nudges, but don't let them feel like they're being pushed hard. They'll resent it. It's one thing to be charismatic. Clients like being around those with magnetism, but they'll want nothing to do with an overbearing nag.

We all get so caught up in our own selfish mission that we tend to forget that the people we're trying to reach are generally part of a big corporate team and they have many internal responsibilities.

State Farm's Ed Gold, one of the real gentlemen of our business, references cold callers' first contact, "First, there is the sponsorship proposal website we utilize. Then, I am open to calls, email and regular mail. But if you email, DO NOT send 5+MB files. Learn to make them smaller. Do not clog up my email system."

To this end, *Fortune* magazine identified practices to make email overload a more efficient communication tool. While *Fortune's* tips are intended to improve email succinctness and efficiency within a corporate team, there's sellers' application too.

To begin with, it's worthwhile to avoid words that will direct your email into the prospect's spam filter. A conversation with your IT department might provide some beneficial guidance to avoid your email landing in the junk file.

Remember that the goal of your initial email is to get prospects to schedule telephone time and, better yet, an appointment. Don't beat around the bush. Once you sense that you've built enough traction to earn an appointment, ask for it.

1. **Hyperspecific subject lines.** They should grab addressees and prompt them to absorb the contents of the message and respond almost immediately. For instance, if you're selling a St. John's University basketball sponsorship package, be clear and concise in the subject line. Don't be cagey. The subject line might read: "St. John's basketball/Burger King. Would like to discuss on phone."

2. **Brevity.** Stop the long-winded pitch. Be simple and to the point. "This is the best opportunity to cross your desk this week. The Johnnies are ranked in the top 10 pre-season. I have a dynamic package that meets your media and hospitality needs. Need 10 minutes on the phone. When is a good time in the next couple of days to talk?"

   If you're struggling to compose something short, sweet and Twitter-tight, Joseph McCormack, author of *Brief: Make a Bigger Impact by Saying Less,* recommends, "write them on a smartphone, for a smartphone." On a first introductory email, be mindful of the fact that PDF or PowerPoint attachments might not be opened. Remember: you're simply trying to entice prospects to engage in a conversation or accept a meeting. You're not selling anything specific yet.

3. **Avoid email that addresses more than one subject or one sales opportunity.** Keep things simple. Executives are inundated as it is, don't be overbearing. You'll undermine your own hard work. McCormack's research indicates that

43% of professionals abandon complicated email in the first 30 seconds. Stick to one topic and one catchy opportunity.

In Figure 5.2, marketers were asked whether they would open an attachment to an email.

Figure 5.2. Marketers discuss email attachments

Tom Peyton HONDA	I only open attachments that are from known, reputable sellers (CAA, etc.). Otherwise give me a link to connect or a good summary in the body of the email. FYI...many unknown sellers with attachments never make it through our firewall.
Anonymous AUTO-RELATED ADVERTISER	No. Make sure everything you want me to know or see is in the body of the email.
John MacDonald ENTERPRISE	Only after the seller convinces me that he/she or his/her properties can have the potential to meet my needs/issues.
Drew Iddings HERSHEY'S	Occasionally. It all depends on the product offering, message content, mood and schedule.
Noah Syken IBM	Perhaps...but if I don't know someone...and the organization isn't VERY familiar...I'm wary of attachments.
Rex Conklin HOME DEPOT	Yes, assuming the email has an enticing headline and customized messaging.
David Lim AMTRAK	Only if the body copy of the email was interesting and compelling. Like the email, I would expect the attachment to be straightforward in terms of what the potential offering is. In other words, don't make me work too hard to understand the value proposition.
Julie Lyle HHGREGG	If it's short and concise and opens/loads very quickly. And it should be tailored to my business. Do your homework. If you just send me a generic corporate identity package, you are expecting me to sift through your products and services to determine if/how you may be relevant to me. I don't have time for that, and I won't do your work for you.
Stephen Quinn WAL-MART	No.
Phil Wang WELLS FARGO	Yes, but keep it short.
Ed Gold STATE FARM	I will open an attachment, but do me a favor and make it as small as possible. Do not clog my email.
Betsy Wilson UPS	Yes.
Paul Hodges	If I don't know you, I will not open the attachment.

Figure 5.2. *Continued*

Mark Eckert EDWARD JONES	If they make a compelling case for relevance, innovation, advantage and/or impact in their email, the attachment provides quick access to continue the dialogue and passively get further into the details addressing what, why, how, etc.
Tim Sullivan WENDY'S	Probably, if the email was intriguing. If I don't know the person, it may make sense to leave a voicemail message giving me the heads-up to the email info.
Brad Barnett NATIONWIDE	Yes, I would likely open an attachment if there is enough linkage to our strategy or approach in the body of the email. While most of the time there is not a fit, I can take the five seconds required to open something and give it a quick review. There's always a chance you let the one great opportunity slip through the cracks.
Michael Robichaud MASTERCARD	Maybe—if I was eating my lunch and something caught my eye!
Ellie Malloy JOHN HANCOCK	I have no issues opening an attachment. Hancock has a pretty failsafe program guarding against viruses.
Jack Hollis TOYOTA	Yes, I'd be inclined to open an attachment if the body of the email is well written, concise and shows clear relevance for Toyota. Both the email and the attachment should also be tailored to address Toyota's business needs. I won't read an email if I don't find the initial information compelling.

Tom Peyton, who heads up sponsorships and media at Honda, also has two strong suggestions for sellers who reach out by email:

1. "Don't send 20 email messages to 20 executives at our company with the same offer. It tells us you're unprofessional and probably not someone we want to do business with.

2. "Don't send it to my CEO. If it's a marketing proposal, do your homework and send it to a marketing executive. The CEO is not the initial decision maker— why bother him, his staff and everyone else? It also tells me that you're someone I probably don't want to do business with."

Starting with a phone call has its place, especially locally where clients are retailers, insurance agents and restaurant owners who interface with the public. They're more likely to pick up the phone and interact with a seller on the telephone.

For instance, if you're selling the University of Miami and you determine to chase Edward Jones because you keep spotting its offices around town, do so by phone. Check school connections. You might find an Edward Jones link to the school. Dig for information. Try to elicit the support of the regional head.

At times, the decision maker is at corporate headquarters in another city, but regional management has the juice to get it done.

If you're selling the Canes and you want to chase down Miami-headquartered Burger King, review the history. Both institutions have been in South Florida forever. If the two haven't collaborated on a sports sponsorship yet, there's a reason. Find out why. Perhaps the dissenter at Burger King who turned it down is no longer at Burger King. It might give you an opportunity to restart the effort.

Once the appointment is set up, you will want to prepare a convincing and well-argued package. This will require the cooperation of various departments within the organization for which you work: research, marketing, public relations, production, sales planning and other support groups. You're likely to call a meeting to brainstorm. You will count on internal imagination and fruitful collaboration to concoct something driving and persuasive. Don't be shy or a pious disciple of routine. You need ideas. Bring a group together out of pragmatism and consensus. Remember, you'll need everyone's cooperation internally to execute a program.

Bringing the team together into one room to collaborate will strengthen your leadership abilities to coordinate the work of various departments. Your leadership in this area is a quality that management will appreciate. Use the team around you as an asset. Work everyone. Internal betrayal can destroy a sales effort. You'll have your team brain trust and a bastion of reasoning in one room. You want to walk out with uplifting suggestions.

Joyce Russell, director of the Executive Coaching and Leadership Development Program at the University of Maryland, makes these trenchant suggestions:

- First, ask yourself whether the meeting can be done by phone. While a bit less formal, the telephone is more efficient time wise. Don't call internal meetings for every pitch that you will make. You want to be taken seriously.

- If you're to meet, keep it short and sweet.

- Feel free to bring snacks or food to a meeting. It shows your colleagues that you care about them.

- Invite only those people who have to be there. Fragile and brittle support staff will weaken your ability to succeed unless you can galvanize them.

- Require preparation from everyone attending. Send out a quick agenda and spell out what you'll be looking for. It will allow the participating departments to contemplate beforehand.

- Send advance materials to the internal participants. For example, circulate a brand brief on the account to which you'll be presenting, a mission statement, goals, previous marketing history, successes and failures. Provide any history that will trigger fertile ideas.

- Provide a firm start and end time for the meeting and a rough amount of time each person is expected to speak.

- Politely ask attendees to silence their smartphones.

- If possible, have an assistant play the role of minute keeper.

- Leave a few minutes to summarize what each person promises to do and a hard deadline of when it's expected.

Andy England, CMO of MillerCoors, makes this clear. "I'd recommend that sales personnel in sports do their homework on what the target company is trying to solve. The vast majority of contacts I get in any form are people trying to sell what they have vs. what's going to help my company. I also think sales personnel need to think about who makes decisions and how they make them. CMOs aren't going to respond to an email from someone they don't know selling something they don't need."

Writing a good business developmental letter keeps you sharp and helps build writing skills. You can be different. Send it with a team pennant, a team photo or a box of chocolates if it makes sense.

Let's go through some basic examples of letters.

Sample Letter #1

This is a rifle approach based on empirics. After committing to a sponsorship that you represent, the decision maker at Company X leaves for Company Y and you now pursue Company Y as a prospect.

HALBY GROUP

Dear Joe,

I trust that you've settled in and all is well on the new job at Company Y.

We are delighted that you have historically valued sports as a powerful marketing tool. What a better testimony than the landmark commitment you made to the Northern Basketball Conference when Company X was under your aegis three years ago. It's going strong as you know.

For many of the same reasons, this is a fabulous opportunity for your new employer, Company Y. The audience and fan profiles are perfectly suited to match the demographic you're now charged with targeting.

You might be happy to hear that since you committed to our league three years ago, our tentacles have extend further than ever and our core competencies have swelled significantly. In other words, we can now build a bond that is unshakable and will unquestionably move the needle.

I will take the liberty to call your office to set up a meeting to explore working with you and Company Y developing a driving partnership. It would be fun.

Looking forward to seeing you again.

Continued success.

David J. Halberstam

Sample Letter #2

Idiosyncratic rifle approach based on my passion for Dunkin' Donuts.

HALBY GROUP

Dear Bryan,

I am a Dunkin' Donuts junkie. If I told you some of the things I've done to get my fix, you wouldn't believe it. I cringe before going to cities west where Dunkin' Donuts doesn't have locations. If I'm in a city where locations are sparse, I will find Dunkin' stores no matter the distance, whether in Atlanta, Phoenix, Detroit, Pittsburgh or elsewhere.

Delta is my airline of preference. They treat me well, except for the selection of coffee. I am thinking of changing to Jet Blue after reading the attached article (about Jet Blue serving Dunkin' Donuts exclusively).

If you don't believe my addiction, ask my staff. They bought me $250 worth of Dunkin' Dollars. I went through the Dunkin' Dollars pretty quickly.

I'm a true fan and look forward to contacting you for a meeting to discuss a partnership with Team X which I proudly represent and which enjoys unsurpassed community support.

Wouldn't it be nice to make Dunkin' the official coffee of Team X?

How's the week of February 15th? Please advise.

Continued success.

David J. Halberstam

Sample Letter #3

Hometown approach: major sporting event in St. Louis.

HALBY GROUP

Dear Pat,

We've been fans of Energizer for many years. For that matter, Energizer has in the past sponsored sports carried by The Biggest Sports Network which we represent.

You know that the tournament championship will be held next year in your hometown of St. Louis.

Interest will be pervasive. To a man, woman and child, the championship consumes America and is a constant subject of conversation for a month; online, on social media, on radio stations, on television, in the newspapers and around the proverbial water cooler. Each team's goal, of course, is to reach St. Louis, home of the national championship and conveniently the home of Energizer.

The fan profile perfectly mirrors the Energizer target. We can support television coverage with hospitality, signage at local popular venues, interviews at Radio Row and through social media and experiential activities.

There are customized ideas that are mutually profitable.

I will shoot you a quick email in the next few days to set up some time to discuss this on the phone.

It's a natural and fabulous opportunity!

Continued success.

David J. Halberstam

Sample Letter #4

A general letter to open a door.

HALBY GROUP

Dear Linda,

I read the attached article about Pacific Life's continued commitment to Indian Wells. It sounds like sports programs are an integral part of the company's marketing plan!

The Sports Radio Network that we represent syndicates sports programming to 7,500 stations and reaches 150 million listeners every week.

The stable of broadcast rights is formidable. It includes football, the basketball championships, baseball, golf and more.

Sports sponsorships transcend media as you well know. In addition to attractive efficiencies, the embedded partnerships incorporate cause marketing, hard-hitting in-game on-air features and compelling merchandising support, a particularly critical element because Pacific Life's agents can make effective use of hospitality and the like.

I'm in the Los Angeles area fairly regularly and hope that you will carve out an hour to explore some outstanding opportunities.

Before heading west next, I will shoot you an email to set up an appointment.

I assure you that our meeting will be fruitful and that it will generate opportunities and ideas that you will want to explore further.

Continued success.

David J. Halberstam

Sample Letter #5

A letter to a marketer whom you met in passing and buys the competition.

HALBY GROUP

Dear Harry,

We met in the Delta lounge at Hartsfield in Atlanta a few months ago, got acquainted and spoke briefly. Both of us were trying to get home and we were fighting our way through weather delays.

Our company is the largest representative of sports sponsorships and sports media. We represent 32 professional teams, 3 professional leagues, international sporting events, college and more.

While we're delighted that your company is buying sports on radio and television and now owns prominent signage in arenas and stadiums, we're also absolutely confident that our represented properties with their millions of fans and pervasive reach would do a fabulous job selling your magnificent services. I don't doubt for a moment that we can embed your brand in the fabric of team programming and foster symbiotic partnerships that work.

I will take the liberty to call your office to set up a mutually convenient time to meet. I assure you that it will be an hour well spent and I will be mindful of your busy schedule. Promise!

Continued success.

David J. Halberstam

P.S. I was at Fenway Park a few weeks ago and picked up a game program. You told me you love the Sox. So please enjoy the publication. Hey, they're in the thick of things this season! Should be an interesting late summer and fall.

Sample Letter #6

Another letter to a top decision maker at a sponsor buying the competition.

HALBY GROUP

Dear Don,

Because my effort to cultivate your company's business began directly with you last January, I am reaching out again to bring you up to speed on our follow-up efforts within the buying hierarchy.

Members of our sales staff in Detroit have had several meetings with your sports marketing agency in Cleveland. They presented our stirring sports coverage and a highly customized program, one that would absolutely move the needle in the marketplace.

John, Steve and Beverly at the agency couldn't have been nicer and more generous with their time. Our proposal is on their radar and under consideration for inclusion in next year's plan.

Peggy of your staff in the home office has also been wonderful and has asked some uplifting questions.

I'm familiar with the great sports sponsorship programs you've authored in the past and I'm confident that we too can get the job done brilliantly and meet your lofty expectations. At this point, I would be grateful if you would be good enough to take an hour to meet with me. I will be in Atlanta the middle of next month. It would indeed be a privilege to visit and get your insight.

We work with many of America's biggest sports sponsors as you know and I would be happy to share case studies that will be of assistance to you in your decision making.

I will take the liberty to send you an email to set up an appointment.

Continued success.

David J. Halberstam

Sample Letter #7

Company X: buying sports on television, not radio.

HALBY GROUP

Dear Martin,

I reached out to you in early January in the hope of securing a commitment from your company to advertise on the national broadcast of the Big Championship. As I mentioned at the time, the broadcast is carried by 600+ stations in 100% of the country.

As it turned out, we reached you a bit too late. Plans were already in place. I know of the annual success you have had the last eleven years running spots in the telecast of the game.

While television coverage is far reaching, radio can be more pervasive. Television requires a deeper spend. There's truly no medium other than radio that better marries a brand with the sporting event and its play-by-play announcers. There's less separation of church and state on radio. Sports advertisers have an easier time bonding with fans on radio.

To be part of the broadcast fabric, radio gets it done! On-air sponsor features are indelible.

Now that it's May, it's time to plan for fall and winter!

As such, I would love to meet to explore the possibility of fostering a unique relationship to cover all of next season. We have the rights to not only the pros, we have college too. These indispensible and powerful sports broadcasts spice things up uniquely! Radio is more than just the AM dial. It's FM. It's satellite, it's mobile devices and laptops. It's local, it's national and international.

I will take the liberty to call your assistant, Jean, to schedule a mutually convenient appointment.

Looking forward to making your acquaintance. Many thanks.

Continued success!

David J. Halberstam

PREPARING TO CONTACT NEW PROSPECTS

Sample Letter #8

A general shotgun letter to an advertiser, otherwise impossible to reach on the phone.

HALBY GROUP

Dear Mr. Jones,

With all the business that you do at retail locations near some of America's great fishing spots, you know that anglers are a special breed.

Our company owns the rights to a weekly television fishing show and the Big Cup next fall. With the help of top professionals in bass fishing, viewers get tips and secrets and watch them put into action. It's insightful, practical information and it's delivered in a completely new format.

We can do a pervasive job, embedding Equipment Store X in many of the features of our programming.

Let me share some quick data:

• People that have gone fishing in the past 12 months are much more likely to watch fishing on TV than other major sports

• The market is massive. Some 50 million Americans participate and generate more than $50 billion in retail sales

• The audience is steady. Fishing and the outdoors are part of the American fabric

• We can offer Equipment Store X prime awareness and features on our telecasts

• Your visibility will be uncluttered. We limit our commercials

• We can offer hospitality at tournaments and events that you can use profitably

If you give me half an hour in your office, you'll be delighted that you did. In consideration of your busy schedule, I will be economical with your time and right to the key points.

I will take the liberty to reach out to your assistant Jodi for an appointment.

Continued success.

David J. Halberstam

Sample Letter #9

Another note to an advertiser buying the competition.

HALBY GROUP

Dear Jeffrey,

We haven't had the opportunity to meet. Yet I trust you know the network we represent. It's the fastest growing vertical sports network in America. Our sport is widely followed, as you know. The sport is about history, tradition and memories. We all grew up with it. It's our national pastime.

The program production is top notch. I challenge any network in America to produce programming as brilliantly as we do. Whether it's play-by-play or in studio shows, the quality is award winning. You know the personalities, the hosts and game announcers. They're all recognizable and best in class!

I see your brand all over sports television so I know that the sports space works for you as a medium. We can do it too, at impressive economies and in captivating fashion! The efficiencies are tremendous and the added value is far-reaching.

Some of the greatest companies in America are our clients. So by association, there's osmosis and a lot to say!

I will take the liberty to call your office to set up a meeting. I promise to be mindful of your busy schedule.

Many thanks. I look forward to meeting you.

Continued success.

David J. Halberstam

Unfortunately, many prospects require unending attention before they reply and establish a degree of interaction. If the idea you're presenting is particularly compelling and one that's a perfectly customized fit, keep plugging. In this case, your note is a respectful call to action.

Sample Letter #10

Trying to get an elusive prospect on the phone.

HALBY GROUP

Jack,

I have failed miserably to reach you on the phone.

I represent The Biggest Sports Network, America's fastest growing cable programmer. We're owned by the most successful teams in the country and a consortium of cable titans.

Can we get a minute on the phone to discuss a specific opportunity around basketball? It's an on-air feature around athletic injuries, sports medicine and more? Sounds perfect for what you're trying to accomplish!

Are you available sometime next week? Need fifteen minutes. That's it. I promise it will be worth your time.

David J. Halberstam

Sample Letter #11

A quick note to a marketing director to request telephone time to discuss a sports sponsorship.

HALBY GROUP

Laurie,

We represent The Biggest Sports Network, America's fastest growing sports cable programmer.

As you likely know, programming is made up of lots of play-by-play and some of the best personalities in sports and sports broadcasting. In addition to traditional commercials, we have the capability of embedding our sponsors organically, in the very fabric of our broadcasts. We're prepared to develop features to create a symbiotic bond between brand and programming.

I'm confident that we can partner on wonderfully unique things. How about product placement? Your office chairs would look beautiful in our studios. They would be nice and comfy for not only our hosts. Our well recognized on-air guests would look wonderful in them too.

Talk about top of mind and interchangeable identification! Can you imagine the visibility this would afford?

Can we get a minute on the phone next week? Would love your thoughts and guidance!

Please let me know what works best. Thanks.

Continued success!

David J. Halberstam

Gatekeepers, while often painfully indifferent, can be your best friends when they want to help. And it's your job to work these assistants through charm and loving care. Find out their birthdays, where they're from, are they married, do they have kids. Heck, it's human nature to want attention. And if they get to like you, they will help get you in the door. Break down the gatekeepers by whatever sycophantic means you choose. Always be respectful.

There are fewer human gatekeepers because of advanced technology and a shrinking workforce. But there's an inanimate gatekeeper called voicemail that has two middle names: Distant and Detached.

Sometimes it's helpful to phone the client's administrative assistant, even after you've left a message for the client directly. When administrative assistants don't pick up their phones, leave messages. Be clear. Kindly ask them to leave a written note with their bosses. It's a gentle command to action that might be acted upon.

Your voicemail messages have to be short, cogent and creative. But again, if a letter precedes the phone call, you're more likely to get through or at least get a response.

We know the old expression. It takes five calls to close a piece of business and most sellers quit after four. The more prospects you contact, the better shot you have of closing. It's a numbers game.

There are many appeals, exhortations and cajoling you can try by voicemail:

- "I know you're a good and caring person and will try to get back to me."

- "We want you on our team."

- "Our broadcasts are ubiquitous and we want you to be a part of them."

- Be unique. If the prospect reads his or her own spots on air, "We want you to read the disclaimer on-air." How about, "I'm Ed Miller, president of Interstate Batteries. During the game, you'll be hearing a lot more about Interstate. Right now, I want to tell you that these broadcasts are the property of 640AM under rights granted by the University of West Florida."

- You can have your lead announcer, a familiar voice, leave a message on the prospect's voicemail. Or you can be creative, "Hi, I'm Chick Hearn, forever the Voice of the Lakers. I haven't been alive for years, but I am keeping an eye on the Lakers from my broadcast position in heaven. The Lakers really want Chili's as sponsors. I'm in heaven where they serve Chili's delicious menu. Would you call my associate David Halberstam at...." Or, "Hi, I'm Chick Hearn. I haven't been alive for years, but I am keeping an eye on the Lakers from my broadcast position in heaven. The Lakers really want Apple as sponsors. What the heck is Apple anyhow? They weren't around when I was alive. Jerry West loves apples. He ate one before every game."

- You might want to send a game program with your phone number on it. It will remain on the client's desk for weeks. At some point, your call might be returned.

- How about leaving some play-by-play highlights on the target's voicemail? Use voicemail strikingly, to energize emotions and stir goosebumps.

Breaking tension and being somewhat disarming are the hardest things to do on the telephone. Humor, of course, can cut right through it when it works. But you don't know the person on the other end, and one person's humor is another's obscenity, so you have to be circumspect. It's risky.

Advertisers' responses on what would they expect to see or hear in a seller's first communiqué is covered in Figure 5.3.

Figure 5.3. Advertisers' expectations in a seller's first communiqué

Tom Peyton HONDA	Give me the key facts and, most importantly, targeting Information. We use experiential marketing to create an emotional connection with a specific customer. Know exactly whom your property reaches is key...more so than pricing.
Anonymous AUTO-RELATED MARKETER	Make sure that you show me you have taken time to know my business or a possible problem or opportunity I may have that you can help. Nothing turns me off more than a communication that was a mass email and you left the wrong company name in the communication, or worse, you used a competitor's name.
John MacDonald ENTERPRISE	Because a seller who does not have a relationship with me or my business will not know my particular needs the first communication should be attempting to start a relationship. In order to start a relationship, the seller has to convince me that he/she or his/her properties can have the potential to meet my needs/issues. Listening, not selling, is required.
Drew Iddings HERSHEY'S	Prove that you have researched my company, understand our go-to market model and can provide value to activate our strategy.
David Lim AMTRAK	A concise message that demonstrates the seller has customized his solicitation to my organization by referencing his organization's benefits to my needs. I would be more receptive to a friendly, respectful tone (not loud car salesman over-promising types) that doesn't appear to be a template for mass emails.
Julie Lyle HHGREGG	Don't be obtuse. It's one thing to try and capture my imagination with how you can make my life easier, save my business money, or accomplish something of real value. It's entirely different to be disingenuous or coy. The latter is annoying and I'll tune you out. Get to the point.
Stephen Quinn WAL-MART	Who you are and what you do.
Phil Wang WELLS FARGO	Basic premise....benefit and rough costs. Not interested in trying to see how much something will cost and finding out it's way out of our budget parameters.

Figure 5.3. *Continued*

Ed Gold STATE FARM	High level overview of the opportunity and why they see this as a fit for my brand.
Betsy Wilson UPS	A thoughtful reason why it would make sense for UPS to consider your property, as well as high-level detail on what you have to offer and the value of it.
Noah Syken IBM	Short...to the point...with some texture and information about a proposal...not just a request to talk.
Paul Hodges REGIONS BANK	That you understand my industry. You know about my company and our marketing strategy. You can demonstrate how your service adds value.
Rex Conklin HOME DEPOT	They need to have thought about my business and how their property can support our business goals.
Mark Eckert EDWARD JONES	Demonstrate an understanding of our business and strategy and how your product/service could be a relevant and impactful asset.
Tim Sullivan WENDY'S	Be brief. Tell me why you think it makes sense for my business. Demonstrate you know a little something about my business challenges. Tell me what makes you unique/compelling.
Brad Barnett NATIONWIDE	If done through the proper channels, I expect to understand the idea quickly, be able to relate it to our strategy, know if it can really be executed and the overall timing and cost of moving forward. In short, I expect to be able to know enough to make a decision and, if necessary, update relevant leaders internally.
Ellie Malloy JOHN HANCOCK	I don't need a specific proposal. Show me a concept, a menu of features and range of pricing. I'll generally respond if the vendor simply says, "I think this will work. If it's not a good fit, please let me know." Be less abrasive and more humble.
Michael Robichaud MASTERCARD	It would have to come through a relationship I already have.
Jack Hollis TOYOTA	The initial communication should demonstrate how your offering is a fit for Toyota, as well as showcase your expertise. I want to see an assessment of my industry, an understanding of my customer—or the challenges of reaching my customer—and my business. If the proposal is in direct competition with an existing Toyota sponsorship or vendor, the seller must include compelling evidence on why we should consider changing our current approach.

Chapter 6

Your First Conversation with the Prospect

Getting people on the phone today is more difficult than ever. Bill Sutton, the accomplished author and sports professor at the University of South Florida, describes how young people view telephones today. "In their world," he says, "the phone is a device for texting, creating and sharing contacts and last but far from least, a magic portal to learn about each other and ultimately connect with each other through social media."

Living and breathing secretaries have gone the way of the two-martini lunch. Friendly telephone introductions have been zapped by caller identification, turning sellers' prologues into distant voicemail messages of cold hard facts.

Today, even telephone calls are scheduled by email, so when you secure these conversations make the best of them.

Before the Call

- Practice into a tape recorder. Talk in front of a mirror. Hear what you sound like. See what you look like. What's your level of enthusiasm? Are you using the right intonations? Are you pausing for emphasis when needed?

- Do you find that when you're talking in front of others it weakens your concentrative powers? If so, talk in front of a mannequin. Don't laugh. It's good practice. It will train you to synchronize your verbal command and thought process while also engaging a live audience.

- You'll be poised and self-assured when you're fully prepared. You'll come across as confident, your tone will be strengthened, and your voice will resonate with conviction. As such, make sure your reservoir of top-of-mind facts is brimming with features of what you're selling and key challenges that the prospect is facing.

- Psych yourself. Whip yourself into a frenzy. It doesn't mean you should sound like a maniac, but you don't want to be sleep-inducing either.

- Passion is infectious but don't scream.

- Call from a quiet area. Avoid ambient noise.

- In general, it's best to call from a well-lighted area. It helps you concentrate on the mission at hand. It promotes a sense of purpose and cuts down outside distractions. Do everything to create a setting that will help you focus imperturbably.

- Unless there is a group of you on the phone, don't use speakerphone. You'll sound like you're talking from deep in a well.

- Set up a list of generally anticipated objections that you might have to field. You will then have some handy responses that you can fluently use to overcome doubts and hesitations.

- When you hear no, think twice. When asked what she finds annoying, the always pleasant Betsy Wilson of UPS says, "[Sellers] not taking no for an answer. I don't mind that someone is trying to be persistent to make a sale, but once the customer says no, you need to back off. It's not good to keep pushing!"

- Always be mindful that your goal is to get an appointment. You're not trying to close the piece of business when you first say hello.

Be Prepared for Objections

Objection: Budgetary
- This is always a difficult objection to overcome. As the line goes, "You can't squeeze blood out of a stone!"

- When you face targets whose budgets might be limited or exhausted, it might be easier to ask, "How do you manage to accomplish your goals, given these limitations? I'm sure it's not easy," instead of saying, "I hope you'll still find a way to include our program in your budget because we're the greatest thing since sliced bread." By positioning your question passively, prospects immediately appreciate that you, the seller will not be judgmental about their buying decisions and that you understand the budgetary hardship with which they have to contend.

- You'll be tempted to say, "Can we present a fail-safe program?" Not only is this highly unlikely to turn a discussion around, it will likely make the prospect feel uncomfortable and think, "Will this character bug me to death now?"

- The right thing to do is be completely disarming. After the prospect shares news of his budgetary restriction, remain hushed for a pregnant pause. Then, continue firmly, almost solemnly, "Understood."

- Instead of being insensitive by whining, sparring verbally or rambling on about the merits of your product, be empathetic. Once you say 'understood,' the prospect feels relieved that the bad news has been shared and that the worst of the discussion is over.

- Ask about the budgetary cycle and whether the accounting is set up fiscally or annually. It will help you map out your calendar for follow up. When you sense that the prospect's interest is sincere, you might raise the opportunity of billing sponsorship packages in subsequent accounting years. These are difficult deals because major companies are uncomfortable doing so. Yet, it might keep the immediate conversation alive.

- Ask whether, in the interest of future opportunities, you can get some simple and quick answers to a few questions. The prospect will probably acquiesce:

  o Find out when marketing planning begins for the next budgetary year so that you can have your presentation in place in a timely fashion.

  o If it's a big company with fluid activities, there are many budgets that support marketing and sales. There are dollars earmarked for sponsorships, for national media of various brands, for cooperative efforts with retailers, for sales promotion, regional funds, discretionary funds and more. Ask whether there are other budgetary sources and, if so, whom to contact. This might result in a lead elsewhere within the organization. We were shot down by a national product manager of a tire manufacturer one year. Yet it was suggested that we see the head honcho for retail operations. Doing so enabled us to secure an order for a proposal we had in place. Don't be afraid to ask!

  o What might also happen occasionally is that the prospect might have suggestions, directly or indirectly, of outside targets you should approach with your proposal. A direct lead might come in the form of a non-competitor. You might be told go see a Harry Johnson at XYZ Freight. The prospect will tell you, "He's a huge fan, and his company is doing well." An unintended lead might be, "I wish I had the money to do more. I know that a couple of our competitors are planning to spend." When you hear this, you'll take note and pursue referenced accounts.

- Finish the discussion by asking for a continuation of the dialogue. "Let's agree on meeting in a couple of months when you'll have a clearer view of future budgets. In the interim, I will send you a brief overview of our capabilities and related successes. If you want to take in a game let me know and we'll get a chance to do so." You're likely to get a favorable answer. You're also finishing up pleasantly. Follow up by sending copies of the deck both electronically and by snail mail.

Objection: Sports as an entity

Prospects demur, dismissing the value of sports marketing, strategically or tactically.

Having studied a target's objectives and recent marketing history in advance of the call, you can anticipate this objection. When there's no evidence of sports spending in the prospect's history, there's likely a reason. See whether the prospect's competitors are engaged in sports and learn the nature of their activity.

Ask for a minute to summarize sports' core competencies. They should be committed to memory.

- Best diversion for the country's constituency in times of war and peace, bad days and good and through economic headwinds and financial booms. Underscore the fact that, more so than any programming or entertainment entity on earth, sports marketing's capabilities are at unprecedented heights. Its tentacles continue to expand, and its reach continues to lengthen. Sponsors now enjoy an unmatched array of touchpoints and a ubiquity of visibility and fan engagement. The gender mix is narrowing, and the age cell of those engaged is broadening.

- If the sponsor's reach has a woman's skew, relate successes. For example, in Cincinnati, P&G's Tide and supermarket chain Kroger each sponsor Xavier basketball. They host basketball clinics for women, engage women and give P&G's buyers and sellers the opportunity to attend, hobnob and bond.

- If it's a health care insurer, for example, share the successes of other clients in the space that successfully use sports. Marketers are always interested in absorbing information about the competition. You'll want to talk about the naming rights commitment Moda, a health care insurer in the Pacific Northwest, made relatively recently to the Portland Trailblazers.

- Powerhouse GEICO sponsors college athletics, big and small, in order to have access to alumni and to offer them special insurance discounts.

- Talk about other companies that in the past have shied away from sports and, after reconsideration, have invested in the space: Chobani, Bose and CDW, to name a few.

- Portray the changing landscape and the technological influences on sports marketing. This is a good talking point if the prospect has been hesitant about sports. It's a capabilities update that the target can weigh as part of a reevaluation of sports marketing.

- A sports team is a piece of the rock, part of the community. The pro franchise or the college institution is viewed as a quasi-governmental entity.

- Sports are enjoyed mindlessly by the passive fan and stimulatingly by the consumed fan.

- Use buzz words like *passion, riveting, fascinating, spellbinding* and *gripping*.

- Programming that's DVR proof.

- Sports bond communities.

- Teams are a constant subject of innocuous conversation.

- Messaging extensions deepen—virtual ads, mobile marketing, real-time tweets, second screens, product placement, digital content platforms, embedded and branded content and other organic opportunities. Sports are not just about television and radio anymore.

- Traditional broadcasts still have mass audiences, and in-stadium signage is unavoidable.

- Talk about the engaging personalities associated with your entity.

- Hospitality and entertainment accesses are great assets to companies that have a layered selling hierarchy.

- Experiential and activation opportunities.

- Sponsors will benefit from emotional and unforgettable experiences.

Objection: Upscale target, we buy news not sports

There are two key points when pitching sports against news. The first is the environment. Sports are often positive. News is rarely. Sports are about engagement and joyous anticipation. News is about negative engagement and worried anticipation. A commitment to news is generally linear. It's a newscast and that's that. Sports are inclusive of a cobbling of broad media, hospitality, promotions, touch-and-feel experiences and digital extensions.

Furthermore, an in-depth analysis of research might prove that sports will reach a more stylish and educated audience. Use the subject to take up the prospect's challenge. Offer to provide a research report juxtaposing the two programming platforms. Suggest that you are prepared to present it at a meeting face-to-face.

Objection: Expensive

This might be a landmine or pitfall. It could be a way of simply saying no or it's the target's euphemism for, "I'll look at something cheap or discounted." This target might take a meeting but will haggle about price. Expensive might also be a code word for inefficient media. The prospect might price-point counter at 'a dollar a holler' and depress you.

Until you meet face-to-face, you won't know. Take the meeting and learn more. In conclusion, your goal is to tease the target sufficiently to earn an appointment. So don't go into a deep dive on the phone; promise more customized information when you meet.

If you've talked your heart out and the target is stubborn, move on. As former President Gerald Ford said, "Disagree but don't be disagreeable." Always keep the door open.

Listen, ask the right questions and get the prospect to talk

Listen! When you get a potential customer to talk or open up, pay attention assiduously. It's critical. Do so with every ounce of imperturbable energy you have. It will pay off handsomely. Prospects will, at some point, identify issues their companies face, programs they pursue, packages that have worked, sponsorships that were disappointing and insights into their decision-making process.

If you have the gift of a psychologist to get people to talk, you're blessed. It's a license to convert intelligence into cash. Getting prospects to provide an overview of marketing goals and of the inner workings of corporate decision making will provide you sufficient informational fodder that should trigger a sliver of an opportunity if not a bright big idea. Use this reconnaissance judiciously.

It might even be a throw-away line like, "Yes, our president went to school with Jay Wright [Villanova's basketball coach]." As a Villanova seller, your mind is already racing. You're saying, "I can't wait to have Wright reach out to the president." Or it might be something like, "We've done some sampling activation to get the young demo to test our product and it's worked." Knowing this, you will want to beef up the experiential components of the package you're concocting. If it's, "Our brand doesn't play well on radio," you'll keep standard 30- or 60-second commercials out of a proposed broader package. Even when the overall tenor of a conversation was cautionary, the copious notes you kept will help you navigate your way through future dialogue. It will tighten your direction on how to put your best foot forward.

In a 2012 *Miami Herald* article, Manny Garcia-Tunon wrote a meaningful piece on how to improve listening, the core to understanding goals and needs, account by account.

Quoting listening expert, Julian Treasure, Garcia-Tunon argues that listening has diminished in a technological world of video recordings, sound bites and 140-character tweets. He says the world favors these means of communications over what he calls an 'oratorical presentation.' Treasure says that, in society today, "We spend 60% of our communication time listening—but we're not very good at it. We retain just 25% of what we hear."

Treasure has developed a list of five exercises to "help us improve and retune our hearing and listening better":

1. SILENCE. Three minutes of silence a day in perfect stillness will reset your ears to better listen to subtle sounds. Digesting the subtleties of a discussion will help you assess your next step. We often make assumptions on what people are saying halfway through their sentences. Listen to the people through the entirety of their comment. He or she may not be saying what you think or what you're assuming. Letting someone finish also gives you more time to plan your response.

2. SOUND MIXER. Take time to isolate and listen to each individual track of sound you hear. It improves listening, according to Treasure. As such when you're in a room, isolate what each person says, who he or she represents, catalog and digest it. When hiring sellers, Bart Foley, VP of ROOT Sports Northwest gets right to the heart of the requirement of an applicant, "The candidate listens more than

talks." It's why Foley measures sales candidates by how they observe, listen and respond.

3. SAVORING. Enjoy mundane sounds, patterns of machines, dryers and washers. Each has a pattern. It's around us all the time. When listening closely, prospects talk in patterns and rhythms. Pick up when the patterns and rhythms change. You'll be able to decipher the nuances of speech that will help you interpret personal and corporate likes and dislikes.

4. LISTENING POSITIONS. This is truly instructive. In conversations, some folks are active and others are passive. Sometimes we are both active and passive in the same conversation. Active might be critical and passive is empathetic. In a first conversation with a client, you're more likely to be passive, more empathetic. You'll then want to be more active, by constructively confirming, affirming or offering counterpoints to what was said by the prospect. But show self-restraint. Wait until you've digested everything you've heard.

5. RASA. This is Treasure's acronym that reminds us to: Receive the information; Appreciate what is being said; Summarize the conversation; and Ask questions. In sales, of course, this means set your next steps. The broad message is understand what's going on in your prospect's world. It will help you construct salable packages.

Building an exchange of trust and developing an earnest commitment

Listening can prove particularly remunerative when you get prospects to open up and take you into their worlds. Like people overall, prospects have personalities. Some are open books. Others are guarded.

Hannah Storm, the versatile on-air television hostess who has keenly hopped between sports and entertainment in stints with ESPN, NBC and CBS, opened up on how she gets interviewees to talk. It's frankly not much different from a conversation you might have with a prospect or client on the other side of the desk.

In preparing to interview, Storm says, "Approach it like an adventure. Don't play out scenarios." For instance, after you complete your first question, let parties talk. Don't think about your next question. The answer to the first might lead to a better follow-up question.

So, if you're selling baseball and your target is in the midst of answering your first question (How do you evaluate sponsorships?), be flexible about your next question (Have you considered baseball?). The target's answer to the first question might lead to broaching a more advanced follow-up question.

Hannah talks about using the "velvet hammer" to ask tough questions, something you'll certainly have to do often with prospective sponsors. If an entertainer, for instance, was criticized in the press for poor off-screen behavior, Hannah might say, "How do you manage to deal with the recent criticism you've been facing?" as opposed to, "Are you actually guilty of the indiscretions the press suggests?"

Like sports sellers who engage in a few minutes of chitchat with prospects before delving into their sponsorship presentation, on-air interviewers spend time trying to find common ground with interviewees in the greenroom. Hannah says she usually asks guests something harmless like where they ate dinner. It enables the parties to share innocuous personal experiences through which to build a bond and set the tone for less defensive dialogue once the interview begins.

In sales, many prospects are less trusting when they feel they are being influenced. When they feel they're being influenced or sold, they'll feel compelled to check and double-check facts before being convinced. Presenting gently, using emollient phrases and turning words outwardly will help you achieve your goal. Instead of "Our sponsorship program is a great fit," you might say, "Have you considered the benefits of developing a bond with a sports property?"

In *Give and Take*, Adam Grant identifies those who employ "powerless communication skills" to achieve their purposes. Powerless communication skills might include speaking softly and respectfully. Grant relates the experience of an optician who, in the spirit of powerless communication, says, "My mindset is not to sell. It's to help." Interestingly, the optician observed by Grant outsells his colleagues who keep trying to hard-sell their wares.

Businessperson, author and speaker Kevin Kruse elaborates on business dialogue.

In a one-on-one sales setting with a prospect, sponsorship sellers might want to paraphrase what prospects just told them, simply to confirm that they perfectly understand the gist of the marketer's comments and directive. It speaks volumes of a seller's professionalism and affirms a commitment to understand the mission and go the distance to make the proposed partnership a glittering success.

Ask for specifics not generics. Instead of asking "What do you think?" how about asking "What did you think of our integration suggestions?" or "Isn't our suggested arena promotion pretty intriguing?"

Conversation Preparation

- Before you pick up the phone, indoctrinate yourself. Appreciate the power of the property you're pitching. The contents and tenor of your pitch have to be so ingrained that, if you're woken out of a deep sleep, you should be as ready and as fresh as a spellbinding preacher. The phone is informal. It's audio only. All you have is a canvas on which to paint a verbal word picture. Be locked in and prepared. Healthy fear or slight nervousness is fine.

- Ray Kroc, the founder of McDonald's, said, "It requires a certain kind of mind to see a beauty in a hamburger bun." Your job on the phone is to convey the roar of a crowd, the heart-throbbing finish of a tight game and the fans' emotional connection with sports and sponsors. If you sound detached and too restrained, you're better off selling Ore-Ida potatoes.

- Prepare a quick outline of what you'll cover. But ad lib your pitch, of course. Have quick attention-grabbing factoids: "Did you know that on any given Saturday in the fall, we have 250,000 listeners to our football broadcasts? Did you know that we have 250 stations on our network?"

- At your disposal, you should always have an abbreviated yet intriguing "elevator version" of your pitch. You never know when you'll be rushed off the phone or you will luckily catch a prospect for a minute on a call that wasn't pre-scheduled. It's always good to have a quickly crafted sales pitch that will earn an appointment. This might even be helpful when you bump into people on a train, plane or, yes, the elevator.

- Before the call, visualize your audience. See if you can get a photo online to picture what the party you'll talk with looks like.

Specific "Target" Example of Preparation

- Sometimes when talking with potential customers, it might be helpful to open the conversation with a cheerful comment about the company. It shows you care and that you're prepared. Do something simple. If you were to have pitched Bose in mid-2014, you would have wanted to jumpstart your discussion by alluding to a bubbly report in *Consumer Reports* about the $300 Bose QuietComfort 15. The magazine said that Bose "is still a top dog among noise-canceling headphones." Historically, Bose used the late iconic radio personality Paul Harvey to launch its first major national marketing campaign. An indomitable radio endorser, Harvey had strong fingerprints on Bose's exponential growth in consumer markets.

Bose's competitors have grown in recent years, including Beats, a subsidiary of mighty Apple. It was likely the reason that Bose had a recent appetite for sports sponsorships, committing to both the NFL and the U.S. Ski and Snowboard Association. These sports sponsorships were bought to fend off youth-centric brands Skullcandy and Beats. Competitor Harman bought the NBA.

Compassion

- If the prospect's company is struggling, be compassionate. In 2014, if you reached out to State Farm, a company based in the heartland and as American as apple pie, you should have been cognizant of unprecedented problems. The insurer suffered a $700 million judgment for replacing damaged parts with shoddy goods, and its life insurance unit agreed to a $100 million settlement for misleading sales practices in California. Know the issues if they come up during a conversation. Forewarned is forearmed.

- Be prepared for all eventualities. In 2014, Congress looked into a 2012 NASCAR sponsorship by the National Guard at a cost of $26.5 million. The net result of the investment was not a single signed reservist. Not one. The Guard did get 24,800 prospects from the program, but only 20 met the necessary qualifications. None signed.

If a savvy prospect reads *USA Today* or other newspapers, this notorious failure might be raised during the phone conversation. Tough to answer, right? NASCAR officials defended the effectiveness of its sponsorship programs by pointing to successes of partners Coke, Sprint and Toyota.

The fact of the matter is that the latter three are essentially promoting their brands. The National Guard, though, is expecting results from a "command to action" program. It wasn't a branding campaign.

ROIs are best measured through a metric taught in Advertising 101. Advertising's mission is to develop awareness. Did The Guard's message reach the preset numerical goals it set? Are NASCAR fans aware of The Guard's offering spelled out in the content of its messaging? The fact is that the visibility drew close to 25,000 Guard applicants. That's not chopped liver.

The achievement of sales goals is evaluated differently. Other factors come into play: What is the value proposition; how much time do I have to allocate to the Guard; what's the pay; what are the results; will this commitment fulfill my military obligation; is there war; will I be drafted?

While all this is good in theory, at the end of the day, the fact that no one signed is tough to defend.

So always be prepared, know current issues and how to react if asked.

Material and being organized for the call

- Have material that you'll need at your fingertips; a cheat sheet on the prospect's history, needs and product lines. You'll, of course, want notes on your own property, subjects you want to address, buzz words and product benefits of a sponsorship with the entity you're representing.

- Keep thorough notes and make sure they're easily accessible. One location might be under contacts in Outlook. If the client mentions a key person in the decision-making hierarchy, his wife's name or a new brand that will be introduced, make sure to mark it down. You'll want to reference it next time.

Personality and breaking barriers of unwillingness

- Be yourself, your authentic self, your unique you. Don't be someone you're not. It will manifest itself immediately. You'll be uncomfortable and so will the potential client. Radiate with confidence in a conversational tone. Don't try to sound like the late sonorous Don Pardo of *Saturday Night Live*. On the phone, you're being judged by word and voice as opposed to in-person visits where face and manners play a role. Be genuine, natural, enthusiastic and knowledgeable. Use individualism, magnetism and charm.

- One thing that might break some tension is a common interest that bonds you and your prospect. Try one or two common threads, restaurants, recent sports development, traffic or weather. If you get pushback on small talk or the prospect is taciturn, segue into the business discussion.

- Don't try to impress the target with how brilliant

you are. A. G. Lafley is CEO of P&G, a company lifer who revitalized the company after some down years. His mantra is plain and simple, hardly anything sophisticated, "Consumer, the Boss." *U.S. News and World Report* quoted an unnamed board member, "Lafley isn't the sort of guy you meet and think 'wow,' but he wears well." So cold callers shouldn't try to overimpress on their first call.

- The phone can be distant. Even a landline is informal. There's nothing like eyeball-to-eyeball contact, where you can reach out and touch the flesh. Try to break the voice-only barrier with a happy telephone face. If you've ever listened to the Hall of Fame sports announcer Dick Enberg, it sounds like he's always smiling when he's talking. People want to talk to folks who are happy. Joy and happiness can be infectious even over a cold telephone line. When you're on the phone, do smile when you talk; your inflections will produce a psychological smile.

- One day, I was sitting in my Manhattan office when this poor construction worker seemed to be hanging precariously from a ledge. I began describing it to a prospect with whom I had just gotten on the phone; it got his attention. Everyone likes a good story, as long as it's short.

The Call

Early in call
- When asked the perfunctory, "How are you?" I might say something innocuous like, "I'm just trying to make a living." The person on the other side of the phone can relate. He or she is trying to do the same thing. It also segues into the serious business discussion you're hoping to have with a would-be prospect. You're trying to break the tension.

- One quick way to forge a connection is asking targets where they are from or where they went to college. It invariably leads to a colorful exchange of memories and reminiscences. Targets love talking about the favorite teams of their youth. If you find out the prospect is from Columbus and a fan of Ohio State, get into it with him or her. If it's a city you're familiar with, bring up a familiar venue that was mutually enjoyed. It would understandably help if you have some of this intelligence before your first vocal encounter. This way, when you ask these questions, you'll be prepared to answer them. LinkedIn, of course, is a marvelous source.

- Don't be limited. Yes, you're selling sports, but if the prospect likes business or pop culture, go in that direction to break the ice. Switch to something innocuous. Find common agreeable ground before getting to the meat of the matter: sports.

- If your instinct says the prospect is distracted, preoccupied and doesn't want to talk, it's best to call back. Ask the prospect when you can call again.

- Unless the target is a busy no-nonsense individual who doesn't have any time to be entertained, you can spice things up with some quick humor. It's difficult to read the person on the other end, but if the response is tepid, be very businesslike. Never be a wise guy.

- Learn fast about who is on the other end of the call. Are you talking to the decision maker? If not, politely and not imperiously ask who else should partake in the call. Naturally, don't ask the question if you're confident that the real deal is on the phone. If you do, you might be pawned off on someone with no power to say yes. In today's world of split responsibilities, sponsorship and media might fall under the bailiwick of two managers with separate titles. As such, you should, of course, contact the appropriate party.

First impressions

- Fast food, fast cars, fast world and fast deals. The first 30 seconds are critical. That's when you'll have the most attention. At the start, the prospect is listening to you carefully.

- Share a quick, hard-hitting but easily understood vision statement, one with a lasting impression and image. It shouldn't be alarming, yet it should perk up ears. For instance, "Our property has five of the most appealing qualities that are on all sponsors' wish lists":

  1. We have a rich tradition, and we win every year.
  2. We sell out our stadium.
  3. Our broadcasts get the highest ratings in the marketplace.
  4. Our sponsors enjoy one of the best ROIs in sports.
  5. Our sponsor retention and satisfaction are the best in sports, bar none!

- "I will take five minutes to provide a little color, and when we're done, I will request an in-face meeting so that we can make a customized proposal."

- Say something uplifting. If you're selling baseball in the dead of winter and there's a thaw in the air, how about a bright reference, "Touch of spring in the air today. Let's go out and play two. Baseball season is around the corner."

Keep your eye on the goal

- Remember the goal. You want an appointment. You want to get in the door. That's it. Seek direction and hope to establish dialogue. Don't try to close the piece of business on the phone. Don't try to hit a home run; you'll strike out.

- Be disarming. Demonstrate a hearty willingness to help and counsel the prospect. It puts the client more at ease and will enable you to allay indifference or antagonism. The first call is about courtship not marriage. You're not selling $10 items on a Manhattan street corner. Sponsorships have big tickets. It generally involves a multi-tiered decision-making process.

- At some point early in the call, be clear about the objective: a face-to-face meeting. The rest of the conversation should be spent reinforcing your intention and strengthening your request for a meeting.

- Accept the fact that the gestation period is a lot longer than a short phone call.

- Forget the play and movie *Glengarry Glen Ross*. It's not ABC (always be closing). You're trying to get an appointment. No more.

Call content

- Orate with eloquence and compelling brevity. Economize the framework of your thoughts. Don't ramble. As Dr. Martin Luther King said, "Eloquence is the stirring gift of restraint." Don't say anything foolish.

- If applicable, talk about product placement to deepen a connection, mention a couple of examples of embedding sponsors and other effective participatory relationships.

- When you're representing a number of different sports properties and the prospect has viewed your menu of offerings and grants you a meeting, ask the client to tighten your direction and suggest where he or she feels the opportunities sit. It will enable you to better prepare a customized deck for the meeting.

- Use magical and galvanizing words. Don't be overdramatic, yet always paint a picture, "We reach the whole market through a pervasive multi-platform program." It suggests a powerful reach, an upbeat sports environment and one-stop shopping. "We'll embed your brand in the sports culture, we'll put together something that's intrusive, something that's driving, a program that transcends media and stimulating elements that are multi-platform."

- Speak slowly, clearly but firmly, fondle your words, like the product you're pitching is delicious. All the person on the other end knows is that you are product X. You want the prospect to think that product X is tasty and sweet.

- Always have diversion tactics ready. If you see that the conversation isn't headed your way, swerve totally off subject and then circle back after the dialogue is a little less icy. If you don't have an answer to an objection, have stock deviating factoids. This way, you'll be able to buy time and prolong the conversation.

- Focus on key issues, but don't fire a fusillade of questions. Ask more open-ended questions and wait for prospects to complete their thoughts. Don't interrupt. After there's some trust and a level of comfort, keep the discussion on track. Be logical and concise.

- Lower your voice reverentially when you're referencing recent prospect developments that made news: earnings, expansion or solid *Consumer Reports'* reviews. "I see where you're now expanding out West. It's impressive!"

- Assure the prospect that your property will have skin in the proposed sponsorship, that there's an equal desire to make the partnership proposal work as synergistically as John Stockton and Karl Malone. Use the word "we" to build the bond. "Together we can do great things." Talk partnership. "We'll partner on great programs. We'll collaborate as true partners. When we meet, you'll hear about what we can do for you and how a partnership can benefit your company."

- Always assure prospects that, if you're granted an appointment, you'll be mindful of their time. It's another disarming commitment that you won't be lounging around their offices endlessly. People are busy.

- Again, never, ever use scripts; you'll sound foolish. The listener will be uncomfortable, and the call will have an awkward tone to it. It will sound lethargic and unnatural. The great announcer, athlete and broadcast coach Marty Glickman saw me do my on-air open to a basketball game by reading it from a direct script. He told me to rip it up and to extemporize. When Mike Shannon started broadcasting Cardinals' games, his mentor was veteran Redbirds' play-by-play voice Jack Buck. Early in Shannon's broadcasting career, Buck sat near Mike in the booth and saw him consult his notes quite a bit. At a commercial break, Buck covered up Shannon's notes, pointed to the field and said, "Mike, the game is down there," suggesting in no uncertain terms that he report what he sees on the field and not count on his notes. In other words, be natural. Sound like a human being, not a robot.

- Sell ideas, not specific packages, on the initial phone call. You can sell specifics at the presentation. The phone conversation is to pique prospects' interest and get in front of them.

After a while, you'll sense where you're headed on the phone. You'll get a "sixth sense" of when to pause, what's working, what's not, when prospects are drifting and how to engage them and reengage them when their minds drift.

- Don't tell them everything that you know. Keep most of the details for the in-face presentation.

- You might want to occasionally throw in the person's name as you talk. "Jim, I've got to tell you...." Don't overdo it because it will get annoying. But for emphasis and to keep the prospect engaged, sprinkling his or her name into the phone conversation won't hurt. If it's a tricky first name, make sure you're pronouncing the prospect's name properly.

- Sponsors like to be in good company. Let prospects know the company that they'll keep. Power by osmosis, whether they're Fortune 500 companies or well-respected local businesses. You might want to list three or four of your sponsors. They're generally big and impressive companies, nationally and locally. For instance, "We would love to have you join Coca-Cola, Cadillac and the Georgia Lottery." Whether the prospect is big or small, it wants an association with winners.

- If the prospect equivocates on granting you a meeting, dig into your bag of tricks. Tickets and sports keepsakes have emollient powers. If you can secure sports collateral of some value, tell the prospect that you will bring some team goodies for his or her favorite charity when you come to meet. Or you might simply offer something tantalizing that can be reduced to one sentence. "When we meet, I'll bring over a souvenir game program from last season that you might want to keep in your office."

Pitfalls

- When the client gives you an appointment but asks to see your presentation or agenda ahead of time, be vague, send bullet points and talking points. Never send pricing. Don't give prospects reasons to cancel the meeting later because of sticker shock.

- Back off when you see a prospect is adamant and won't meet, don't try to elbow your way in. Be amicable. As Stephen Quinn, CMO of Wal-Mart said, "I've had people get very angry that I'm not interested, begging the question, Why did you go into sales?"

Silent prospect

- Just as when you present in person, don't get trapped or intimidated by prospects' stoic silence. Make points enthusiastically and await responses. Don't be afraid to pause. Know when to shut up. If you ramble, you'll stumble right into trouble. Just ask specific questions for specific direction or probe through open-ended questions to find more opportunities.

- The sonorous Harry Kalas, longtime voice of the Phillies and NFL Films, was known to economize his words. When asked about it, Kalas said, "If I have nothing to say, I just shut up."

- When you get someone on the phone who's terse, don't be intimidated and don't try to be cute. One man's lyrics are another's obscenities. Be different and be creative. Don't ever resort to dirty or racial jokes. That's an absolute no-no. Years ago, unfortunately, it was routinely accepted. Remember the Polish jokes on *The Tonight Show Starring Johnny Carson*? Times have improved.

While you don't want to be intimidated by silence on the other end of the conversation, don't be terrified to say something spontaneous. Study politicians on the stump. Memorize aphorisms—innocuous or bold, relevant or extraneous, heartwarming or pithy—expressions that will help you connect with the target. The late author and poet Maya Angelou said, "I've learned that people will forget what you said, people will forget what you did, but people will never forget how you made them feel." More than anything, you're selling yourself. That's paramount.

End of conversation

- Find some common ground of a personal nature that you can use to maintain future dialogue before you say your good-byes. If you later see something of interest about the prospect's competitor, send it. If there's something you can share judiciously without betraying a confidence, call, email or text. Build trust and respect! Over time, it will pay dividends. Don't dwell, agonize or harp. Don't despair. Move on. Just make another call, research another prospect or write another email or letter.

- At the conclusion of the call, when prospects share views that are not particularly gratifying, be nonjudgmental, "Thank you. I appreciate your overview and your objectives. I will think about our conversation and get back to you."

- Learn from each experience. You just don't want to make the same mistake twice. Did you get the prospect to engage? How did you handle the interaction? Did you sound rushed because the prospect sounded busy or preoccupied? Did you use the right buzz words? Were you warm and engaging? Did you address the prospect's goals? Did your ideas resonate? Were you able to get the appointment? Was there something you could have said that wasn't said? How do you follow up?

- Even if you didn't get the appointment, you might eventually win. If the prospect encourages you to stay in touch, it's a good first step.

Voicemail

- If the call was not pre-set and you're still attempting to reach the prospect for the first time, leave an enthusiastic message, and leave your number twice. Phil Wang at Wells Fargo will tell you that one thing he abhors about sellers is "they name drop other executives in the company and think that is the way in." Be humble.

- Don't give your number so fast that it can't be digested or written down. Tell the prospect that you'll call again. This might say to the target, "If I don't call back, I'll get another 20 messages." After you've left a voicemail, you might also send an email to the prospect saying that you left a detailed message on the phone and you look forward to a return call.

- If need be, leave voicemail at odd hours. Call on weekends leaving messages on office lines. Your message should be clear. Let the prospect know that you're calling on Sunday morning because you care and you wanted to share a helpful thought.

Chapter 7

Making the In-Face Presentation

Not everyone gets in-face dates. Jack Hollis, vice president, marketing, Toyota Group, suggests alternate ways to communicate. "There is less of a need to meet in person. These days, I like to familiarize myself with sellers and their product offerings by visiting their websites, participating in WebEx's, using their databases (if a research company, for example), watching their industry videos, and checking out their social channels. Word of mouth and referrals from colleagues in the industry also go a long way."

In other words, consider yourself fortunate. You've worked hard to earn this date, be buttoned up. It's your day for a hearing.

Do Your Homework

- Confirm your appointment and scout your audience. If your boss or someone senior is joining you, you don't want the embarrassment of showing up and finding out that the decision maker isn't available. If you are bringing senior members with you, let the prospect know. Two or three of you walking into an appointment might be overbearing to a prospect sitting there alone.

- Have the key points of your presentation deeply ingrained, both the selling qualities of the entity you're pitching and the solutions you're proposing to help the corporate target attain its marketing goals. How do you plan to keep the prospect and potentially a room of people focused? Feel it and play it out in your head.

What to Include in a Presentation

Presentations are like clothing. Everyone wants them to look beautiful but beauty is in the eye of the beholder. You might or might not have the capabilities to present an extraordinary deck replete with bells and whistles, yet the flashiness of a pitch is generally commensurate with the tag price of the sponsorship proposed. If you're asking for a seven-figure deal, stapled sheets of paper placed in a manila folder won't do.

You control the substance of the presentation. Consider this punch list for starters:

- ✓ Activation schedule
- ✓ Brief history
- ✓ Case studies
- ✓ Competitors of prospect in space and with your entity
- ✓ Components and breakout of each element (media, tickets, hospitality, appearances, signage, etc.)
- ✓ Core competencies
- ✓ Creative requirements
- ✓ Exclusivity provisions
- ✓ Explicit social media proposal
- ✓ Gauge ROI
- ✓ Growth—exposure of sports property, ratings, circulations, digital reach and the like
- ✓ Hospitality
- ✓ If media entity, proposed program schedule
- ✓ In-facility promotion and visibility
- ✓ Intellectual rights and restrictions
- ✓ Experiential activity plan
- ✓ Qualitative data to support compatibility
- ✓ Seasonality and timing
- ✓ Substantiation of audiences
- ✓ Tag price and terms
- ✓ Value proposition

Psychological Preparation

- On the morning of the presentation, when you're showering, shaving or exercising, picture yourself in front of the target. It might be with the one person with whom you've set the meeting or a larger group made up of members of the marketing team. Envision the scene. How will you respond to the setting, whether it's just you and one prospect or you and a room full of prospects? Often, if there's an official calendar invitation sent to all attendees you'll have a handle on who'll be there. You might want to look up the titles of those attending so you'll know what each person does. Doing so, you'll be prepared.

- Ease up. Be natural. Sponsorships are hardly an exigency. Clients don't have to engage in sports marketing. You're not selling medical equipment, file cabinets or needed parts for a Boeing jet. The company you're pitching can fly with sports or without it.

- Be in command like a pioneer, a crusader and a spellbinding preacher at the pulpit. Commit presentation points to memory. You don't want to have to glance at a cheat sheet every minute. Plan an arsenal of words to describe various points in your pitch. Yes, don't be reluctant to study a thesaurus. If you use a fresh word, you might keep the room engaged longer. Find and memorize synonyms for common words that are often overused. Include metrics, analytics and other support data that are product generic and prospect specific. Understand key elements in depth so that you'll strike your audience as being astute.

- Be prepared to address unenthusiastic questions or downright expressions of doubt. As heavyweight fighter Mike Tyson said, "Everybody's got a plan until they get hit." How will you counterpunch challenges and doubts that are raised at the presentation? Anticipate these vagaries a day or two in advance of your meeting with management and sales-support departments in your office.

- Be rested. Get a good night's sleep. If you have a presentation, rehearse it over and over. Envision what the conference room will look like, where you'll sit, what you'll say and how you'll say it. If you can role play internally with your teammates, do it in a similar setting in your conference room.

- Selling is a natural extension of who you are. Have faith in your ability to sell the virtues of your product. A Miller Heiman study revealed that 66% of sellers overall completely believe in the goods, products and services they sell. Perhaps. Yet when you walk in on the call, you better demonstrate that you're 100% behind the product. Give examples of how you and your on-air talent, when applicable, believe in it. In New York, legendary broadcaster Marty Glickman touted Hess on Jets products. With permeating conviction, he would read scripts. "Hess, for quality gasoline and service, you'll like them for the little things they do!" It made listeners, many of whom were on the road, keep an eye out for the next Hess station. After all, when a beloved and respectable figure like Glickman speaks compellingly about Hess, how can anyone go to a competitor? Show you believe and why, how other sponsors believe and how they've put their budgets behind the product you're pitching.

Bring with You

- If you're representing a team or a league, bring some paraphernalia—T-shirts, caps and goodies—that will serve as reminders of your offering. Dr. G. Clotaire Rapaille, a sales psychologist, points out that, yes, the prospect uses the cortex, the intellectual side of the brain, to know that the T-shirt is a ploy. Still, the prospect's limbic, the emotional side of the brain, is indeed influenced by the thoughtful leave-behind.

- Bring some cookies or other sweets. There's no better way to reach prospects' hearts than through their stomachs.

Attire

- No one sells alike and no one buys alike. But don't dress ostentatiously or iconoclastically. Dress neatly and fashionably. Wear well-tailored clothing made of quality material. Don't get hung up on brand names. The prospect won't be searching your attire for labels. If you look good, you'll feel good. It builds your confidence. If you feel successful you'll be prosperous. If you have issues with body odor or bad breath, address them before you walk into your appointment. Mints and deodorants should be part and parcel of your work bag. Tie sales in America have dropped like a brick. Still, wear one unless you're told in advance not to overdress and that the dress code is business casual. If so, look the part. Whether you're wearing a neat pair of jeans, khakis, an expensive dress or a three-piece suit, carry yourself with a military-like posture. Your shoulders shouldn't be slumped. It gives off an impression of a wimp.

Transportation

- This sounds trite. Be on time. I can't tell you how many young sellers underestimate the time it takes to get from here to there. Leave loads of time for traffic or getting lost, GPS or no GPS.

- If you will drive your clients to lunch in your car, make sure the interior is clean and neat. It tells them who you are. If your car exterior is dirty, make sure it's washed beforehand. If you need gas, fill up. Make sure your tires are not low on air. The devil is in the detail.

- Don't count on a two-seater or Smartcar. In Houston, Texas, on one of my career's early calls, I took a new client and his agency contact to lunch in a rental car. I tried to save my company money, so I rented a sub-compact. It wasn't a good idea. The client was tall and broad shouldered. It pained me as I watched him from the driver's seat. His knees were crunched against the dashboard and his shoulders were stiffened uncomfortably. Through it all, I'm trying to make conversation with someone I'm meeting for the first time while glancing at a guy squeezed like a pickle into a tight jar.

- Don't drive like a maniac either. On that same Houston call, I didn't realize that I was driving like one whose roots are indeed in New York. When I accelerated on a right turn to beat a pedestrian to the crosswalk, the client sprung upward grazing his head against the car ceiling. "You can get arrested down here for doing that," he bristled. My driving didn't win any brownie points with him.

- You never know. Over the course of a career, many odd experiences occur. One snowy day in Detroit, my client's car got stuck in a heap of snow in an open parking lot. The car wouldn't budge out of the spot. I had to get out and push the vehicle from behind while my client maneuvered the steering wheel. The good news was that it worked. The bad news was that slushy snow spewed all over my suit pants and dress shirt. I had a dinner engagement that night, so we had to stop at a dry cleaner in the Fisher Building where I sat half-stripped for an hour while my clothing was dry-cleaned. Funny, these unforgettable experiences can sometimes build bonds too.

Before Walking through the Prospect's Door

- Before you walk in, pump yourself up again. Broadcaster Marty Glickman would read Chaucer before going on air. He did so to warm up his mouth in advance of having to pronounce tongue-twisting words while calling a fast-paced game. It's all about preparation and execution. Be convinced that the components of the proposed package are perfectly suited for the prospect. Instill this in yourself first. If you're not convinced, how will you sell it effectively?

- Don't cross the prospect's entrance half-asleep. Walk in with enthusiasm and with alacrity. The presentation isn't a solemn pageantry—it needs life. You don't want to preside over a soporific.

When You Arrive

- In the waiting room, befriend the receptionist. Glean what you can from conversations in the visitor's waiting room. Knowledge is powerful! There might be other sellers in the waiting room as well as sports and ad agency personnel. Build up your Rolodex.

The client isn't available
- When you walk in, you might have the misfortune of being told by the receptionist that the prospect has been called into a meeting and will be unavailable to see you. You're informed that an associate will take the meeting. Instead of seething, knowing sadly that the associate or underling doesn't have the power to purchase the goods you're peddling, take the meeting. Yes, you don't want to be relegated to a staff member incapable of making a decision, but show equal enthusiasm. Make sure the decision maker is copied on follow-up notes.

Find a reason to schedule a second meeting that includes the decision maker.

- Another approach is to take the meeting with the underling and use it simply as a fact-finding mission. In other words, ask questions to learn more about the prospect's goals and objectives. In such a case, don't make the presentation you've prepared, keep it in your briefcase. Opt instead to reschedule the presentation itself for a later date with the decision maker. Use the meeting with the underling as an informal exchange of ideas and to understand the prospect's mission. This might actually be a blessing in disguise. You'll pick up intelligence from the underling in the first meeting and use the reconnaissance you picked up to tweak your presentation for the second visit, which will include the decision maker.

- When in doubt, if given the choice, the best thing to do is to reschedule and, if possible, to do so right then and there with the decision maker's administrative assistant. You have to play it by ear.

- When you learn upon arrival that the meeting is abruptly canceled, never, ever lose it. As crestfallen as you might be, wear a smile and don't let your energy wane.

Leave nothing for chance
- Make sure your electronics work. You don't want any glitches when you set up your presentation in prospects' offices or their conference rooms. It's nerve racking and terribly unsettling. You'll want to throw yourself under a desk or table. You created a polished and bright presentation. Don't let it implode on you because you forgot an accessory or the conference room isn't equipped with Wi-Fi.

In client's office

- When you settle into the prospect's office, take an inconspicuous look at pictures on the wall, on bookshelves and on credenzas. Pictures tell stories. They break the ice. You'll see not only what the client's interests are—skiing, photography or golf—but also diplomas, plaques or other accolades. If there are sports pictures on the wall, you'll quickly learn the target's rooting interests. It is said that Lou Lamoriello, the glitteringly successful New Jersey Devils executive, discouraged his employees from posting family pictures on their desks. He expected an unbending focus of Devils' employees while they were on the job and wanted no distractions and no diversions. But Lou's view is the exception, not the rule. If there are family pictures, they speak loudly about the person you're visiting and often serve as common ground to launch small talk. Memorabilia and other personal effects strike a chord too. Take note.

- Read backwards but be discreet and subtle about it. You might see the names of your competitors on the prospect's desk, whether it's a PowerPoint deck or a trinket. Never ever touch anything on your host's desk, but be quick to observe notes, files and decks of interest without violating a visitor's code of behavior.

- In today's setup, particularly at ad agencies, the physical configurations of offices might resemble classrooms. There's row upon row of counter space. Often, media people are cramped into a row separated by glass partitions at best. There's full transparency and little room between neighbors. Meetings with vendors are held in conference rooms or elsewhere. So, trying to figure out what makes people tick through pictures and such is more difficult today.

Office or conference room

- When presenting to one or two people in an office, it's a little less formal and the setting is more relaxed. You can truly present conversationally unlike in a conference room where one way or another you're 'presenting.' But nowadays, because of the open space offices, it's most likely that sellers will be steered into a conference room even if a meeting involves only one or two members of the prospect.

- The two challenges a seller faces in an office are interruptions and finding the right angle where prospects can comfortably see the presentation. The distraction issue is inherent in the very setting of being in a private office. Phone calls, email and folders on a desk catch the prospect's ears and eyes disruptively.

- You might want to suggest a trip to the office cafeteria, especially if it's not lunchtime.

- In a room full of people, all you need is one antagonist to poison the presentation. In a quiet office, it's easier to warm up an individual client to the idea of a sports initiative. The limitation is that, in the corporate world today, decisions are often made by informal committees through a multi-layered hierarchy. You would like to present to all decision makers at one time.

Settling in, the first greeting and the presentation

- Start with a firm handshake. Don't squeeze the client's hand into submission. Don't extend a limp hand either, the one that feels like a wet rag. You'll give off a weak impression. Tell the prospect that you're honored to be there.

- You can open with a striking comment if appropriate. If, through prior email or telephone communication, you were given a set of criteria to cover, address issues germane to the request. You might say, "We won't talk about challenges and opportunities today, rather, solutions!"

- If you're being joined by a senior member of your management team, let him or her provide industry trends. When MLB Network was my client, we were chasing Subway's business. I brokered a lunch date with client Tony Pace and MLBN president, Tony Petitti. Pace appreciated Petitti's 30,000-foot view of the vertical sports networks and his early vision for MLBN. It helped us firm up a lasting partnership.

- Before you begin a slide presentation, which is very impersonal—the *Wall Street Journal* calls it 'corporate karaoke'—warm up the party with brief, simple and innocuous conversation. The operative word in today's efficient environment is *brief!*

- As folks settle in their seats, try to bond through common geography and sentiment. Maybe you root for the same pro team or college. Maybe you live in the same neighborhood. Maybe you put up with the same traffic pattern every day.

- In the right setting, and if time permits, one emollient question in a one-on-one meeting with a vice president might be, "How did you rise through the ranks?" People love talking about their accomplishments. It breaks the ice.

- If you yourself came out of the buying side, at either an ad agency or sports marketing group, let the room know that you can see the world from their buying lens. It will build your credibility.

- You might tell a quick success story about a sponsor that the attendees are familiar with or a colleague who's mutually known.

- In a one-on-one, you'll be able to tell in the first couple of minutes by quick assessment if the client is distracted, distanced or tuning you out. You might want to say, "I'm happy to reschedule when you'll be less pressed."

- Often presentations to a group will include top people, associates and underlings. There will be good cops and bad cops. Be prepared. Disarm your challengers. There's often someone who will give you pushback and put you on the defensive. Don't ever sound self-protective or engage in debate. Show self-restraint even after innuendos and insinuations. You can apologize from time to time, but don't sound weak and suspicious either. You can underscore facts and leave the determination to those attending your presentation.

- Sometimes the prospect's challengers in a room are needy and are looking for some attention. You can adroitly throw them off-kilter by saying that they're raising good points. Tell them you're happy that they raised the issue and continue by addressing the point raised.

- You might want to use some innocuous humor but be careful—comedians flop too. Comedians will tell you that the business of comedy is hardly a laughing matter. If you want to crack a joke, the least risky ones are those that are self-deprecating.

- A presentation to a room, unlike a one-on-one directly with one prospect, is much like public speaking. It's more impersonal. It's like a congregant's relationship with a priest or minister, it's through the pulpit.

- Command the room. So check yourself in the mirror beforehand. Speechwriter Alan Perlman suggests that presenters be aware of their posture and never pitch their heads in front of their shoulders. Most importantly don't jingle coins in your pocket. Not only is it distracting, it makes everyone nervous and uneasy.

- In any setting, eye contact is important. Fix your eyes on the entire audience, occasionally stopping to look at just one attendee.

PowerPoints, Data and Graphics

- Data visualization is compelling. It makes prospects feel more comfortable about pulling the trigger if their guts say do it. The numbers serve as substantiation that defends buys. Include relevant research, but slides shouldn't be full of arcane or detailed data. Keep things simple. As Perlman laments, "Elaborate, attention-grabbing visuals undermine the unique power of a speech as one of the human-to-human communication forms we have left." Perlman suggests that when a PowerPoint is used "keep the number of slides and the amount of graphic ornamentation to a minimum." He adds, "PowerPoint must complement and supplement—never repeat—the words coming out of your mouth." Numbers are often impossible to digest from a screen, so leave copies behind for everyone, but don't distribute them until you're done. You don't want attendees jumping ahead of your slide-by-slide PowerPoint. You might also follow up by sending electronic versions.

- If the presentation is similar to the ones you've given recently, spice up the slides. Uniformity might lead you to uninspiring repetitiveness, which can weaken the vim and verve of your pitch.

- Use the data slides as further evidence. For instance, "Let me again show you why the proposed package is on target with your goals and why it's unassailable." As you get to the next slide, again slowly and not overbearingly, "Once again the data is convincingly impressive!" When you present a profile of your fans, "The qualitative is a perfect fit. The research is overpowering." Engage your audience. "Aren't you impressed? It's eye-popping!"

Short pause, "Think about it for a moment," while pointing to a compelling number.

- Yes, 75% of what we learn is visual. Experts say that it doubles the length of time we remember things. Words with pictures are six times more likely to be effective. But stay away from complexities. Leave it for later, to the folks at agencies who deal with the tapestry of measures. They're like the gremlins who oversee the procurement process, otherwise known as torture. No matter the verbal embroidering, the buyers will pick apart the numbers.

- In this millennium, attention span is short. Use quick factoids and short sound-bites. Don't overdo it. Less delivered means more is retained.

- Think of the play-by-play announcer, firing a fusillade of stats. His game call is rhythmic and almost musical. But the play-by-play announcers who aren't very good spew so much data in a heartbeat that the listener has a headache digesting it. Most importantly, the listener won't remember a thing the announcer said, perhaps not even the score because there's just a flood of statistical data.

- German psychologist Hermann Ebbinghaus uses some compelling numbers of what audiences forget:

  o 40% of what they hear by the end of the presentation

  o 60% by the end of the day

  o 90% by end of the week

Ebbinghaus claimed the numbers are even larger when under stress. He said, "Messages should be simpler, catchier, distinctive and have immediate relevance." Think of the great sports broadcasters again; they don't spew stats throughout a broadcast. Who in the world will remember them? The great ones, like Vin Scully, Red Barber and Mel Allen told a couple stories that are ingrained in listeners' and viewers' minds. Audiences are more likely to remember information that's vivid or material that's traumatic. Say things that are succinct and memorable. Don't make the mistake that the motor mouth announcers make or as the late Bob Prince said, "They stat you to death." Worse yet, on the sales side, your target's mind will drift. You'll lose his or her attention. The client is a human being not a computer.

Video

- Video is fantastic. If you're representing a television network and you can demonstrate an overview of your entity in animated form, perfect! Do it, though, within time constraints. If there's a feature embedding a sponsor and it's cutting and driving, by all means show it. If the prospect and potential dollars are sufficiently large, convince your management to mock up a customized feature involving the prospect. It will excite some people in the room. There's no better tease. When MLB Network presented a package to Ace Hardware, it went through the effort of creating a customized and suitable feature that made the client's toes tingle.

- If you're reaching out to executives who've been around a while and are sports fans, think about invoking an applicable old highlight or two. Show the video or, if you have audio only, play it against old still photos. A trip down memory lane about a team or sport the prospect loves is an uplifting reunion with good times gone by. The potential client will emerge out of the meeting refreshed and more upbeat.

Trust and Watch What You Say

- Speak with a smile. It sets a positive aura. Be disarming. Speak with conviction and out of pragmatism. Don't sound overly serious; be agreeable, upbeat and understanding.

- Mark Twain said that he could live two weeks on a good compliment. So can prospects. If you can, compliment a client in as sincere a tone as possible. It might be when you see pictures of a prospect's children or are aware of a recent promotion.

- Remember that the client isn't always right, but the client always makes the decision. So you'll be fighting a delicate balance particularly when the client has the equanimity of a cold disposition or an inscrutable personality and challenges you during your presentation.

- Because your own believability with prospects is vital, try to make an emotional connection at the presentation. To that end, don't exaggerate or use hyperbole. One slip up on a fact or detail, and the prospect will question everything you've said.

- Once prospects feel comfortable that you've studied their businesses and that your presentation reflects the homework you've done, you can ask in an open-ended tone, "Why do you buy marketing and media packages the way you do, and what are you trying to achieve by doing it that way?" People love to talk about their jobs, their accomplishments and their missions. Once they open up, glean assiduously. Don't interrupt. Interpret nuances and keep copious notes.

- Don't bad-mouth your competition. If you don't have anything nice to say, say nothing. People won't trust you. In the words of former Defense Secretary Donald Rumsfeld, "Trust leaves on horseback and returns on foot."

Tenor

- The fact that you're already sitting in a client's office or conference room is the clearest indication that the target has an understanding for sports. Otherwise it's unlikely that you'd be there. The tone of the meeting will, as such, likely be energetic, stirring and encouraging.

- In sports, more than any other form of entertainment or media, you're selling hope and anticipation! You're selling an unending plot. It's DVR proof. Personify the enthusiasm and gusto. Play up the unknown. Characterize what the proposed relationship will be like. Paint a picture. "You'll bring your customers to a hospitality suite or the ball games." Show pictures of the suite. Talk about prospects striking deals with their own new prospects in the suite. "It's like a golf course. You'll have your customer's ear a whole night. You'll have contests and your names on the scoreboard. It's absolutely driving!"

- Think of magical words to pierce home the value of osmosis. "By associating with the Yankees, you'll galvanize your distributors and you'll have an interchangeable identification with a team that has the greatest heritage in sports." Take three or four words to use in your presentation to punctuate a point and raise heads. Words that resonate include recognition, solutions, respect, exalted company, building internal morale, winning environment and owning a piece of the rock.

- If you will talk about on-air drop-ins on either radio or television (e.g., "The second quarter of today's game, the second 15 minutes played, is sponsored by GEICO. A 15-minute call might save you 15% on car insurance."), underscore it. It's intrusive. It's inaction. It's an organic sound bite, the mind doesn't drift. We're living in a short-bite world. The message is delivered hard and done so multiple times.

It helps build the sponsor–team bond! Play samples of recordings.

- Keep the discussion on track. Don't digress much. People don't have time. What you find interesting anecdotally, others might not. Be upbeat, interesting and succinct at the same time. Translate compelling developments into common denominators, those that are measurable. So, for example, if a pro team has promising draft picks, you can talk about more newspaper coverage, a buzz in the community, higher broadcast ratings and a run on up-front ticket sales. You might illustrate your point by using numbers mirrored elsewhere, in other markets where high draft picks resulted in better ratings and greater turnouts for sponsor programs.

- Bob Costas says that "sports is drama without a script." Don't read your presentation from a script or stick to an inflexible agenda. Don't memorize a speech or make it sound like you're reading from a teleprompter. Be yourself, even if you occasionally stumble over words. It beats sounding stiff.

- Do things within your sphere of understanding and within your comfort zone. Be realistic and not overly optimistic. It's difficult to gain confidence and be persuasive when a client doubts your claims or your ability to deliver.

Presenting to a Group

Decisions to purchase sports are often fueled by emotion and sentiment. If you're meeting with lone decision makers predisposed to sports, you'll naturally be ahead of the game from the moment you shake hands. These prospects are more likely to digest your presentation with their hearts and an appreciation of the robustness of sports sponsorship's tentacles. They're eager to make a bold statement, to do something different.

But be prepared when you're escorted into a conference room populated by team members. They're generally number crunchers and emotionally distanced. Team members don't easily embrace new ideas or change. The status quo is convenient.

Getting a room of team members to think against the grain is a seller's nightmare. Asking team members to express individuality in front of their comrades in an open room is a crucible. Suggesting to functionaries that they include a sponsorship on a marketing plan is like asking them to underwrite a trip to Mars.

In a 2007 column in *SportsBusiness Journal*, John Genzale wrote about "team players"—like those conference room attendees digesting sales presentations. He noted that they contribute to the mission of a business but seldom inspire excellence. Doing something *different,* like sports sponsorship, takes confidence, leadership and gumption.

Genzale writes that "team players don't inspire organizations, bright ideas do. Different isn't always better, but better is always different." In other words, the room won't be filled with the *different* who lead. It will be filled with 'team' players who will cast doubts. The 'room' won't buy into the intangibles and emotional value of sports. The room will see shortcomings and inefficiencies. If the team isn't convinced, you'll suffer the pain of their bureaucratic paralysis.

Prospects often won't buy sponsorship programs because of their fear of failure of new ventures. As such:

- Downplay risks, an anathema to those often caught up in doing the same old, same old.

- The pitch has to carry a fail-safe theme, through reach, activation, affiliation and efficiency.

- Assure prospects that the ROI is plausible and that their investments are unimpeachable and irreproachable.

- Case studies instill confidence. Use empirical success by similar businesses in the sports space. Sports sponsorships are not inexpensive, so talk about the trappings of achievement elsewhere.

- Find the protagonist in the room to lead the charge and to help you navigate the program through the buying channels. It takes the paragon of persuasion to turn around an embedded way of thinking, one that does not include sports.

Additional Thoughts When Addressing Multiple People at Once

- If there are a bunch of participants around a conference table, get their names, roles and titles. Get business cards. Your capital is your network. Don't be afraid to ask who does what.

- Be uplifting, express to the audience that you're seeking a unified commitment from everyone around the table.

- Be consistent. Don't send mixed messages. Make a statement and lay out the proposal. Pause. See whether there are questions. Don't prattle and babble. Young sellers have a tendency to do so. It shows strength and maturity when you don't.

- If the room has few questions, create one or two to trigger dialogue.

- Read the room. If they're tuning out, either speed things up or wind things down.

Engaging

- Sound like a partner, not a pitchman. Couch your language and facial expressions and construct your language in a collaborative manner. Function with dynamic energy and unshakeable endurance. Show that you're generous and have a hearty eagerness to make a symbiotic program work. Light up the room.

- Although you've done your homework and your customized presentation addresses the mission that is spelled out in the prospect's brand brief, still ask the questions, "What's your problem? How can we help?" It shows you care.

- Make sure to get good seats near decision makers where they won't be distracted. The mere fact that you're sitting nearby where you can make helpful eye contact will help you build a bond.

- Don't shake your chair back and forth or twitch your legs. Look loose. You want the prospect relaxed and focused on what you're saying, not on how uncomfortable you are.

- Take a pair of tickets to an upcoming game. You might want to promise to leave them behind if the attendees put away their phones during the presentation. You can also promise to keep the presentation down to an absolute minimum number of minutes by coaxing attendees to completely engage.

- Once you've made the presentation and clients acknowledge your familiarity with their business, you might pose a simple question like, "What do you need from us?" or "What would you like to see from us next?" You might even say, "Fill me in, please, on a sponsorship program that worked and why it worked. What were some of the components that were fruitful?" or "How do you go about evaluating sponsorship opportunities?" It's always helpful to get the decision maker to talk.

- Listen. Listen. In the words of former Secretary of State, Dean Rusk, the man who was America's top diplomat at the height of the Cold War, "The best way to persuade others is with your ears."

- Part of listening is observing. Watch movements. Inscrutable faces are hard to decipher, but various postures might be indicative of clients' points of view. They're not always reliable signals but do take note. Some physical gestures might provide a constellation of symptoms. Observe the non-verbal response when you talk about hospitality at big sporting events, connections with popular athletes, names on stadium scoreboards or creating interchangeable partnerships with local sports institutions. Exaggerated movements by prospects might be an expression of passion or interest in the emotional subjects you're addressing. Then again, prospects tapping their feet or rubbing their knees might suggest that they're growing impatient and want to end the meeting. Rubbing their noses might mean they're not being completely honest with you. It's tough to know for sure, but observe body language.

Visualize Success

- Show examples of what it is like to have the target's product on the scoreboard.

- Demonstrate social media success through contest interaction on mobile devices in a stadium or elsewhere.

- If it's a partnership that allows the use of a team logo, show examples of success.

- When you present case studies, go through program implementation.

- Show that your entity has produced more than it promises, overdelivering program elements and media rating points to existing sponsors currently on the roster.

- Use testimonies by other clients.

- Use video or slides of experiential activation.

Underscore the Uniqueness of Sports

Talk about the prospect's competitors and what they've done in the sports space. Ears will perk up. So, if you're going in to see Haggar Slacks in Dallas, tell them what Levi's and Wrangler are doing without betraying confidences or sharing spending levels. (Also see "Objection: Sports as an entity" in chapter 6.)

Keep stressing the positives, the uniqueness of sports.

- Sports afford sponsors an opportunity to activate cause marketing, enabling advertisers to raise money for charities while at the same time fostering a bond with millions who will view sponsors as responsible corporate citizens.

- Promotional opportunities forge bonds between brand names and top-of-mind sporting events.

- Sports are upbeat. News often produces lachrymose moods. Many entertainment programs are not efficient against men.

- Keep talking about the abundant and cherished resources of your property and the reach and popularity of the personalities associated with your franchise. Personalize it. For example, "To me, growing up in Chicago, Wrigley Field was the Sistine Chapel. To have an interchangeable relationship with the Ivy Wall is powerful!"

- Camaraderie-building parties prior to games build momentum within the channel of distribution and are perfectly suited for internal incentive programs.

- Communities, big and small, love sports. Sponsors will be interwoven in the activity of team-beloved institutions.

- Imperturbable fans hang on every development in the stadium, every angle the camera delivers, every word the announcer utters. They devour everything they can in social media and on sports news websites.

- Remember to point out that radio, still vibrant, was the original social media vehicle.

- Play-by-play commentators are gripping and commercially cogent. Often their very voices are implicit endorsements for advertisers' products, goods and services.

- On television and radio, customized features embed advertisers into the fabric of the action.

- Teams and leagues have rich heritages. Talk about sponsors historically wrapping their brands in teams' and leagues' logos.

Bumps on the Road and Caveats

- Don't be intimated by silence, even when it's stony cold. If you're out of material, don't say anything. Silence is a powerful tool. Don't buy into it by saying something regrettable or damaging. After a few seconds of silence around the room, you can humbly but comfortably chuckle out loud, "I hope you're mentally all saying yes or it is a pregnant pause of silent affirmation."

- If you feel that you have to say something to keep the conversation going, reinforce something generic like, "There's no better way for you, the potential sponsor, to understand your own customers than through sports where you'll have unmatched access, entertainment and hospitality opportunities."

- If it sounds like you're presiding over a soporific and few seem engaged, ask for a show of hands once or twice when you're making a group pitch. "Has anyone had a chance to see our telecasts?" "How many of you are Lakers' fans?" If there are some compelling numbers you're presenting, you might say with excitement in your voice, "What do you think of those numbers?"

- Like chess, be prepared for how you'll answer objections, doubts and hesitations. Anticipate them and retort confidently. If you're running out of answering runway, something generic will do. For instance, "We'll have to get you out to a game and let you experience things for yourself so that you can envision what it will be like to be a part of our family."

- You might be able to assuage a doubt or answer a quick question. Be very familiar with all the core competencies, research and capabilities of your entity so that you can respond alertly and pertinently.

- Remember that you'll be dealing with an assimilation of two sets of thoughts. The emotional and visceral involvement of sports will often galvanize the room while the numbers, efficiencies, affordability and question of overall fit of a sponsorship will get the room into their game faces. The latter will be a harder component to tackle. But sell through all of it—the emotion and the qualitative and quantitative values— with equal zest. Make the bean counters and gremlins in the room feel comfortable.

- If you've presented a compelling merchandising element, for instance, fix your eyes on one party in the room and ask "Is that important?" If there's a suggestion to alter a specific component, say fine and promise to send a modified version of the presentation after the meeting. And by the way, anything you promise to do at the meeting, you better do it. And get to it with alacrity. It's just another way you'll be judged on your reliability.

- When there are specific questions or potential objections that were raised in conversations leading up to the meeting, address them without being prompted to do so by the prospect. Don't wait until they're brought up. Get them out of the way. Don't try to hide them under the rug or kick them down the road. You won't get an order until these issues are satisfactorily resolved.

- Don't think of the prospect as an adversary. Walk in thinking about a win-win. The pitch isn't a debate. Don't try to outwit and outsmart prospects and certainly don't underestimate them.

- Come with a few timed presentations, a longer one, a moderate one and a shorter one. Often, when you walk in you'll be told that you have a hard stop in 30 minutes. Don't panic. Be ready. Sometimes you'll want to be up-front and say this will be a 45-minute presentation so no one will start staring at their watches and make you feel uncomfortable.

- If the client launches a fusillade of objections and it's obvious that there's no interest, be graceful. Chock it up to a tyranny of the status quo. If there are objections that you just can't answer, say, "I'll get back to you" and then kick yourself in the behind that you were ill-prepared to answer them immediately.

- Learn to tell the difference between a target agonizing, harping and dwelling about the negative and a target haggling and quibbling about components and the tag price. The latter might be buying signals and the former might mean the prospect doesn't want to move forward.

- When you're in front of the group, let the people in the room feel that this is the most important thing you'll do all day and that you're excited and privileged to be there. As former Vice President Hubert Humphrey said, "Don't talk about your father on Mother's Day." It's the prospect's Mother's Day. Talk about nothing but the prospect. Make everyone in your audience feel special.

- Never take customs for granted. While jet travel and the immediacy of the Internet are closing gaps on regional nuances, what's accepted in New York might not be conventional elsewhere. Just because it's moderately acceptable to push your way onto a New York subway car, other cities would find such action repulsive.

- If prospects say they will mull the proposal internally and with their agencies, don't push for an answer. Ask for a timetable and if there's anything more that they need from you.

- If you sense a genuine interest or incipient buying signals, begin to convey a tempered sense of urgency. If nothing more, it might help you set up the next meeting or agree on imminent next steps.

- If the presentation went exceedingly well, come on a bit stronger. "Please let me know what's needed to get the order," or at least, "When do you think we'll be able to wrap this up?" They'll respect you for asking without nagging. Leave it there. Remember that the seller proposes and client disposes. Don't make prospects uncomfortable.

- If they ask you for a "drop dead date" on a decision, give them a soft one. It buys you time and options to use later. You can also suggest a "hold," which gives the prospect the inventory until a specified cutoff date. It gives the target time to get all approvals in place. Historically, a "hold" is somewhat of a verbal commitment that precedes an official "order."

- Sports media is unique in that often no signature is required for single silo deals, from multimillion dollar Super Bowl television buys to local media sports sponsorships. It's a word-of-mouth industry. One critical piece of advice: word of mouth in the sports business travels quickly. Keep your word. If not, it will kill your reputation. Socrates said, "Regard your good name as the richest jewel you can possess."

Jargon and Language

- Yes, be current. Know today's media and sponsorship nomenclature, but limit your jargon and acronyms when first visiting a client. Arcane acronyms will sound presumptuous and turn prospects off. Your audience might not know every buzzword, and if they do, they'll say to themselves, "Who is this wise guy?" Be modest.

Assessment, Departure and Follow-Up

- Before you conclude the presentation, do a brief summary that starts something like, "Let's talk about the takeaways from our presentation." When you're winding down, thank the participants and tell them you are looking forward to doing business. It's a gracious and strong valedictory.

- If the presentation doesn't work out, be cordial. Just keep the doors open and keep thinking of how to make it work. Life is a journey and selling is a destination.

- As a follow up, send testimonials from current satisfied clients who will extol the effectiveness of your product and will sing your praises as a trusted and caring seller and as one who watches over clients and all components of a sponsorship program.

- Sports are partnerships of joy and happiness. Yes, the backroom and agencies often have to sign off, but the rigid rules of engagement or procurement *generally* don't apply. There's a softer feel. Prospects can be less unbending when they assess the value of qualitative and intangible components of sports packages. The exercise allows for subjectivity. There's no absolute formula. It's more art than science.

- After the first presentation to a prospect, it's good to internally brainstorm additional deal points if the proposal has to be beefed up to close the deal. It's called hip-pocket assets. So, if and when momentum slows, there are new elements you can broach to reenergize discussions.

- In 1969, when Buzz Aldrin was settling into the rocket capsule for his historic voyage to the moon, word is that he sarcastically quipped, "It makes me feel very comfortable knowing that every part on this spaceship was bought in compliance with rules of governmental procurement, buying at the lowest price!" So, there is Aldrin putting his life in the hands of a governmental functionary who was out to save a penny. The sports decision-making process is more emotional because of added-value, hospitality and promotional undertakings. Thankfully, not life and death.

- If you were unsure before the meeting how the prospect felt about sports marketing, and you left the meeting with the sense that the target is indeed convinced that an affiliation with a major sports institution is worthwhile, you're ahead of the game.

- There might be others involved in the buying process of the company you're pitching. You'll want to cultivate them too. Don't be afraid to ask your contact if there's someone else within the organization that you can call, one who will influence the decision. Don't let your contact pass along the deck blindly to that person and have it evaluated on its bare merits. You want to pitch it. Knocking on the door of a secondary party at a prospect with the referral of your first contact makes it easier to get an appointment. Referral calls are always easier than cold calls.

- Labyrinthine companies will sometimes have several pools of budgets that can be tapped. Getting steered in the right direction by the advertising contact will help. For instance, Nissan corporate bought a national Olympics package one year using a budget committed for regional use. With some urging by the seller, the regional head used his discretion to cobble regional budgets to make national buys.

Yes, there's nothing like pressing the flesh. But, as Jack Hollis of Toyota said, he welcomes participating in WebEx's. WebEx provides videoconferencing and more, an ability to include a deck in the video presentation. So, if your target is reluctant to take an in-face meeting or your boss won't pay for you to travel out of town, video beats audio! You can sit at your desk in a UPS golf shirt if you're pitching UPS. You can sip a cup of Dunkin' Donuts coffee if you're pitching Dunkin'. It adds a personal and warm touch. It produces the face behind the voice. Video conferencing is also available by Skype, Facetime, and Google Hangout. To use video effectively be sure to have proper lighting to reduce shadows, a good mic, quality in-ear headphones or a wireless headset, a steady surface, the right height and closeness, and the necessary trappings and accoutrements.

Ask good questions and keep plugging!

Chapter 8

Overcoming Objections and Rejection

From Henry Fielding, "He that can heroically endure adversity will bear prosperity with equal greatness of soul; for the mind that cannot be dejected by the former is not likely to be transported with the latter."

Accept it as a given. In cold calling, the frustrations come at many fronts and they come incessantly. Some sellers are dealt better hands than others, but no one has it easy.

Fears of Cold Calling

We all have our fears. For some, it's going to the dentist. I have had 12 implants. Not easy. In the early years of cavities and root canals, my dentist gave me laughing gas. When people tell me that they're afraid to cold call, I ask, why? The prospect won't extract any of your teeth.

Hard Work Pays Off

For runners, it's painful to get up at the crack of dawn when cold winds howl. The last thing runners want to do is put on their running shoes when it's 20 degrees. What motivates them is the thought of that wonderful high they'll enjoy when they're done with an arduous five-mile jog. Similarly, if you as a seller, keep your focus on the magnificent high you'll enjoy when you do close a new piece of business, it will get you through tough times that lead up to the big moment. Think of what it will be like to have praise heaped upon you, the respect you will be paid around the office and the commission check that will follow.

Challenges Run the Gamut

Where do the issues begin? These are just five of too many to enumerate.

- "I can't get decision makers on the phone."
- "They promise to get back to me and they don't."
- "They assure me that they'll see me and then they duck me."
- "I show up for an appointment and they're not around."
- "I finally get the client on the phone after two months, and he tells me to call back in the morning. I call back in the morning, and the voicemail message says he left on a business trip for a week."

Developmental orders don't come in daily. When you score, you'll be serenaded. Big cold call orders make careers. They're uplifting. They're springboards to promotions. They get the recognition from the big boss.

Tough Objections and Difficult Times

Be positive and match the right industries with the right economic times.

- If you're in front of clients who oversee marketing for high-end items, remind them that the wealthy buy luxury items during recessions too. They do so to better cope through disheartening stretches. In 2010, for example, when the country was tiptoeing its way out of the greatest economic collapse since the Great Depression, *Fortune* ran a headline, "Record Sales for Recession-proof Luxury Cars." The article reported that Mercedes' sales climbed 15% in the first half of the year and BMW's sales were up 13% for the same period.

  Not to say that teams didn't suffer during the Great Recession and that there weren't significant layoffs, yet sellers had opportunities to refocus their directions, chasing advertising categories and industries that were a beacon of hope in economically restrained times.

- There are businesses that flourish in difficult times and will consider resourceful packages. They include auto-after products—tires and batteries, for instance—and the retailers that sell these items, like AutoZone and NAPA. When fiat currencies come under pressure, there are those peddling gold. There are bankruptcy attorneys opportunistically selling their wares. Credit card companies might step up their spending. Zappos, the Las Vegas-based e-retailer enjoyed a 20% sales increase during the crippling economic downturn of 2008. Keep your finger on the pulse and your eyes on the industries that are likely to succeed under varying economic conditions.

- Most importantly, during challenging markets, teams, leagues and rights holders need good sellers, those who can develop new business to replace sponsors that are forced to bow out.

- If you haven't gotten a firm response to your proposal, remain patient and encouraging as long as there's positive sentiment within the buying hierarchy. Don't give up either if the prospect is still visibly engaged in sponsorship and advertising elsewhere. For instance, when the company is running an ad campaign, the theme of which is compatible with what you're offering, keep clawing away. If you're thrown out the front door, try the back window.

- If you feel that the momentum of your discussion is slowing, find out why. If possible, ask the prospect what is necessary to bridge the gap. Address solutions. Get to the root of the problem. Address key objections. Remain positive. Use phrases like, "When we partner," "Let's think about this" or "Let's revisit it and maintain ongoing dialogue."

What Not to Do

- Objections of all sorts will always surface. Prospects will tell you that their budgets are completely depleted. They might tell you that they don't buy the core sports medium that you're selling—be it signage, television or radio—or that they completely stay away from sports sponsorships.

  These are difficult objections to overcome in the middle of the budgetary year, once marketing goals, partnerships and formatted programming are in place. Don't sit there and debate or engage in polemics. It won't work. You'll just annoy the target. Some sellers will go on using these scare tactics:

  o "You'll be dropping your best salespeople."

  o "Why are you giving your competitor an opportunity?"

  o "Out of sight out of mind."

  o "Companies don't grow by saving dollars."

They can alienate the prospect.

Instead, be positive. Suggest revisiting the opportunity during the budgeting and planning process of the next budgetary year. Talk about starting discussions afresh.

Redirect the conversation. Remind the target that sports historically have been a magnificent diversion in good times and in bad. During World War II, many of the world's best athletes honored their country by joining the ranks of the military. The NFL was, for that matter, depleted of some stars to the point that two teams had to consolidate. The Steelers and Eagles merged in 1943, and the Cleveland Browns actually suspended operations.

During the height of the war, there were forums around the country to decide whether or not to shelve sports' schedules entirely. It was determined that sports were a beneficial distraction for the psyche of the American citizenry.

So no matter the challenges, politically or economically, sports are warmly received by corporate America and the country's population.

Don't Lose It

In the years I was selling baseball on radio, Cruex struck me as a good target. Heck, the brand's selling season peaks during the warm summer months and Cruex is a male product. It took me a lot of time to track down the elusive brand manager who was then based in Rochester, New York.

Once I did, he told me that he was coming down to New York to see the ad agency and would 'happily' meet with me then. Long story short, we agreed to have breakfast in the Roosevelt Hotel dining room.

Fifteen minutes after our scheduled appointment, there was no sight of him. I called his room, and he picked up in what seemed to me to be a stupor. I immediately suspected that he might have gone out on the town the night before. He apologized perfunctorily and promised to be down in 15 minutes. After another 30 minutes and no brand manager, I called his room again. This time there was no answer. So I checked with the front desk and was told that he had checked out. Nasty!

Fuming, I ran over to the ad agency and pulled him out of a meeting. I wanted him to know that what he did was despicable. While I didn't raise my voice or use profanities, he got the message loud and clear. I wasn't going to allow anyone to step all over me and get away with such shenanigans.

Frankly, what I did was wrong. There was little to be gained by storming into the agency. Although I got the anger off my chest, I could easily have done some long-term damage and then heard about it from my bosses. It would have been best to bite my tongue and move on. The prospect had to live with his insensitive action.

Lobbying for Support within and Outside of the Prospect's Structure

Always study and be mindful of the prospect's organizational chart. Without offending the decision maker at the corporate office, lobby sideways within the company, the prospects' own customers or other influential executives in the decision-making chain. Call up distributors, retailers and jobbers. They can provide your sales effort a lift by putting in good words to decision makers or sharing with you some of the decision maker's hot buttons. Be selective and don't be overbearing. If you are, you will either get a kick in the behind or your effort will backfire.

When Madison Square Garden Network pitched Gulf Oil a Rangers' sponsorship, the owner of the brand in Massachusetts, Cumberland Farms, made it clear that it would use Rudy in Long Island as a sounding board. I don't think Rudy ever had a last name, but he owned a couple of key filling stations off the Long Island Expressway. They were apparently pretty important to Gulf and Cumberland. Rudy must have liked the deal because Cumberland corporate approved it.

Once the deal was done, MSG Network was instructed to send all tickets and goodies to Rudy. When Rudy was on the phone with MSG Network, he would often talk while he was at the cash register or between conversations with customers filling up their cars. Heck, Rudy helped get the order. MSG treated him like a king.

Referencing Other Successes

In bad times, potential sponsors can be reminded of an historical empiricism. Kellogg and its competitor Post cereal were neck and neck in the early 1930s at the start of the depression. Post cereal cut back and Kellogg remained visible. When the economic slide ended, Kellogg had the loyalty and emerged dominant.

Remember that great leaders like Ray Kroc at McDonald's and Lee Iacocca at Chrysler commanded, "More advertising," just when times were slow and market conditions needed it.

In the dark days of 2008 and 2009, Tom Murray, CEO of Perio, owner of Barbasol, maintained if not increased his advertising and sponsorship expenditures. The decision paid dividends, as his business continued to grow. RE/MAX, the national realtor, continued to sponsor sports as the real estate market tanked in 2008.

Locally, if it's a matter of budgetary constraints, suggest to the potential client that the difference between a big store and a little store is the size of the ad budget and the opportunity to build a bond with great sports institutions.

David vs. Goliath

When you're pitching against a bigger company, a more popular sport or a more heavily followed team, convince the client to "bet on the jockey not the racetrack." Convince the prospect that you'll give it your all, that you'll go the distance for the account. Look prospects straight in the eyeballs and promise not to let them down. It will go a long way. You'll be the big fish!

Specific Media Objections

If you're selling signage in a stadium and a prospect says, "Outdoor isn't part of our strategy," don't fight it. It's a decision the company made after lots of deliberation and internal discussion. Just position it differently. What you might want to do is say, "OK. I got it. It might not be part of an approved strategy, yet it's effective tactically. Unlike other roadside billboards, ballpark signage is truly a command to action. A stadium holds a captivated audience. There is a natural connection. Your restaurant chain offers discounts to stub holders, folks you hope to lure from our facility to yours," or "it reinforces the related longer messages that you run on television and radio sports programming. It's thus not a standalone or isolated sign. It's part of connecting the partnership dots."

Talk about how signage at a ballpark tells an emotional story that roadside billboards don't. "A sign on a busy roadway is associated with irritating traffic. A sign at our arena is a reminder of pulsating excitement and winning plays."

In a similar objection, prospects might say, "We don't do radio. It's not part of our strategy." Well, if you're selling the NFL, keep hammering home the power of the brand not the medium. "You're buying the NFL. This isn't a radio market buy. You're associating your brand with America's most popular sport." Hyundai, for instance, doesn't generally do national radio but does buy college football nationally on radio for just this reason.

Volvo has in the past bought the NCAA Tournament on radio. It bought an event not the medium. The event happens to be carried on radio. It afforded Volvo, whose marketing budget pales to the bigger autos, the opportunity to promote an NCAA sponsorship through its dealer network.

By buying the tournament on radio, Volvo captured the all-important *osmosis by association* without having to spend a boatload of television money. Although radio isn't part of Volvo's strategy, it justified its use tactically.

One common objection today in sports sponsorships and media is that the landscape is littered. "The space is too cluttered, we can't stand out," is something marketers will say. Be quick on your feet to reply, "Well, it's apparently working for everyone else!" It's like the Yogi Berra line about the restaurant. "No one goes there anymore because the lines are too long!"

From a Client's Perspective

Innately, people do want to help. Targets are paralyzed by their legacy for toughness and inaccessibility. Truthfully, they're swamped. The same way that sellers have pressure to produce orders, clients have pressure to be efficient, to meet deadlines and turn around struggling brands. The grass is always greener on the other side. But marketers contend with shorthanded staffs, pressing issues and projects that constantly have to be completed. Be mindful, too, that marketing departments in many companies are underappreciated. They're often not considered a part of mainstream, not sales and not production. They, too, have internal battles that they're waging. It's always good to understand what clients are up against emotionally before you pitch them something. Understand how the world looks from their perspective.

Prospects are absolutely inundated by an overwhelming number of phone calls and email messages. From their viewpoint, your call or email is just another extraneous request with which they deal. Just as it's a seller's job in many ways to be hardened to unreturned calls, clients become hardened, too, not prioritizing sellers' voicemail and email. For this precise reason, your messages and email should be concise and Twitter-like, limited to a set number of voice characters. Get to the point in a hurry!

Julie Lyle of retailer hhgregg doesn't beat around the bush. "The caller on the phone tried to engage me with social chatter about how my day is going, etc. Even worse, some callers don't even think about my business before dialing. I actually had two cold call salespeople call me the day before Thanksgiving. Is there really anybody on the planet that doesn't know that is the busiest time of year for an omnichannel retail executive? If you are that out of touch with my business and industry, then there probably isn't a win-win relationship in our future."

People remember what they accomplished. They also remember how they helped others, whether it's a marketing director hiring a young executive who proceeds to have a glistening career or, yes, giving junior sellers their first orders. The giver remembers it as much as the receiver. People do like to help, and it's always beneficial to let the prospect know how important this order would be to you.

What Does No Mean?

Dr. G. Clotaire Rapaille consults Fortune 500 companies about the mistakes salespeople make. He says, "The greatest salespeople are always happy even when doors are slamming in their faces. Strive to be a 'happy loser.' Rejection is actually inspiring because it allows the game to continue, and all the true salespeople love the game." A no is never a permanent answer. It's just an extension of the process until they say yes.

When you do hear no and it's an irreversible no, at least at that point, respond three ways:

1. Ignore the emotions. Admittedly, this is difficult but becomes easier over time. Confront negative feelings head-on without letting them overwhelm you.

2. Let it motivate you to work harder. Life is about second chances and certainly another cold call.

3. Treat the experience like it's your special piece of history. Like any piece of history, learn from the experience.

Keep remembering that all it takes is one fresh phone call. Think of the Nets' seller who called Barclays Bank and got a $200 million deal for the naming rights to their new arena. Yes, a cold call—for the naming rights!

When No Is No, At Least for Now

These are times to be voracious. When there's hope and you're in the mix of consideration, go for it. As long as there's a fighting chance, push hard. Use all arsenals at your disposal.

Annoying and Overbearing from a Prospect's Perspective

Sponsors and advertisers comment on what they find annoying and overbearing in Figure 8.1.

Figure 8.1. Marketers' examples of sellers' overbearing tactics

John MacDonald ENTERPRISE	Assuming I will have an interest in the property when they obviously know nothing of my business' current maturity state, business objectives etc.
Drew Iddings HERSHEY'S	Asking me about our strategy and future plans. Any non-confidential information that we would be willing to share is easily accessible on the Internet. It's not my responsibility to spend my time helping you sell to me. Do some research.
Tom Peyton HONDA	I'm ok with someone following up on a communication once...but after that, if we don't respond, there is generally a reason.
Rex Conklin HOME DEPOT	Not taking "no" for an answer and/or asking me to spend time to share my business goals and strategies.
David Lim AMTRAK	When the seller doesn't understand the basics of "need satisfying selling" and thinks if he/she should jam their proposition through, by talking fast and over me.
Julie Lyle HHGREGG	I try to be open and fairly accessible to suppliers. However, when I say "no," I mean "no". Stop pushing. And when I say, "I have passed the information on to the appropriate members on my team and they will follow up if there is an opportunity." Stop hounding me, and don't try to find out who I've passed the info to. As a leader, I set the tone and expectation for my team members to be respectful and accessible (as much as possible) to suppliers. I expect suppliers to be the same with me and my organization. A seller who copies 4, 5, 6 people on a cold call email or leaves voicemail for multiple members of my team infuriates me. Sellers who won't do their homework or don't have the patience to try and strategically reach the individual to whom their "value-add" is most relevant, demonstrate to me that they will take unnecessary short cuts and not be respectful of my team's time and priorities— before they even win our business.
Stephen Quinn - Wal-Mart	Constantly finding a way to get to me to tell me they have the solution to my problem. As in: Them: "In attracting today's teens, Xtreme sports are highly engaging". Me: "I'm not trying to attract teens." Them: "Well extreme sports are growing in popularity with all age demographics". Me: "Ok...." I've had people get very angry that I'm not interested begging the question "why did you go into sales?
Phil Wang WELLS FARGO	More than three attempts and no answer means there's not a fit. Move on.
Ed Gold STATE FARM	Call stalking. Seriously?
Betsy Wilson UPS	Not taking no for an answer. I don't mind that someone is trying to be persistent to make a sale, but once the customer says no, you need to back off. It's not good to keep pushing!
Paul Hodges REGIONS BANK	Depends on the seller. If you are trying to find solutions, I can handle the calls. If you trying to sell me something I don't need and you have no idea about our industry and existing marketing plans, then I have no patience or time for your calls.

Figure 8.1. *Continued*

Mark Eckert EDWARD JONES	When you politely tell someone, "No, we're not interested, and here's why..." yet they continue to pitch and/or adopt a dismissive attitude thereafter. If I'm kind enough to entertain your call/pitch, the seller needs to be respectful of my judgment and time.
Tim Sullivan WENDY'S	Acting like they know me to get me to take a call. Acting like we are buddies when we don't even know each other. Being long-winded. Using my competition as a reason why we should be doing business with the company. Leaving multiple messages. Not getting the hint when I don't call back. Using other senior "names" at the company to try to get to me. Being long-winded. Knowing nothing about my business. Not getting the hint. Being insincere.
Brad Barnett NATIONWIDE	Emailing every contact a person has at one time in the same company, starting with the CMO or CEO on an opportunity vs. day-to-day leaders, going around the agency when told no, or continuing to contact after being told "no."
Michael Robichaud MASTERCARD	People that act like I don't understand the value of a partnership just because I don't take their call or meeting. I don't need to spend 30 minutes on the phone with someone to know that a beach badminton tournament does not fit the MasterCard strategy. I understand sales is tough, especially for junior people getting into the business, but if you are dealing with a senior person at a brand, we've seen it all. We can probably do the pitch for a junior person better than they can. When I was first starting out in sports marketing someone told me, "it's a small world and forever is a long time." If a sales person wants to have a long career, they should focus on building relationships, not closing sales.
Ellie Malloy JOHN HANCOCK	When I pick up the phone and the seller starts and won't come up for air, just talks and talks and talks. Be respectful. Ask me whether I have a few minutes to talk? Don't assume. When a seller keeps forwarding me the first email he or she sent or when I've said no and they keep pushing to no end. We've had the Boston Marathon for a while. Some people call and lecture me on how to market the Boston Marathon. Sellers should appreciate that we know this space. If there's something tactical they want to propose in support of our strategy, that's fine.
Anonymous AUTO-RELATED MARKETER	Emails, followed by phone messages, followed by snail mail. You are cold calling. If you do your job and peak my interest, I will respond. If I don't there is a reason! If I do respond, and it was that I have forwarded the information on for someone else to review, don't come back and ask for a name or put me on a follow up.
Jack Hollis TOYOTA	Be considerate of your audience's time. Lengthy messages that get into too much detail without an understanding of your audience is a turn-off. It's also important to customize and proofread your communications. Copying and pasting can lead to calling someone by the wrong name or addressing the wrong company, which looks unprofessional and shows me that you didn't do your homework.

Other tactics to avoid:

- Labeling your solutions "turnkey."

- Aggressive and excessive follow-up calls and email.

- Employing the shotgun or blanket approach whereby cold callers contact several people without a clear understanding of those associates' roles within the organization. This typically leads to a loss of credibility on the part of the seller.

- Asking for a meeting during your initial communication when you're told, "If your proposal demonstrates value to our business, we'll request time to meet with you."

- The double-whammy approach where sellers send an email followed by an immediate phone call to inquire about their email.

Perfection, Excellence and Being Realistic

There are times to be realistic. Ask yourself, "Have I done everything I can? Have I run out of tools?" If so, put down your arms and just move on. When you're convinced that the dollars have been spent, that the budget has indeed been drained, that the client is intransigently convinced that your sports product is not the right fit, forget it. It's a waste of time and emotional energy.

The landscape is littered with other prospects.

In *Forbes* magazine several years ago, author Steven Berglas did a piece on steps preventing executive burnout. He explained that hard-driving entrepreneurs and powerful executives constantly chase perfection and only rarely, if ever, do they achieve it. Berglas suggests that failure to perfect saps them of their self-esteem.

In sales certainly, setting unrealistic high goals will lead to burnout. There's no way you'll ever sell everyone you call. Because the hit–miss ratio is so lopsided, accepting nothing short of perfection is a prescription for despair. In cold calling sales or any sales for that matter, temper your own expectations or you will end up in the loony bin.

Berglas described how Pablo Picasso dealt with burnout, "He made sure his atelier teemed with projects in various stages of incompletion." For sellers, there's always another account to pitch, another account to get in to see and another one to close.

Stay driven. Pursue perfection and accept excellence.

Inspiring Stories

- The MLB Network was launched in 2009 in the thick of the Great Recession. In the fall of 2008, network television veteran Bill Morningstar and his small sales team peddled spots and sponsorships to the backdrop of once-esteemed institutions like Lehman Brothers and AIG going belly up. Nonetheless, the network exceeded its budgetary expectations and continued to grow through America's worst financial crisis since the Great Depression. In many ways, Bill and his team were cold-calling, pitching a brand new network, asking cash-strapped corporations for a leap of confidence. Sports will do it.

- Feeling you're a victim is a prescription for failure. There are people who've tried hard, failed and felt worse. Think of Scott Norwood, who missed a 47-yard field goal attempt in the 1991 Super Bowl. Had he nailed it, the Bills would have won their first ever title. He missed it infamously.

  After football, Norwood went to Northern Virginia to make a living selling real estate. He told *Sports Illustrated* that he lives with a combination of burden and opportunity. When couples to whom he hopes to sell homes recognize his name and his unforgettable kick, there is an understanding and sympathy. Norwood says, "That could help cajole a couple into bidding on a split-level colonial at the end of a cul-de-sac."

  Just as kickers Jim O'Brien and Adam Vinatieri won Super Bowls, this fellow lost one, Super

Bowl XXV. Norwood carries a humiliating load but never asks for pity. Some never bounce back. *Sports Illustrated* described Norwood's resilience, "failure, and the redemptive success of overcoming that setback."

It is how we deal with these deflating moments that makes us who we are, and that is the American measure of success. To fail is to pick yourself up and try again. We are a nation of losers made good. To fail is not American, it is human. But it is American to overcome failure.

Yes, negative news can be eviscerating, but don't ever let it temper your resolve. Think of the long-term goal, the resolve to succeed. Show the prospect the passion you have for the product that you represent.

In late 2008, at the depth of the Great Recession, stock markets were tumbling. It was a frightening time for our great country. Many lost much of their lifetime savings. Seemingly, every day, there was news of deep trouble. Big banks and financial houses were on the brink, stock markets took another rocking hit and the government had to bail out the mighty. On December 29th of that unforgettable year, *Barron's* published a human interest piece about the agony of those suffering and those people who dealt with it through denial, claiming that they had sold their stock portfolio before the market collapsed.

Joe Queenan wrote in *Barron's*, "It's an example that psychiatrist specialists refer to as retroactive pre-science or rear vision Cassandraism." This is a mindset in which people who have been victims of catastrophes seek to mitigate the trauma by denying that it ever happened.

Similarly and strangely, we too, as the years go on, have tendencies to remember big sales hits, those that propelled our careers, just as we reminisce about the great times of our marriages. We forget all the unreturned calls, all the pleading, the dismissive nature of prospects just as we do the troubled moments of long marriages, any of which, even the best, are never straight lines.

Sometimes we truly feel that these elusive targets are misanthropic. You wonder whether they really exist. You have a sickly taste in your mouth. It's okay.

Misery loves company Queenan wrote in *Barron's* about those gloomy days around Christmas 2008, "People living through dark times derive solace from trading hair-raising anecdotes; the sense that we are not the only victims or suckers in town makes hardship easier to endure." It's why it's important for you to fess up to your sales colleagues and them to you, not so to create a negative setting, but to endure together. In the words of the stately Winston Churchill in those harrowing early years of World War II, "Never despair."

Regional Cultures

As you deal with people of all walks of life, either from around the country or around the world, you'll find that they are different in cadence, tempo and attitude. You may have to adjust your own pace and rhythm, bouncing as you will from one culture to the next. There will be attitude nuances and behavioral differences. You'll have to be sensitive to regional idiosyncrasies and unacquainted styles. Sometimes you'll have to light up a room, sometimes you'll be better laid back. You'll always want to be articulate, knowledgeable and sophisticated. You'll always want to demonstrate expertise, be quick on your feet and learn to read people. It's imperative that you're confident, a self-starter and self-motivated. Don't count on anyone winding you up every morning. Either you're ready or find another occupation.

Keeping a Journal

One therapeutic practice is to maintain a journal, more of a private diary where you would document your personal feelings, nothing business specific. Don't date the pages. You'll then feel compelled to update the journal every night. The journal is helpful for moments when you feel especially bad or especially good. At mediocre moments too, if you have a second, and you're in the mood, add thoughts to your journal. You'll be surprised. Doing this, will enable you to reflect and see how you're coping.

Keep a diary and regularly jot down notes. It's important to continually evaluate your own performance. After a call, ask yourself, what you might have done differently. What would have helped? Don't agonize, harp and dwell much because in many cases, P. T. Barnum wouldn't have converted a stubborn prospect. But replaying sales calls in your head will help prepare you for your next call.

Is it better now than before? Is there something you learned from the last time you were in the dumps? Chances are you'll better accept setbacks as a matter of routine, a matter of the process. You might also want to mark up the front of your journal with rejoinders to help you dig out of the malaises that are part and parcel of sales.

Thinking about Challenges When You're Relaxed

As absurd as it might sound, take the challenge with you when you go to sleep. When you begin to relax and the burdens of the day begin to fade, you'll think clearer and fresher. You never know what will emerge from an unsullied mind.

Improving Effectiveness

It's also worth sharing your experiences of what occurred on difficult calls with veteran colleagues, sellers or management. Remember that they have a broader body of experience; their intuition is scented by many more years of sales interaction, and they can provide fresh takes.

The great bandleader Benny Goodman was as popular in his heyday as the Rolling Stones were in theirs. "The King of Swing" made it big before Big Band juggernaut Glenn Miller. As a fledgling musician, Miller beseechingly reached out to Goodman for counseling and encouragement. "What should I do Benny? I can use your advice to advance my career." Goodman paused as he usually did before sharing his opinion. "I don't know what to tell you, but don't quit, Glenn." The rest is history. Miller became the best-selling recording artist in America from 1939–43.

Budding sellers must also fight their way through bumps on the early road to success. As Benny said, "don't quit."

In his 70s, Goodman said, "I still love to play [the clarinet] and love to work at it." Sellers must also have a natural lifelong love for their work and should never cease striving to perfect their craft.

In my years doing NBA play-by-play on radio, I listened to recordings of virtually every one of my broadcasts. If I made mistakes, I replayed them over and over until I wouldn't make the same mistake again. Mike Breen, ESPN's voice of the NBA, keeps notes of dos and don'ts in his wallet. Like play-by-play, selling is an art.

Motivationally and Psychologically

- Make it personal. Think of your grandparents, many were immigrants who might have toiled in unpleasant conditions in factories, six days a week, doing hard labor, working in steamy plants, taking home little more than meals for their tables. And if your father was a Holocaust survivor, like mine, you think of the horrors they suffered in places like Buchenwald and Flossenburg. When I was really down, I remember thinking of my dad and the number branded on his wrist by the Nazis like he was no more than cattle. Now that's work. A turndown in a sales effort is not a life-threatening experience.

  A bad day is just that. Keep going. Be impervious to a day's failed attempts. They're not even a career's undoing.

- Judith Sills, a Philadelphia clinical psychologist, has a number of suggestions for professionals during hard economic times. They're easily adapted for sales:

    a. Keep your big picture in mind. What are you doing? Why are you doing it? What are the alternatives?

    b. Ask yourself what about sales you do best. You'll think productively, and it will steer you to the right mindset.

    c. Think of why you're in sales. Think of the dough that you can make. Think of the alternatives. Think of what the repercussions are if you fail. You'll go back to doing something else, something that doesn't pay as much, something that might be tied to a desk.

    d. Say yes to every opportunity to go the extra yard. Raise your hand often. Build bridges with your co-workers on the company's sales support staff.

    e. Draw on support from your friends, family and colleagues to recharge your thinking. Let them share stories. Laugh a little. There's no better cure.

- *Psychology Today* suggests that "happiness lies in the chase." Appropriately, "Action toward goals other than happiness makes us happy. And it's not crossing the finish line that is most rewarding; it's anticipating achieving your goal."

Inspiration and a Shoulder to Lean On

Sellers respond differently. Like athletes, sellers respond to a softer approach, others to a stricter approach. It's seen so often in coaching. Cowboys' owner Jerry Jones brought in Wade Phillips to coach, hoping that an easier touch would inspire the team. It worked for a while.

Some sellers need kicks in the backside. Others need compliments and pats on the back. What everyone needs is to be appreciated. When you're facing a challenge and you've been tagged with repeated bad news, don't be afraid to initiate a conversation with your manager.

When you need a shoulder, a sounding board, engage in conversation with your manager. Ideas might emerge. If nothing else, your manager will know that you're doing everything humanly possible to make things work. Bosses hate surprises. Be transparent. You'll generally walk out of there feeling better. The worst you can do is share half truths with bosses. Be forthright. No reason to fool anyone, especially your sales manager. We all need empathy. It will come from a variety of places, conversations with your manager or your significant other. It might come at a sales meeting when you're all in the same room, brainstorming how to overcome common objections. It goes without saying that you should never post negative comments on social media that reflect poorly on the hand or industry that feeds you.

All this is to make a key point. In the words of William James, "The deepest desire in human nature is the craving to be appreciated." A good manager will nurture and guide a seller through the process, kick you in the behind when deserved and extend a hand off the mat when that's what's needed.

But most of it is you. You have to remain positive and active throughout. As the incomparable coach John Wooden would say, "Make each day your masterpiece."

There are all sorts of issues. In sports, decisions on sponsorships and media require a process, a long and agonizing one for a seller and a deliberative one for the party determining whether or not to buy. You'll work in the business for forty years, an entire career, and won't believe what you'll experience. In many ways it's part of the fun. You'll also meet tons of people and make interesting friends.

Eye on the Prize

Many obstacles can be overcome by hard work. If you're fighting through clutter, be imaginative and keep knocking. Use all the avenues available to you—letters, email, handwritten notes, caps, voicemail or letters by coaches, players and popular talent. Eventually, the squeaky wheel gets the grease.

Your early sales experiences will harden you. Your cynicism will swell as you leave a growing number of beseeching messages that are callously ignored. You'll learn painfully that there's little protocol of common decency in sports and media sales. Marketers will unsympathetically ignore your customized messages. Months of being summarily and regularly dismissed have an insidious effect. It might forever taint your trust of others. You'll never again count on returned calls from anyone, other than your mom.

Rule one is to keep your eye on the prize. Think of the heightened rewards you'll enjoy once you close a new piece of business. It is all you need to lift your spirits. The emotional high will be unmatched. Station brokers, those who bring together buyers and sellers of radio and television stations, might close one or two deals a year, but the payoff is big. There's a lot of suffering between deals. There's a lot of time between drinks. But those drinks taste good.

Becoming a winner is not a magical overnight accomplishment. Even the great ones—Michael Jordan, LeBron James and Kobe Bryant—fought through rites of passage early in their careers. Precocious young sellers also go through rough baptisms early in their pursuits. They learn from disappointing experiences and perfect their skills.

How Do You React at Moments Like This?

You've made progress developing a piece of business and you have the ball first and goal; all signs are pointing to a successful finish. The prospect is promising to call you imminently with an order. Days go by, momentum slows. You're dying a death of a thousand cuts. If only the pain could talk, it would tell of dyspepsia and anxiety. You finally get the ugly word: you've been turned down.

You're carrying the burden of wanting to succeed and the angst of coming up empty. You're feeling directionless and bankrupt of salesmanship.

You pick up the paper and read Dan Le Batard's column about Kenny Anderson, the former NBAer who squandered his millions. "He had to crawl around in darkness to find perspective." You too feel like you're crawling around aimlessly through dark spaces after weeks of downbeat results.

Be bold and tough-skinned, otherwise you'll rot in loneliness. It's then that the good sellers differentiate themselves from the mediocre ones. They remain ravenous and voracious. They will continue to strategize and dig. They go out there and write another email, dial another number, knock, post and blog.

When you cold call, you're generally free to move around more freely than sellers assigned active accounts. It gives you the flexibility and resiliency to distance yourself from discouraging news and to uncork hope by immediately pitching brand new business.

Never allow setbacks to temper your enthusiasm. In the overall scheme of things, be mindful of the fact that a sales career is an eternity. Even the jokes of great stand-up comedians occasionally fall flat. It's how comedians handle these moments that help define their careers. Jay Leno was marvelous upon these occasions, poking fun at himself in his years on *The Tonight Show*. Yet what a legend he became!

Turndowns are no more than a small measure of the process. Don't fret over disappointments. Think of the great Warren Buffett. His Berkshire Hathaway buys companies for the long term. He doesn't rush to judgment after one quarter's earnings. Evaluate your sales results over a body of time. Just as Buffett outperforms most others over time, a dedicated, committed and determined cold caller will make a healthy living and serve admirably. It is like a baseball game. The game isn't over after the first inning. Tomorrow is another day.

Be different. Everyone sends email or leaves telephone messages. Vow to undertake new practices. Become an inveterate letter writer. Make your mailman bowlegged. Write as opposed to type. Yes, a handwritten note to clients personalizes messages and shows clients that you do care. Make it heartfelt and reference the prospect's favorite hobby or team:

> *Bob, I know you cherish the company dollars you spend. You've done an amazing job building awareness for the products you market. If you give me a hearing, I'll give you three fresh ideas that I know you'll appreciate and that are in line with strategy.... And, yes, go Bruins. How about that win on Saturday! It was stirring!*

You're Not Alone

You are working a tough emotional fault line. Failure precedes success. So many successful sports and public figures first suffer setback after setback. Digest these when your call isn't returned:

- On a table behind the desk of the late mercurial George Steinbrenner was a picture of him in his days as a halfback at Williams College. Reaching for a catch, he was elbowed and knocked flat on his back. His message was, "A man could take a hit."

- Humbled? How about Charlie Weis? He was turned down many times before landing his first major head coaching job. Weis was an assistant on Bill Parcells' Jets' staff when Parcells quit to become the team's general manager. Assistant Bill Belichick replaced Parcells as coach but bolted immediately for the Patriots. Weis then pleaded with Parcells to promote him to head coach. As the story goes, Weis was not only thrown out of Parcells' office, he was fired on the spot. Landing as an assistant in New England with Belichick, Weis thought his hefty weight was one reason he couldn't get a head coaching job, so he went to the extent of having gastrointestinal surgery for obesity. After Super Bowl success in New England, Weis finally landed at fabled Notre Dame. Some things are worth the wait.

- Christopher Columbus was turned down several times by Portuguese and Spanish kings before he secured the funding for his voyage to the New World.

- In 1962, two years after narrowly losing the presidential election to John Kennedy, former Vice President Richard Nixon ran for governor of his home state of California. He lost. Crestfallen in defeat, Nixon's political career was at a low point and seemingly over. At the post-election press conference, he told reporters, "You won't have Nixon to kick around anymore." His future expectations were dashed.

    What followed, of course, was remarkable. As the *SF Gate* wrote decades later, "He accomplished one of the great resurrections in American political history, winning the presidency just six years after announcing his own political obituary."

- Joe Paterno was an assistant at Penn State for 16 years before he finally got the head gig.

- You might laugh about failures too. In their Super Bowl win, 14–7, over the Washington Redskins on January 14, 1973, the Miami Dolphins capped a perfect 17-0 season. With the score 14–0, the Fins' late kicker, Garo Yepremian, attempted a 42-yard field goal. The kick was blocked but picked up by Yepremian himself. Instead of falling on the ball, he threw it downfield, and it was brought back for a Washington touchdown. Although Miami won, the play is always remembered as 'Garo's Gaffe.' Shortly before his death in 2015, Yepremian posted on Twitter, "42 years later I realize I should have deflated the ball to get a better grip on it" (in reference to Tom Brady's 2015 New England Patriots).

- Michael Jordan, arguably the best NBA player ever, was cut from the varsity by his high school coach Clifton Herring and sent to the junior varsity. He later was selected third in the NBA draft. Jordan's drive is fueled by his own failure. He himself said it best:

> *I've missed more than 9,000 shots in my career. I've lost almost 300 games. Twenty-six times, I've been trusted to take the game winning shot and missed. I've failed over and over and over again in my life. And that is why I succeed.*

- Matt Millen thought he would be banned from football after his disastrous tenure as the Lions' general manager. His last Lions team went an ignominious 0–16. Instead he was picked up by ESPN and the NFL Network to serve as commentator.

- Hitters in baseball go through terrible slumps. Even the best of 'em! It's inevitable. Easy to fall into and hard to get out of, a slump is like a soft bed. Gil Hodges suffered through a forgettable 1952 World Series with the Dodgers. He was 0 for 12 and called a bum in Brooklyn. In his four subsequent World Series appearances, he hit .337!

- Frank Gehry was told by a professor at USC that he had no future as an architect. Gehry's career has been legendary.

- Oprah Winfrey was fired from her first television job in Baltimore. Her subsequent career as a glittering television hostess is conventional knowledge.

- The iconic kids' writer Dr. Seuss was rejected by 27 publishers before getting his first book printed.

- Floyd Layne was suspended from City College's basketball team for partaking in a point shaving scandal that rocked the athletic world in 1951. Amazingly, 23 years later, he was hired as the school's head coach. When he accepted the job, he uttered the words, "The shortest distance between two points is a straight line, and I've come full circle."

- Suffering from cancer, Hall of Fame women's basketball coach, Kay Yow said, "When life gives you a kick, make sure it kicks you forward."

- An executive framed on his office wall the words of the indomitable coach Vince Lombardi: "The spirit, the will to win and the will to excel are the things that endure. These qualities are so much more important than the events that occur."

- When ESPN launched on television in 1979, few gave it a chance. And here it is today, the industry juggernaut. For all the success of ESPN Radio, it was a long road to profitability. There was Enterprise Radio, a pioneer all-sports network in the 1980s, which failed. In fact, it took years for ESPN Radio to take hold after it started with just weekend programming. Patience and persistence!

Overcoming Adversity and Tough Days

- Sellers can learn from Isiah Thomas' attitude on the eve of being fired by the Knicks, "I've had my high points and I've had my low points. But none of it is permanent, you keep moving forward."

- Rejection is overcome by drive. Thomas Edison worked relentlessly on one electrical invention after another, the phonograph, the carbon microphone and nickel iron batteries. He didn't let failure weaken his resolve before he invented the incandescent light bulb, his most famous creation. "I have not failed. I've just found 10,000 ways that won't work," he famously said as he persisted, adding, "Many of life's failures are people who did not realize how close they were to success when they gave up."

- Failure and rejection are a prelude to success. Michael Jordan's numbers improved by the year, his skills sharpened through practice and sheer will.

  Michael Jordan watched his game films, replayed sequences and reanalyzed plays.

  Sales are about numbers, the ground you cover. The more calls you make, the better your odds to succeed, not only because you're hitting more targets but because the interaction with every new account improves your skills.

  Never let a setback temper your enthusiasm. A 'no' is just that; don't be afraid of it. When you leave the office, the world will still be functioning. The sun will set, and it will rise again in the morning. As Jordan said, "Limits, like fears, are often just illusions."

- Lewis Schaffel, a former managing general partner of the Miami Heat, did a brilliant job launching the franchise in 1988. He was asked why he's successful. He said simply, "If I am, it's because I try lots of things. If one thing doesn't work I'll try another." Entrepreneurs are often successful because of their focus, stick-to-itiveness, patience and determination. They don't throw in the towel at every bump.

- Rejections are more difficult to overcome when they come in droves. You'll feel as though it's a slow death. You'll begin to question not only your luck but also your ability. You'll think that the process is clinically fractured. It's not. It's part of sales. It's natural. Don't ever question your luck because in sales, it's easily conquered. Make more calls, work smarter and be better prepared than the competitor.

- If you're playing with flowers, in this case money, you'll have to deal with the thorns. Prospects will disparage you and your product. Deal with it. Pitching radio one day, I was abruptly told by a target, "Radio is for squad cars and ambulances, not for advertisers." The naysayer then proceeded to cut me off. When you get your next order, you'll remember that Cassandra and other dissenters. Train yourself not to look back. You were born with eyes in front of you for a reason, not in back of you. Don't let negative thoughts corrupt your brain. Be prepared with retorts and recourses when invectives are cast. Don't be discouraged.

- After suffering a setback, you're being tested. How will you respond? Former Notre Dame football coach Lou Holtz says, "Life is 10% about what happens and 90% about how you react."

- Sometimes, the mere interaction of a prolonged and failed dialogue between buyer, seller and agency, produces a lasting personal bond between all parties. Stay in touch with these people. Good might come out of a 'no' down the road.

- I think about how much better off I am than others. During my years in New York, I had plenty of trying days. In the winter, I would look out the window and watch construction workers working precariously on a two-by-two beam, the wind howling and the temperature in the twenties. Now that's work. I would look down at the street and watch peddlers selling all sorts of trinkets in the ice cold. I started appreciating the kind of work I was doing. These folks were just happy to get a fair day's pay. From that perspective, account turndowns become less traumatic.

- Sometimes you get so down that you think you can't even sell a handkerchief to a pal with a cold or you get so down on your confidence that you feel you would screw up a one-car funeral arrangement. Don't take everything personally. There's no room for self-pity. There's more room for introspection.

- Don't look for sympathy from prospects. Let prospects feel your pain but don't make them feel guilty. Do so in an irreverent, eccentric, or unconventional manner.

- At the end of the day, this is America, the citadel of democracy and the stronghold of capitalism. Even in the worst of times, no one starves to death. Don't let an unreturned call by a prospect get the better of you. Other opportunities loom!

- Loosen yourself from the grips of heartlessness by incommunicative prospects. Fight your way through the next step using another one of those assets in your bag of tricks. As stated, cold calling is war. You can't sanitize war.

- When you're turned down by an account that you thought you would land, it's okay to show your peers and your management that it hurts, especially if it's an account many in your office knew was pending. But don't appear lugubrious or disconsolate. Show you're mature and tough. Remember that suffering is temporary and that hope is eternal.

- Envision the future with aspiring ideals. Keep smiling.

- When you get down, just remember that it takes one big hit, one big order and your mood will change in an instant. Your confidence will be a mile high. It won't get any better. With every failed attempt, think of the numbers game. One more failure means that the law of averages dictates you're getting much closer to that big hit.

- There's a reason you go through these issues. Most companies will pay sellers more to develop new business. The commission rate is higher. You're being paid to deal with more aggravation.

- If you can emotionally handle these day-to-day vicissitudes, you'll succeed. Remember it's darkest before dawn.

- Don't despair, everyone's been there. There will be times someone will have to talk you off the cliff. Tommy Lasorda says, "When in doubt, when in fear, be aggressive, commit yourself and never look back."

- Gregg Popovich, the accomplished coach of the San Antonio Spurs who has guided his teams to several NBA titles, is a voracious reader. He found a passage that caught his fancy and, as he told *Sports Illustrated*, it's more meaningful than "there's no 'I' in team." So he hung a copy of Jacob Riis' classic *Stonecutter Credo* between the dressing stalls of stars, Tim Duncan and Manu Ginobili:

    When nothing seems to help, I go look at a stonecutter hammering away at his rock, perhaps a hundred times without as much as a crack showing on it. Yet at the hundred and first blow it will split in two, and I know it was not that blow that did it, but all that had gone before.

    How true for cold call selling or for any business development process for that matter. There's a gestation. Just stick with it.

Chapter 9

Learning from a Wide Range of Leaders

Success is not an accident. There are sales takeaways from leaders in a variety of fields, spanning many disciplines. Be eclectic. Pick things up from everyone anywhere.

Authors, Bios and Books

In *Fortune*, Sharon Anderson Wright (10.6.14) referenced three titles and what to learn from each of them.

Walter Isaacson's biography of the late Steve Jobs of Apple got wonderful reviews. Jobs followed his instincts irrepressibly. Instincts are internally fueled. Instincts are a product of enthusiasm. In turn, enthusiasm is infectious. Have prospects buy into your enthusiasm.

In Harper Lee's classic *To Kill a Mockingbird*, the author's message is, as Wright put it, "Stand up for your beliefs, in spite of opposition." Crusade! Let your presentation drip with the perspiration of passion. Champion the powers of sports and the sponsorship program you're selling. You might get pushback on price or suitability, but never ever back down on the potency of the theme of the package presented and the bonding powers of sports. It's the life you've chosen and the industry you've embraced.

One major takeaway from Maurice Sendak's *Where the Wild Things Are*, according to Wright is, "Be adventurous." Find and go after new prospects in novel ways. If it's hard to get an appointment with them during work hours, find them where they'll be found after work hours. It might be the lounge at the airport, the ticket counter at the train station, at a gas station or while they're walking their dogs. Maybe even through a spouse with whom you can start up a conversation. If you can't get in the front door, use the backdoor.

Broadcasters

Marty Glickman - iconic broadcaster and athlete

(This article by David Halberstam was written for and first appeared in *SportsBusiness Journal* on November 11, 2013.)

A Road Map to Life

Pick yourself up off the mat

In 1936 in Berlin at age 19, Glickman was denied a once-in-a-lifetime opportunity to compete for an Olympic gold medal. Allegedly, U.S. Olympic head Avery Brundage didn't want to discomfit Adolf Hitler by potentially having a Jew excel on German soil. Crestfallen, Glickman bounced back resiliently, resuming his football career at Syracuse, serving his country in World War II and launching a glittering broadcast career.

A setback is not a disaster. Use it to strengthen character. Keep pursuing goals. Keep going after new clients.

Execution is the result of preparation

Glickman learned this painfully early in his announcing career when he didn't completely do his homework for a track broadcast hosted by Ted Husing, then the nation's No. 1 sports announcer. The lesson was lasting. He later read Chaucer to warm up his mouth.

Be ready, know your product, prepare your presentation over and over, role play so you're ready for objections so you'll be drilled sufficiently for your assignment.

Volunteer

Marty took blind children to the circus, put headsets on their ears and richly described for them the colorful festivities — the high-wire acts, the animals and the clowns. It brought him great joy watching sightless kids laugh and smile.

Give of yourself to the unprivileged. You never know whom you'll meet and ideas you'll come up with.

Mentor and inspire the young

As a budding broadcaster, I was introduced to Marty shortly before he was to broadcast a Giants football game. He not only let me tag along, he invited me to join him in the press dining room and sit with him in the broadcast booth. It stimulated my career. He was equally as generous with many dozens of other aspiring broadcasters.

Nurture those aspiring to get into the sports business. Encourage your clients and bosses to do the same.

Enjoy life

As I got to know Marty through the years, I asked him about his approach financially. He told me that if he could plan it, he would spend his last dime on his dying day.

Have a thirst for life.

You'll be convincing when you sound passionate and genuine

Marty did commercials cogently for a haberdashery in New York, Buddy Lee's. When future announcer, Spencer Ross, turned 13 he was so convinced of Buddy Lee's that he asked his father to buy him his bar-mitzvah suit there.

Galvanize your audience when you present.

Whether it's the technician or the doorman, treat people with respect. Don't be haughty.

Marty addressed many in all walks of life by name and with an engaging smile, from the security person at the stadium to the clerk at the newsstand.

Treat the little guy right.

Don't whine

When the team he covered was being outplayed, Marty didn't denigrate the team or its players, he usually praised the performance of the opponent.

Win or lose, up or down, exude a positive experience.

Have an end-game. Your career won't go on forever. Don't retire from, retire to!

As his on air career wound down, Glickman became a broadcast coach, sailor and world traveler. He never retired per se.

Broaden your interests. It will help you get up every day with a mission the rest of your life.

Beef up your descriptive powers

Marty suggested two helpful exercises to sharpen communication skills. Try to describe for yourself what you're seeing when walking down the street. What do the buildings look like? How do the people on the street dress? What's the weather like? Doing so builds vocabulary and the ability to articulate points. Marty also suggested talking into a mirror to feel more comfortable speaking in public.

Learn to paint a powerful word picture. Critical in sales - you want to mesmerize your prospect.

Chuck Todd, NBC, moderator, Meet the Press

At University of Miami commencement exercises in December 2014, Todd attributed the continued growth of his personal career to five key practices:

1. Using handwritten notes on important occasions to communicate with others whether they're internal or external.

2. Pay attention to detail.

3. Take risks early in life.

4. Show willingness to grow by saying 'yes' to assignments whenever offered.

5. No buts. Just get it done.

Each one of these suggestions is applicable to sales, particularly the one about taking risks early in life. When you start your career, you're generally younger and have less financial responsibility. Your income will be a function of your ability to drive sales. If you can't hack sales, you'll know it early enough in your career to change course. You'll still be young enough to find your niche.

Lowell Thomas, broadcaster

The great broadcaster was asked how he survived for so many years on-air in the national spotlight. He said that he attended as few meetings as he had to, and when he did, he said as little as needed. The lesson is not to be intrusive, or in today's vernacular, "Stay in your lane."

Neal Pilson, former president of CBS Sports

Employee morale can be hurt unnecessarily by failing to reach unattainable goals. So Pilson feels that management should set deadlines and goals that are realistic and achievable.

Unfortunately in sales, expectations are often unreasonable. It's part of the game. There are pressures from Wall Street to grow stock prices. There is debt service that has to be paid and increased revenue that is needed to grow and expand businesses.

A company is not a democracy where the constituency puts leaders in place. It's not managed down-up. It's closer to a dictatorship that's managed up-down.

Cold callers must accept this premise as a given. As such, sellers have to manage up sufficiently to cultivate the support and understanding of management. In other words, it's imperative to have the confidence, faith and trust of your bosses.

Management must completely understand the ins and outs, the frustrations and stresses, of sales development. It has to accept the fact that closing new business is often an unending ordeal. It's imperative for sellers to make sure their bosses are well aware of their toiling efforts. Communicate with them often. Updated reports should be submitted regularly in summary form. Sellers should be upbeat but realistic. Arm them with solid and promising reports, ones that realistically grade the likelihood of closing pending accounts and project decision dates for booking business. It's fine for bosses to be demanding. Yet, they have to understand that it's a gestation. It will require patience. It's your job to sell management on the importance of your role. New business is the last line of defense.

When sales managers get impatient about the progress of your accounts, strike at the core goal. Talk about the role you play and the sense of a shared departmental mission. Remind the powers that be that you're implementing management's innovative sales strategies and that every single day you're getting closer to the positive impact being envisioned. Accentuate to your bosses the strategies and tactics that, in time, will enable you to exceed management's expectations.

Lon Simmons, legendary San Francisco sportscaster

"When you're young, everything means more."

The wins in sales and new orders bring a tingling sensation. The losses, turndowns and unreturned calls, feel like death. As you grow older, you put things into their proper perspective. You judge things through a body of time. Don't rush to judgment. Just keep going.

Dick Enberg, iconic broadcaster

Reaching his 80th birthday, the Hall of Fame broadcaster, among the best of all-time, says he's still motivated, going into the booth to do the elusive *perfect* broadcast. Imagine, this on-air icon who has presided brilliantly over Super Bowls, NCAA title games, Wimbledon, Olympics and more, still feels he's never done a game perfectly. Good sellers, too, are similarly motivated every morning with the hope of closing every account on earth.

Joel Hollander, former president, CBS Radio

Hollander nimbly built consensus among Emmis Broadcasting's management to do something that had never been done in the history of radio, turn a station into an all-sports format. In doing so, he had his fingerprints on the founding of WFAN, America's first all-sports radio station. WFAN went on the air in New York in 1987, survived steep bumps early before Emmis sold it to what is now CBS. By 1998, Hollander built WFAN into a $50 million a year behemoth.

He opened meetings in grand style whether it was with an advertiser, a one-on-one with a sales manager or the rank and file sellers.

"How can I help you?" was one of his opening questions.

Similarly, in individual meetings with sales managers who reported to him, the question invariably was, "What do you need to succeed?" Is it merchandising, adding a seller to the staff or a bigger entertainment budget? Hollander generally accommodated the requests that his managers made.

By doing so, the message wasn't quite as subtle. Hollander in essence was saying, "I'll give you what you need, but you better make your budget." It left the sales manager little margin for error.

On calls with the sellers, Hollander would enthusiastically tell advertising decision makers that he was there for only one reason: to help them. "What can I do for you?" resonated. It was a disarming way to start meetings. He would generally come with goodies, tickets, WFAN paraphernalia and more in hand. He asked how prospects' businesses were doing, and he had a knack for showing that he cared.

By his mere presence in their offices, clients and prospects felt that they were being invited into a glorified world of sports broadcasting, one that Hollander oversaw; personalities like Mike Francesa, Chris Russo and Don Imus and broadcasts of the Mets, the Knicks and more. It created a healthy quid pro quo.

Hollander would occasionally walk into a sales meeting, take cash out of his pocket and offer $1,000 to the first seller to get an order for a challenging package. First thing in the morning, it got sellers' attention.

Hollander had another gift. He made advertisers and sellers feel they had special relationships with him by sharing nontoxic information in semi-whispers or behind closed doors. In fostering this kindred spirit, advertisers and sellers didn't want to let him down lest it would weaken their 'special' relationship with his world of sports.

Team Sports Owners and League Administrators

Paul Tagliabue, former NFL Commissioner
In 2007, the Georgetown alumnus provided *SportsBusiness Journal* with a tutorial on five lessons for success. Cold callers can chew on each for its helpful equivalent in improving sales.

1. If it ain't broke, fix it anyway.

It's about improving, not status quo. Don't get into a rut. If you're using the same old lingo, spice up your sales vocabulary to stay sharp. Are there new buzz words you need to know to stay current? Keep asking yourself how you can get even better. If you're closing one new piece of business a quarter and you're happy, make it two and you'll be even happier.

2. Learn from others outside sports.

Tagliabue preaches from his own experience. In his two decades before becoming NFL czar in 1989, he served two decades at Covington and Burlington LLP in Washington, D.C., where he did lots of legal work in areas completely unrelated to sports.

As a seller, you'll reach out to a circle of contacts outside of sports. Prospects will represent an array of industry groups; retailers, insurers, banks, fast food companies, airlines and other diverse industries. You'll want to feel comfortable talking their language. Ask people of all sorts of industries how they handle their sales. Spend a summer working outside sports, interning in the marketing department of a fast food or accounting company. Spend a day working the grill preparing hamburgers at McDonald's. There's no bad experience. You'll learn from all of them.

3. Have strong partners.

Tagliabue says, "You can't do it all alone. There's more and more specialization." Indeed, sports properties now have specialist departments that weren't dreamed of years ago: digital, dance teams, community outreach, facility rentals and more. Count on these experts. Make friends with them.

4. Pay attention to strategy, but don't forget that execution is the most important thing.

Selling is more art than science. Don't be rigid or married to a textbook approach of how to sell. Strategy is great but sellers and buyers aren't robots. Be flexible and nimble in the way you pursue business. Use common sense.

As golfers might tell you, "It's not how you hit it, it's how it arrives."

5. Have a high tolerance for conflict.

Tagliabue says that conflict creates energy, ideas and new ways of doing things. There will always be different approaches when the sales team sits around the conference table. Make your point firmly and politely. Good ideas will come out of meetings.

David Stern, former NBA Commissioner

Never miss an opportunity! Always sell, especially when you're chief honcho. Years ago at a Madison Square Garden post-game party honoring broadcaster Marv Albert, I introduced Commissioner David Stern to Jim Gordon, Chevron's advertising director. Chevron was a sponsor of the Knicks' broadcasts that particular season. Stern, in his inimitable style, immediately bellowed an impromptu sales sermon to Gordon, whom he had just met, on why Chevron should become a national league-wide official sponsor. He got his point across in 30 seconds and before Gordon could even respond, Stern moved on, glad-handing the next party reveler and continued to work the room.

Ewing Kauffman, former owner, Kansas City Royals

The longtime owner of the Kansas City Royals, Ewing Kauffman, built his pharmaceutical empire with an unshakable spirit and irrepressible determination to sell vitamins. He started by peddling his wares physician to physician.

In his 1977 book, *The Rich Who Own Sports*, Don Kowet said Kauffman cold called doctors at their practices and bellowed excitedly about the merits of his vitamin called Vicam. Kauffman swore it cured common fatigue.

Back then, in the 1950s, vitamins were not yet consumed en masse by the general public. It was well before they were accepted as daily health supplements.

Kauffman would plunk down his large bags of vitamins, each pill enormous in size, and yap about them endlessly and exuberantly. Puzzled doctors, their foreheads puckered, watched him pop pill after pill without the aid of an ounce of water. Now that's selling.

Kowet notes that Kaufmann had to be careful because Vicam didn't only cure common fatigue, it was a laxative too!

Religious and Academic Leaders

Pope John Paul II
In the business pages of *USA Today* in 2005, there was a feature on Pope John Paul II and the lessons business people can learn from his leadership in the Vatican. "Be not afraid" was one of his favorite sayings. In a less heavenly or divine way certainly, sellers too can find corresponding qualities in their day-to-day missions from Pope John Paul's courage and backbone. The article was written in the aftermath of one of the country's greatest corporate scandals, Enron.

The lessons from the pope that have business parallels can be reduced to sellers at any level:

1. **Sacrifice.** Exemplary CEOs according to Warren Bennis, author of *On Becoming a Leader,* renounce or abstain from satisfying their personal needs to serve their constituency. Selflessness is a great attribute that, if demonstrated, will win you friends, clients and new business. Honesty and integrity are qualities that seasoned marketers and buyers recognize. These characteristics foster believability, a genuineness that will enable a cold caller to get a hearing, attention and consideration.

2. **Be genuine.** Stephen Covey, who wrote *The 8th Habit,* says the pope loved people, and it softened a lot of opposition to his position. How true in sales! Win a client over with your honesty, caring and generosity in addition to your intellect, industry knowledge and understanding of prospects' businesses. At the end, the confluence of these qualities will help you win over customers.

The pope appealed with passion, encouraging from the heart, to win over leaders who might rely strictly on reason. Genuine leaders, like Pope John Paul II, stick to their beliefs and convictions. Frankly, you should sell with a blend of passion, sincerity and pragmatism.

3. **Be courageous.** The 1981 assassination attempt on the pope's life didn't temper his world travels. He maintained his convictions. The message to business leaders is to take on tough issues without regard for risk. Sellers too can learn to sway people and fight tirelessly on behalf of embedded beliefs. If it's your passion, whether it's soccer in America or the NFL in Europe, don't be afraid to go against the grain. Your zeal and excitement will be infectious.

4. **Lead by example.** "John Paul walked the talk," according to Dartmouth's Paul Argenti. He didn't ask anything of anyone that he wouldn't have done himself. Have the self-discipline exemplified by the pope. Be the doer. Don't go around the office snapping out commands to the underlings.

5. **Be knowledgeable.** The pope set aside time to reflect and contemplate. Sellers too should strive to grow and broaden their base of knowledge, industry by industry and prospect by prospect. By assimilating streams of thoughts and mixing the right selling blends, sellers can paint cogent stories. If sellers are not comfortably prepared, they should delve deeper until they are sufficiently satisfied that they're able to make the pitch coming out of a deep sleep.

6. **Communicate.** An applicable note for sellers is what author Sharif Khan points out about the pope. He didn't use a "dignitary tone." He connected by speaking from his heart, from the gut, soul-to-soul. Sellers too are most effective when they sell concepts by genuinely encouraging from the heart.

7. **Be inspirational.** Like the pope, make people feel that they are part of something bigger. Sports are about magic, about connections. Convince targets that sports are a part of something larger, something greater than the inanimate product or service they represent. Sports bring products to life. Communicate a vision greater than the individual or the company you're pitching.

Rabbi Edward Davis, Young Israel of Hollywood, Florida

I've watched the clergy communicate with the grieving, with the ill and with mourners. These are helpful personal touches some of which sellers can apply in their day-to-day interaction with prospects and clients.

- "The greatest strength that we show is not in stoic silence. Showing and expressing emotion is healthy." Now that doesn't mean that you sit in front of a busy marketing executive and ramble on as though you were opening up to your psychologist. Yet, showing emotion humanizes the process.

- "Be a good listener" is everlasting good advice. When a prospect talks, note nuances in addition to mainstream marketing goals. Serve as a problem solver. Address the challenges that the prospect encounters. Leave the meeting positively. Say, "I think we can help you. We'll be back with suggested solutions."

- "Offer comfort and support." Be reassuring. Show the client that you're supportive. Do it in a personal way. Something like, "Thank you for having me today and taking me through the company's issues and goals. I promise that we will work hard on your behalf."

- "Make good eye contact." There's no better bond-building, whether it's with a griever, patient, prospect or client. Richard Dulaney of the St. Petersburg Bowl, currently sponsored by Bitcoin, says that, because millennials do the majority of their communicating electronically, they're uncomfortable making eye contact.

- "Rubbing an arm or a warm handshake." Whether it's the infirmed or a sales prospect with whom you've spent some time, the message is, "I'm here to assist." Naturally, use good judgment before rubbing a wrist or arm. Yet a warm handshake, when the opportunity presents itself, will go a long way.

- "Be encouraging." Rabbi Davis says that when patients are ill, be encouraging but don't assure them of divine miracles. When clients complain about issues of any sorts, the people they work with, the people they work for or being overworked, offer encouragement. Say, "I understand. It's not easy. What can I do for you?" But don't make unattainable promises.

- "Don't contradict." When there's anger from a mourner or from a prospect in the mundane world of sales, deal with it in a similar manner. Empathize. Even if the anger is directed at you, just listen. Don't contradict. Just as a spiritual leader or family member is advised to offer encouragement, you, as a seller do the same. Clients may tell you that sellers keep nagging them; don't get into a verbal spat. Show you care and understand the situation from their standpoints.

- "Travel down memory lane." It might bring back recollections of better days for the bedridden or you might have mutual interests that trigger a laugh. It's the same thing on sales calls. Sports in particular generate great moments and fond memories. Find some common ground. Reminisce about a team you liked, a Super Bowl you remember, a coach who was a character or an announcer you both enjoyed.

- "Don't overstay your visit." When visiting mourners or clients, give them the opportunity to talk and communicate. But have a sense of when it's time to leave. Once a prospect expresses his feeling, makes his point and gets a bit fidgety, move on. You've done your deed and made your pitch.

Robert J. Kibbe, former chancellor, CUNY

A cold caller never has a perfect day. I often think of the words I heard Dr. Kibbe repeat more than once. They reverberate after sales losses and routine mishaps, "It's not a disaster. It's only a setback. Tomorrow is another day."

Entertainers

Lead Singer Bono

Bono exhorted world leaders to forgive debt owed by the poorest countries. He also worked presidents and governmental agencies to step up relief for AIDS. Now that's selling! Be inspired. That's a heck of a lot harder than selling sponsorships, partnerships, sports media time, suites or game tickets.

Ed McMahon, television host and commercial spokesperson

McMahon was Johnny Carson's sidekick on *The Tonight Show*, a prime-time television pitchman and a household name for decades. Before his success on television, McMahon peddled everything from vegetable slicers on Atlantic City's boardwalk to pots and pans door-to-door.

He differentiates sellers from the rest of the working population, "You motivate yourself."

Yet it's McMahon's comments about humor that truly resonate. "There is no doubt in my mind that if you can lighten up and learn to laugh in spite of your misadventures and disappointments, you'll sell more, earn more and live longer."

The late McMahon leaves sellers with an inspiring message, "I'd venture to say that if you're now performing your selling act straight—that is, with little or no humor—you can increase your income substantially by building a few lighter moments into your spiel!"

Benny Goodman, King of Swing, clarinetist

Benny Goodman was practicing his clarinet one day when a stagehand asked him, "Benny, you're the best. Why do you keep practicing?" He answered, "If I am the best, it's only because I practice." Or as the golfing great Gary Player said, "The more I practice, the luckier I get."

For sellers, the practice court is the world of knowledge. Learn new things every day about the capabilities of your product and the businesses of your prospects.

Politicians and Captains of Industry

In the spring of 2014, *Fortune* recognized some of the world's great leaders. Inspirational sales lessons can be learned from many of these noted personalities.

Alan Mulally, former CEO Ford

Mulally's leadership kept Ford afloat during the Great Recession. He did so without declaring bankruptcy or accepting government bailouts.

He changed the mindset of employees, turning it from a CYA (cover your ass) culture to one that inspires innovation and teamwork. As Sarah Miller Caldicott said in a *Forbes* blog, before Mulally arrived at Ford, employees "practiced self-preservation over collaboration."

Stop leaning on the corporate manual. Stop having the thought process of a functionary. Stand up for what you think. Use ingenuity. Be different. Be resourceful. Fight hard for what you're selling.

Warren Buffett

Like good investors, remain patient. Don't bail after the first objection. Make a plan and stick with it. Buffett has bought companies that take time to meet expectations. In sales, fostering relationships is a process. Follow a sound strategy and don't alter it at the first sign of doubt. Buffett's investments pay off in time and so will well-planned and executed sales strategies.

Sellers shouldn't feel doomed when tough questions surface from prospects, no matter how harsh or aggressive. "Oh no! They're asking us about our audience numbers. They're not great. What do I do?" Never panic. You'll work your way through them.

Keep focusing on the positive.

Buffett also lives a modest lifestyle. The best nourishment is the kind for the mind, whether through learning, earning or producing sales. So, when you're a young seller not yet making big money, don't start running up your credit cards and burning big holes in pockets you don't yet have. Don't spend commission checks you project but haven't yet earned. Don't delude yourself.

Bill Clinton, former president

He's advocated successfully on behalf of global causes from HIV/AIDS to malaria. On the money-raising trail, he's a crusader, a man on a mission.

Bill Clinton personifies sophistication. He's as comfortable talking to the auto repairman under the hood as he is the head of the philosophy department at Harvard. He has diverse talents because he's curious, likes people, is well read and grew up poor. Broaden your comfort zone. Work on feeling more comfortable with all sorts, from fast talking New Yorkers to prospects with southern drawls.

The former president will tell you that, when you're on the stump, you should be able to clearly articulate a vision. Sellers should articulate the vision and goals that prospects can expect. What are the partnership objectives in year one of the sponsorship? How about year two? Spell it out. Paint a picture of the sponsorship two years down the road. How many of the fans that follow your entity will identify the prospect as a sponsor in two years? How many customers will the prospect be able to entertain at hospitality suites in the first couple of years? How many impressions will the media you're proposing generate? What kind of response do you project the prospect will get from the company's channel of distribution? How do you foresee weaving in the prospect's retailers if applicable? What other cheerful synergies can you envision that will stimulate the target?

Mr. Clinton will tell you that "trying and failing is far better than not trying at all." Always give it your best effort.

Jack Ma, CEO, Alibaba
Founder of Alibaba. We can all learn from the motto that Jack Ma preached to his employees: "Think big and work for your dreams." Those principles and pursuits produced the world's largest online business and the biggest IPO in 2014.

Ken Chenault, CEO, American Express
Fortune sings Chenault's praises for keeping Amex "non-controversial, strong, stable and admired"—key goals to achieve, too, for sellers. Sellers should not be too flamboyant, particularly around the office. Co-workers and managers might view such behavior as immature. Stay out of people's way and off the radar. Demonstrate strength, stability and respect. Stay in your lane.

Eric Greitens, Founder and CEO, The Mission Continues
The former Navy SEAL identifies true leaders as those who confront fear, embrace pain and welcome hardship. It's under these trying circumstances that Greitens says leaders make differences.

When closing pieces of new business after long stretches in which they coped with emptiness and unfathomable hardship, cold callers enjoy a sense of enriching fulfillment. In the words of philosopher, Friedrich Nietzsche, "That which does not kill us makes us stronger."

Cold callers are the SEALS of the sports sponsorship world: Sellers Enduring Agonizing Labor in Sports!

Eric Schmidt, Chairman and CEO, Google

Schmidt told *Fortune* magazine in 2009 that venture capitalist John Doerr recommended to him that he seek a coach. At first, Schmidt resented the idea. He questioned himself. After all, I am a CEO. Is Doerr suggesting this because I'm underperforming or underachieving?

Schmidt finally accepted the fact that a business coach is someone who looks at things with another set of eyes, bringing upside potential to the decision-making process. "They get to watch you and get you to be the best." Bill Campbell, the "secret coach" of Silicon Valley, chairman of Intuit and former longtime board member of Apple, served in just that role as an effective and informal mentor to Schmidt.

If Schmidt can use a mentor, so can you. Once you've settled into your job, develop internal relationships with senior members of the company. See whom you can trust. Let someone you're comfortable with serve as a sounding board. It might be a manager or a senior seller. It doesn't even have to be someone at the company you're working for; it can be someone in the industry who works for another entity, someone seasoned and someone you respect.

Find good listeners, industry experts and good advisers. They'll have been through good times and bad. They'll help steer your career. Once you're successful and comfortable on your own, don't forget your mentor. Keep him or her in the loop throughout your career. Don't forget your roots and certainly don't forget the people who helped you up your career ladder.

When your career matures, reciprocate when the less experienced come by needing a guiding hand. Helping others is rewarding. The feeling is wonderful. You'll make a younger colleague's day. You'll contribute to the greater good of the sports and media business. Being generous, even with your time, makes you stress less and boosts your own work satisfaction.

Heroes

Chesley Sullenberger

As Wall Street companies and bankers selfishly betrayed shareholders at the height of the Great Recession in January 2009, Captain Chesley Sullenberger courageously landed a doomed US Airways flight out of New York's LaGuardia in the icy Hudson River. Amazingly, all passengers and crew survived. As the plane sat afloat, partially submerged in the icy waters and in arctic temperatures, Sullenberger dutifully didn't leave the aircraft until he was sure that everyone was off the aircraft safely. It was an inspiring, feel-good story of heartfelt heroism at a time the country needed a stimulating shot in the arm.

In a matter of less than an hour, Sullenberger went from unidentifiable stranger to American hero. When he took his seat in the cockpit of the Airbus, it was just an ordinary day. Sully was no different from the many hundreds of pilots who amble down airport concourses wearing ubiquitous uniforms, blending in subtly with busy airport crowds. An hour later, he was Superman. Without any warning, at the Super Bowl a few weeks later, Sullenberger and his crew were introduced to a rousing stadium and to a teary-eyed audience of millions at home.

Sellers can learn lessons from this touching story—preparation, going the distance, teamwork and gracefully transitioning from anonymity to American hero.

Like Sullenberger, sellers never know what each day brings. Cold callers often sit anonymously with many others in the sales bullpen, swinging away, hoping to hit one out of the park. In the morning they're almost nameless in an office full of people. If one of them closes a six figure deal that day, the news travels quickly down the corridors into the suites of executive decision makers. The seller is no longer unknown. In sales, thankfully, you don't need a doomed carrier to become a hero, just hard work.

Going the distance as Sully did, walking up and down the aisle of the slowly sinking aircraft to make sure that all passengers were off safely, shows sellers to never leave anything to chance. Whether it's life or death or fulfilling a mundane promise to a client, it takes an extra step. When you leave tickets for a client at will-call, call the window before the game to reconfirm that they're there. If the tickets aren't there, you may lose a client forever. Don't take chances that can easily be avoided.

Be prepared. Sully became an expert on water landing, assiduously studying the practice via instrument. When the moment called for the exigency, he handled it with grace, determination and composure.

My wife's nephew learned the Heimlich maneuver and retrains himself every few weeks. He sells clothing for a living, and if the maneuver is needed around the family table or at a restaurant, he's ready. My wife, Donna, who's a pediatrician, my children and I were out several years ago at a Japanese restaurant when a man sprung from his chair and made guttural sounds. He couldn't breathe. I watched Donna virtually save the gentleman's life by applying the Heimlich maneuver. We should all identify one area of emergency care to help others when the need arises. Imagine if you saved your prospect's life when out to lunch. My goodness!

Teamwork was critical too. Sullenberger worked symbiotically and in lockstep with his co-captain, the tower and his flight attendants. At that special Super Bowl moment, the whole crew got the well-deserved attention of millions. Sellers, too, need support staffs to take them through the gamut of preparation and the excruciating gestation. Work well with your team and show appreciation.

Doers

Vincent Flaherty, former columnist Los Angeles Examiner

Flaherty personified the look of a 1940s and 1950s sports writer. He wore a fedora and, as *Sports Illustrated* noted, 'gaudy ties.'

"Everybody said Los Angeles was not ready to be a big city. Not ready for Major League Baseball," said Kenny Hahn, then Los Angeles County Supervisor.

The columnist began his effort to cultivate support for bringing the Dodgers to Southern California in the 1940s, working gratis for the Los Angeles Citizens' Committee for Major League Baseball. The committee included star-studded names like hotelier Conrad Hilton, movie mogul Louis Mayer and industrialist Howard Hughes. Flaherty wrote upbeat stories that made Southern Californians dream about getting big league ball there.

Walter O'Malley, who moved the Dodgers from Brooklyn, credited Flaherty's columns for developing the fan support required to make Major League Baseball work on the West Coast.

Flaherty also traveled to New York to visit O'Malley and wrote him endless love letters. When O'Malley finally showed up in California in January 1957, Flaherty chauffeured him around town and showed him the plot of land at Chavez Ravine, which eventually became Dodger Stadium. He told the Dodgers owner, "You can call your shots, and L.A. will give you damn near anything."

"Absolute fan and everything he wrote, thought, and talked about was about bringing the Dodgers to Los Angeles," Hahn said.

Of course, no one man gets a team to move coast to coast. There were teams of people in Southern California who worked feverishly, both visibly and behind the scenes, Hahn being one. Meanwhile, of course, New York power brokers wouldn't accede to O'Malley's request for a new park in Brooklyn to replace Ebbets Field.

This story demonstrates that a crusade, whether for sales dollars or for community action, supported by teamwork, patience and persistence, pays off. The Dodgers left Brooklyn in 1957.

Athletes and Coaches

Peyton Manning
When the NFL's Peyton Manning was recruited out of high school, a ton of college coaches knocked on his door expectedly. When asked why he chose the University of Tennessee, Manning said that the Vols' coach at the time, Phil Fulmer, sent him handwritten notes. Clients, like athletes, like to be recruited. Handwritten notes are different from the mass of email prospects receive regularly. Don't be afraid to open up and send a personalized heartfelt note. Unlike email, handwritten notes will sit on clients' desks for a couple days and be remembered. Meanwhile, email will be deleted or forgotten as recipients continually scroll down to their newer messages.

Yogi Berra
Yes, cold callers can learn from Yogi too.

"Nobody goes there anymore; it's too crowded." When everyone's pitching an account, don't say, "They have their buys done for the year. It's not worth trying." Go anyway. You never know when discretionary budgets avail themselves and if not, next year is sooner than you think.

"Baseball is 90% mental. The other half is physical." Selling requires smarts and a strategic sense. You also need to be in physical shape. Clients respect the sharp, the groomed and the fit.

"It was impossible to get a conversation going; everybody was talking too much." Correct. A seller should listen and glean. Information is knowledge. Knowledge is the engine to help you sell.

"If you come to a fork in the road, take it." Yes, if one way doesn't get you in the door, go the other way.

"It ain't the heat; it's the humility." In sales it's both. Sellers suffer a lot of humility and have to bite their tongues. They're also feeling the heat to get appointments and to produce dollars.

Phil Jackson

You can go in with the best-planned strategy, but at the presentation you're thrown a curveball. It happens invariably. When record-setting coach Phil Jackson addressed management at a corporation, he said, "You do have a game plan, but still, you can't use preset plans for every occasion. You've got to continually improvise, respond quickly and anticipate changes." As you get more comfortable in these situations, through experience and product knowledge, you'll become quicker on your feet. It's why you should always have diversion tactics and backup plays in your hip pocket.

Derek Jeter

The retired Yankee had an old school approach. Lesson learned is to never offer excuses or give less than a maximum effort. When a sales effort fails, ask yourself why. Did I answer all questions astutely? Did I follow up in a timely fashion? Be introspective. Was the presentation hard-hitting enough? Did I effectively maximize all the resources in our bags of tricks? Did I overestimate the likelihood of the prospect ever committing? Should I have spent my time going after another target instead? Don't be afraid to admit your mistakes to yourself and to learn from them. It makes us intuitively stronger.

Billie Jean King

When you have the uneasy feeling that traction for a sponsorship package you presented is waning, whether it's becoming more difficult to reach the prospect or it's that the tenor of conversations is redolent of weakening enthusiasm, dig deep to rekindle momentum. Do what you have to do.

When you truly feel that it's Hail Mary time, scour your bag of tricks to reinforce excitement about the merits of your proposed partnership. Take a calculated risk, including potentially going above the prospect's head.

Billie Jean King said that the reason she took a risk, agreeing to play Bobby Riggs in her famous 1973 network television "Battle of the Sexes" was, "There was more risk not to do it, than to do it." Her eventual victory helped recognize the achievements of women, and it contributed to gaining approval for the NCAA's Title IX, anti-gender discrimination law.

Be sensible and aggressive when need be.

George Kennedy, head coach, John Hopkins University's swimming team

His resume is sparkling. He's won 23 conference titles in 28 seasons. It is said that he changes things up not only every season but also for every meet.

Sellers, too, shouldn't have a ubiquitous agenda. Changing things up sales call to sales call might mean tweaking the deck, presenting something unique and finding new descriptive words. It will stimulate and keep you sharp. Your delivery will have a fresh enthusiasm. You won't sound repetitive, and you will be more alert and completely immersed.

Remember that no two buyers buy alike. Each wants to be pitched differently. Some are more patient; some are less so. Some will interrupt; some won't. Some will give you their undivided attention. Others will keep looking at their phones. Be prepared. That's why it's good to have various versions of the presentation.

Magic Johnson

Magic Johnson was talking warmly in the corridor of an arena with Heat Spanish-language announcer Jose Paneda, TV announcer Eric Reid and me. When another gentleman came by and gave Magic a hug, the Hall of Famer felt compelled to introduce this individual to the rest of the group.

But Magic knew none of our names nor the name of the gentleman who hugged him. That might happen to anyone in a room full of people, and it's uncomfortable. Names are the hardest thing to remember, especially when you're stopped a thousand times a day.

Magic handled it gracefully. With his famous big and bright smile, he turned innocently to the fellow who came by and said, "I know these three guys," gently pointing at Jose, Eric and me. "Why don't you introduce yourself to them?" As the words left his mouth, he motioned to a buddy down the hall and headed for the exits with the savvy of a man in the prime of his game of life. He never knew any of our names but made us all feel like we were long lost pals. Any wonder, Magic was so silky smooth on the basketball floor?

Chapter 10

Halby's Tips, Tricks and Snippets of Helpful Information

How do you keep the client focused on the proposal?

Under the right circumstances on days after presentations, it might be a good idea to pick up the phone and call the target. The prospect's team had a night to sleep on the proposal. A day later, you might get a knee-jerk reaction on consensus and next steps. While the presentation is still fresh, ask whether there are any questions covering any of the elements or components presented.

If there are any questions, answer them firmly. Use the opportunity to agree on a timetable for the evaluation process. This is just another way to maintain a wave of enthusiasm. In a private telephone conversation just after a meeting, you will likely get a clearer understanding of approvals necessary and more insights into the personalities of those in the decision-making process. It will help you not only strategize but also be better equipped to gauge the chances of closing the sponsorship.

***

After presentations, send all the attendees that represented the prospect at the meeting a thank you note and promise to enthusiastically fulfill all exciting elements presented: public relations, experiential, promotional, hospitality, media and more. Have it signed by everyone on your team, including the support staff, the receptionist, head of traffic, the mailroom, the broadcasters and more, everyone who will be involved in servicing this potential client. It demonstrates to prospects that a large and committed team will be at their service. It's impressive.

***

If prospects tell you to call back on a particular date for their decision, call a few days beforehand to remind them that you'll be calling on the date prescribed and ask whether there are any questions that need to be answered in advance thereof. Of course, if you don't phone, you can do so by email.

***

When you're getting close to nailing down an account, send over a pie from a local bakery and have a piece cut out. On the inside bottom of the cardboard box, leave a message for the prospect, "You'll have the whole pie and own a piece of our team when you place the order." Cold calling can be tedious, but it should generate a chuckle too.

How do I remain visible with a long-term prospect?

In your travels, if you catch things of interest to particular prospects, take pictures on your phone and send them. So if you're in Barcelona on vacation and run into a few KFCs, take snapshots and show the prospect that you're thinking of him or her.

You might post success stories you're enjoying with recently closed prospects. These posts can include tasteful photos and images of the partnership. Yes, a picture says a thousand words. It also triggers interest. Success spawns success.

Even if it's a flattering article about the prospect's prime competitor, send it anyway. It will be appreciated. When you see that a big spread in *Fortune* ran on the growth and history of Levi's, send it to the ad director of Wrangler and Lee's. It still shows you care. They might have missed the article.

Make friends and build your Rolodex. I noticed an article on shoe manufacturer, Allen Edmonds, in the local newspaper. I sent it to the company's president, and I received a nice note and a brass shoehorn. Class act. Too bad that Allen Edmonds wasn't advertising at the time. Years earlier, similarly, a story on Tom's of Maine

Toothpaste appeared in the area daily. After sending it to the company's owner, I got a box of toothpaste that kept my family brushing for years. Nice.

***

One other idea that works is developing a brief newsletter, short and to the point, that you can get out regularly via email blasts. Maybe it includes a success story with a client or recently signed clients. Email blasts are easy and they help maintain dialogue with your targets. Give the newsletter a catchy name. If your name is Green, call it the Green Sheet.

Why is LinkedIn so helpful in cold calling?

LinkedIn is all about cashing in on common acquaintances and mutual colleagues. Often, these are names you'll use as third-party references. They might attest to the effectiveness of the sponsorship program that you're selling or serve as character and business references on your behalf personally. Should the prospect respect the endorser, it will help get you in the door.

It's always best to personalize your message when communicating electronically. It can be done a variety of ways, whether it's touching targets' hearts through something near and dear to theirs or just letting them know something personal about you that will trigger a return call.

LinkedIn is no more than a preexisting, rich fountain of information that, in analog days took forever to build. It spews electronic 'hot buttons' that were as powerful then as they are now. We knew through the grapevine then that Norm Varney, who ran the Champion Spark Plugs account at J. Walter Thompson, was a member of the team that hired the first trio of Mets' announcers. We figured he would be positively predisposed to sponsoring every Major League Baseball team's local radio broadcast. We put together a compelling package and sold him a productive two-year deal. In other words, try to call on someone who appreciates the product you're selling because of a past positive experience.

How do I learn and improve?

Take your sales manager on sales calls. The good sales managers will allow you to make the presentation. Show your boss how well you present and how effectively you can run a sales call. Some bosses have tendencies to take over the meetings and make the pitches themselves. When this happens, urge your boss to allow you to make the presentation yourself; otherwise, you'll never learn.

What should I be mindful of when in front of a prospect?

Be respectful in the presence of a prospect. There's an old line. True or not, the person with the most money always thinks he or she is the smartest one in the room. The client brings a big fat checkbook.

How do I show clients that I care about them?

Stay in touch with clients who are between jobs. Give them leads on employment opportunities. Make them feel good and important. It will pay healthy dividends when they do land.

What might happen if I stay in touch professionally and in measured intervals?

"Nothing great has ever been achieved without enthusiasm."

For about four years, I unsuccessfully pitched Lowe's a network radio sports package; NFL, NCAA, Notre Dame and more. The client, Kevin Cleary, based in Lowe's North Carolina headquarters, would always see me and ask good questions. But, I could never get him to push the approval button. One day, unexpectedly, Cleary called to tell me that Lowe's would be buying network radio for the first time. His heads-up enabled my New York colleague to get a leg up on making a sports presentation to the planning and buying group at the ad agency.

The Lowe's experience was a good example of developing a relationship and staying in touch. Cleary didn't have to call me. We could have gotten on the buffet line with the rest of the network purveyors once the agency issued its RFP to the stable of vendors. In time, the prospect does appreciate your effort and will reward you accordingly. The lesson is to always be helpfully visible with a potential client.

How do I earn a client's trust and build a relationship?

Become a target's "trusted advisor," not an "untrustworthy peddler." That's why a consultative approach is less deterring to a prospect and often more sustainable over a course of time.

***

Don't be negative and don't betray confidences of others.

In other words, don't share with a prospect something that was said to you in confidence by the prospect's competitor. Be prudent and circumspect. You want clients to trust you. Don't divulge information you shouldn't. If you do, you risk never being trusted. Be careful.

Showing the target that you're knowledgeable about industry events and developments is one thing; being loose-lipped will accomplish little. Be judicious. Share information smartly.

Ripping the competition is never healthy. Clients won't trust those who decry others. It's unproductive. There are ways to juxtapose entities, products and services that politely demonstrate superiority. There's always a qualitative, quantitative or efficiency niche that you can sell, but negative selling leaves a bad taste in prospects' mouths.

You can occasionally take another angle by posing questions. Ask prospects whether there's something they like or dislike about your competitors.

***

On the other hand, if the prospects' kids are college students, see what they want to do when they graduate school. Perhaps you can set them up for an interview or an internship. Do good things for others. It will never hurt you. Many who are about to get out of college are enamored with sports.

***

Hosting a party? When your persistence isn't effective, you can email your prospect, "Mr. Smith, here's a golden opportunity to experience firsthand the benefits of associating your company with our fine program. It won't cost you a dime, and you'll have a great time too. Come to Sponsors Day at football camp and hobnob with our coaches and team officials." Copy the executive's assistant too. If you feel it would help, invite the assistant. It will pay off in the long run.

If there's an event that involves old-timers and former stars of the team you're selling, the prospect will have a grand old time and will appreciate the invite. Reunions with days' past remind us of the diverse world in which we live and the benefit of building bonds through these communities. These events foster happiness, laughter and great memories. They're great ways to show your property's wares. It reinforces the power of sports.

How do I show gatekeepers that I appreciate their help?

Send a note or a memento from the goodie closet to gatekeepers after they have helped you set up an appointment. Gatekeepers can be great friends or an irritating thorn in your side.

How do I differentiate myself?

Brand yourself in your email signature. It's especially good for social media. It could be "The Sports Nut" or "The Zany Fan."

****

Use your on-air talent if you're selling a broadcast package. Team announcers are generally well known and well liked. Their names and voices are synonymous with their beloved teams. Bring them out on sales calls. This has been working productively for many years. The legendary Marty Glickman, when he was broadcasting Jets games, was told that Blue Cross and Blue Shield was considering a sponsorship package. Glickman suggested to the seller that he set up a lunch meeting with the client. The client was so impressed to have Glickman at the lunch that they closed the deal on the spot.

***

Have your coach or popular on-air talent reach out and leave a voice mail. "Joe Dixon of our sales staff tells me that he reached out to you about sponsoring our team. It would be wonderful. Let me know if there's anything I can do personally to make it happen."

If you're afraid that the prospect might not listen to voicemail, use the administrative assistant's phone number. The coach can then say, "Nancy, this is Coach Rivers. Would you please pass along this voicemail to Mr. Jones? I want to make sure Mr. Jones hears this message. Thanks much."

***

Sending scanned articles that are of tailored interest to targets is usually appreciated, even if it's done regularly. It tells the clients you care, you're thinking about them and you would like to see them succeed.

Articles, though, of general interest, particularly those touting the product you're selling, should be sent only in measured intervals. Yet you might consider adding these articles to your blogs and posting them on LinkedIn, Facebook and Twitter.

Sending an audio or video link that's dubbed strikingly to grab a prospect's attention might work if it's indeed special. For example, if there was a sponsor reference in a telecast that involved an unpaid and unprompted ad-libbed plug, send it to a prospect to demonstrate how sponsors are embedded in programming. On an ESPN broadcast, play-by-play announcer Mike Tirico, who lives in Detroit, made a casual comment to the effect that Delta Airlines was his hometown airline. The ESPN seller servicing the account would have been smart to send the video clip to Tim Mapes at Delta in Atlanta. Tim would have appreciated the free shout out.

Whatever the subject matter, the key is to customize the short accompanying note. For instance, your cover note to Schick or Gillette might simply say, "I'm not sure you had a chance to see this article in the *Boston Globe*. It's interesting; it's about consumer trends involving razor and dispenser purchases. It addresses the impact of casual dress in offices on the frequency of shaving." The Schick or Gillette prospect will appreciate the fact that you sent the pertinent newspaper story.

****

A handwritten note is also powerful. In addition to cracking the clutter of phone calls, it captures some of the emotion of the power of the sports entity when the note is written on the property's stationery and is accompanied by popular sports logos and related trappings. It also tells the prospect a little more about you. As ridiculous as it might sound, your handwriting drips with personality. It resonates. The note sits on the prospect's desk for a day or two. The message sinks in and the prospect is more likely to respond or pass it along to the right party.

Is there something that I might be doing that's overbearing?

Don't get in people's faces. Give people their physical space. Don't stand inches from prospects' faces when talking to them. It might work on the basketball court if you're an NBA defender but not at a conference or party during a pleasant exchange. If you happen to have bad breath, bad body odor or are doused with perfume or cologne, look out. The people you'll be talking with will be looking for the closest exit sign.

Give me an example of how I can avoid being overbearing.

Once you've established some dialogue, space your calls and missives.

The trick is to get a sense of when you're beginning to be overbearing. Be tenacious but don't be insensitive. We've talked about pleasant persistence. Phil Wang of Wells Fargo says, "More than three attempts and no answer means there's not a fit. Move on."

Don't send boilerplate material very often. Too much of anything and you'll lose your credibility. After a while, even snail mail notes will find the trash can with the speed of a big league fastball.

Give me an example of something I will pick up eclectically.

I was sitting in my periodontist's waiting room one day while he was consulting another patient on a potential implant. When the doctor came out to greet me he overheard the patient asking his dental assistant specific questions about immediate care after implant surgery. How long will I have to ice my mouth? How long before I get a permanent crown placed over the implant? The dental assistant replied to each specific question with lengthy discourses on the long-term advantages of an implant. Hearing this interaction from afar, the periodontist hollered to the dental assistant in the other room, "Just answer his questions!"

It was a lesson for all of us in sales.

Don't go on long-winded, unprepared dissertations when asked something specific. "Answer the question" with specific answers. Don't overtalk or oversell. No screeds, no lengthy speeches. Questions are to be answered concisely, firmly and confidently. If you don't have the answer, say so. Otherwise, your rambling will be construed as a diversion or sales tactic. The prospect will then begin having doubts. When asked, "Will our sponsor tickets be courtside?" answer yes, no or "I will have to get back to you." Don't go on a long pitch on the virtues of every seat in the building.

What are some suggestions on best use of email?

These are fifteen of mine.

1. Introductory email messages should be worded economically, boldly, encouragingly and stimulatingly. Customized, of course, they should read like the best pieces of advertising copy that serve as a command to action.

2. Assimilate a prospect's needs into a condensed text like format.

3. Remember that recipients cannot forward email internally or to agencies with the same personalized touch of a physical document that you send by snail mail.

4. Email is viewed as somewhat more of perfunctory templates as opposed to well-written and customized letters.

5. The recipient might not always open attachments.

6. Email is better for posing questions that will trigger a quick yes or no. "Can I call you tomorrow to discuss an idea? Can I come over next Tuesday morning? What time works for you?"

7. Email is not as entrapping as telephone calls, particularly when a prospect picked up the phone while

deep in thought on an unrelated subject. Prospects can plot responses to email that they can't during the immediacy of an unexpected phone call.

8. Mass email messages rarely work. If you're fighting the clock and are desperately trying to move inventory, you might try this Hail Mary approach. Otherwise don't resort to it.

9. Email is inherently self-contained. But to help locate, organize and isolate email connected to specific targets, slug the subject with the company's name. As such, when using search for info on specific accounts, the program will spit out all pertinent correspondence in a heartbeat.

10. Weekends can be viewed as intrusive. The issue should be pretty important if you send email on off-days. Some clients might be repulsed. There are others who work weekends or at least catch up then. They might not mind. You might notice a news story on a weekend that's related to clients and you can choose to send a scan, link or PDF of the online version. Because email is accessible 24/7, sending email on weekends or off hours Monday through Friday is more likely to trigger responses because the potential client might have a second to breathe. Do so only selectively when all other means have failed. Solicitations are often considered annoying and 'interruptive marketing,' so intruding on weekends won't always be appreciated.

An example of good weekend use of email entailed an article in the *Miami Herald* one Saturday about an increase in men's skin cream and hair products. I immediately sent it to the Nivea prospect, and he responded with a thank you note. The Nivea client would otherwise never have seen the article and, as such, was appreciative. You might also see a CEO of a prospective sponsor interviewed on television on a Saturday or Sunday.

You can then send the marketing or advertising director information summarizing what was said. Again, it will be appreciated. Furthermore, if you're pitching a competitor of the CEO you saw interviewed, you can similarly summarize highlights of the interview and email it over the weekend. Use good judgment. So much is basic common sense.

11. Never send hasty email responses, especially when you're angry. Write them and leave them in your saved drafts. To avoid accidentally hitting the send button, you might want to leave the "To" field blank. Review them the next morning. If the response is acerbic, you'll realize the email has to be tweaked, and you will likely tone it down. The exercise alone of drafting nasty responses when prospects have been dismissive is by itself cathartic. But wait and think about it very carefully before you hit the send button. In the interest of future opportunities, bite your tongue. Don't do anything you'll later regret.

12. If you're pitching baseball to an athlete's foot product, Lotrimin for example, tease the common seasonality in the subject line of the email. In the body of the email, compose a short paragraph referencing the compatibility of the two products, *baseball and fungal issues during summer*. Don't beat around the bush. Ask for the meeting.

13. Everyone loves a deal.

   A subject line with one sentence, "Here's the best opportunity to cross your desk!" is always intriguing. It can be followed in the text with a direct request, "Can I get a minute of your time on the phone to discuss something special?" You then add a simple sentence. For example, "Jim Rome loves Halby Soap. He won't wash his hands with any other soap. I would like to talk with you about working with Jim." As Tom Peyton at Honda says, "Make it simple and direct: 'Gator Bowl Title Sponsorship Proposal.'"

14. By email, try not to use attachments that are not of tailored interest. So many prospects use smart-phones. They'll likely not open it. For example, a press release should be in the visible text, the main body of the email.

Sponsors and advertisers are split on whether they open attachments. For instance, Ed Gold at State Farm will tell you, "I will open an attachment, but do me a favor and make it as small as possible. Do not clog my email." Paul Hodges at Regions Bank says, "If I don't know you, I will not open the attachment." Rex Conklin at Home Depot qualifies his decision, "Yes, assuming the email has an enticing headline and customized messaging."

15. *Fortune* wrote that email and text messages have produced a world of quarantined cubicles. Businesses are beginning to recognize that software developers lack emotion and empathy. Brad Smith, the CEO of software maker Intuit, marks up software he tests with happy faces or puzzled faces to humanize sentiment.

You might want to try using smiles, frowns and tears to depict your emotion in your correspondence with prospects. It's a quick and pervasive message that might draw a response.

Lewis Schreck of the Redskins network, one of America's great cold callers, shares his observations on email effectiveness. "The downside to technology is that no one gets on the phone. Yet emails save sellers lots of time. I have put together great door opening emails tailored to catch people's attention and say exactly why I am calling and what I am capable of doing. If the person opens it and reads it and is not interested, I have saved myself a ton of time. If they respond they are interested. It allows me to cover much more ground and try with many more accounts."

Whether it's email or any mail, an epistolary relationship is nice, but it won't put the meals on the table. There has to be a command to action.

What's one thing that's old school that should never be done today?

Not too many years ago, it wasn't uncommon to hear executives shout demeaning commands to their secretaries, "Honey, get me a cup of coffee, please." If that wasn't enough, when assistants brought their bosses coffee, executives might make inappropriate comments about their assistant's look that day. Obviously, don't go that road. There are generational differences. Folks in the workplace who are in their 50s, 60s and even 70s have to be particularly sensitive to correctness in today's office environment. But don't try to bridge the gap by awkwardly using what you think is the vernacular. Be respectful but be yourself.

The world is indeed changing. In a sales book written in the 1950s *How to Get More Business by Telephone*, the author shares tips on getting past gatekeepers when asked, "Who's calling?" or when a secretary says, "I must know what the call is about." When all else fails, the author suggests that the cold caller simply say, "My dear young lady, will you please connect me with Mr. Jones without further delay?"

If anyone does so today, the game is over, and you'll be selling pencils on the street corner.

How do I deal with someone terse?

When dealing with one who's terse, get right to the purpose of your call. For example, "I want to get fifteen minutes in your office to talk about our college football team and some potential partnership opportunities. Can I come by next Wednesday? I will make the time worth your while."

Any thoughts on getting through by phone?

If you're ready to tear your hair out because a prospect has been impervious to your messages, leave another. Say something like, "I know you're a nice person. I'm just beginning to feel a sense of despair and hopelessness. May I kindly ask you to respond? Please be sensitive to an eager seller who wants a minute of your time." Or, "Please don't be so impervious to my cries!"

Unless the client is the type whose pants burn and won't yell fire, you'll probably get an answer. When I don't, I channel my anger through my pen. I would write down words in my journal articulating how I feel. Words like dismissive, disheartened, slighted, worthless, dispirited, demeaned, neglected, unsympathetic, humiliated, heartless, soulless and disdained. There were other words, too, but they're not fit to print. I would look at these words every now and then and read them to myself.

I employed a line on an elusive target that I heard used by the incomparable Vin Scully, voice of the Dodgers. "Mr. Jones, I feel like the guy in the balcony winking at the showgirl. I can't get you to respond." When a manager in the dugout failed to get the attention of an impervious umpire in the din of a crowded stadium, Vin said, "Tommy must feel like the guy in the balcony winking at the showgirl."

***

It's different today now that assistants have caller identification. If you keep calling, even secretaries' phones will jump to voice mail. Some assistants are more helpful than others. Some are impervious. Some can be both, depending on the day. By nature, some are indifferent, presenting challenges and obstacles that are murder to overcome. Cold calling can't be sanitized. Different people take different angles. Frankly, not getting calls returned is more exasperating than being told no.

Caller ID is meant as a shield but it's become a sword. It's a tough battle, but we fight on, convincing ourselves that tomorrow will be a better day.

In sales, the mood swings are trying. So when you're down, just make another phone call. Remember it's a numbers game and another sales call is the best therapy. Like a running back who is dragged down play after play and carries on, you, too, should get up with alacrity and fight one more time.

***

Voicemail in many ways is easy. It gives you a license to get to the point without any foreplay, but it's distant and detached. Oftentimes, you'll wonder whether you'll ever be heard. Don't think you're being singled out. All sellers suffer the pain. You're not alone. Believe in yourself and pop off the mat. You won't sell anything with your back on a mat.

Yes, voicemail messages are often dismissed today. Many people, clients or doctors, don't listen to their telephone messages. They see who called through caller identification and choose whose calls to return.

***

Doug Brand of Campbell Soup says that he gets so many voicemail messages, it's difficult to listen to all because callers ramble and don't get to the point. Product managers like Brand are busy. They're consumed with internal and agency meetings from dawn to dusk. It's impossible for them to interact with every seller who reaches out. Brand says just economize your message in as few words as possible. "Tell me how you can wow me! If I think you really can, I'll call you back." He discourages verbose voicemail messages that include perfunctory and disingenuous salutations. He exhorts sellers to be on their game!

Should I ever try a client at home?

You never know when you can reach a client. There's little to lose making a call early, late or on weekends. Early in my career, my colleague, Gil Miller, an eccentric seller, would occasionally call clients at home. He dug around and would somehow find their phone numbers. Gil was a nudist and walked around the office with his shoes off. We were working for a big and conservative company too,

Katz. Yes, Gil was different, but he could throw people off as well as I've ever witnessed. He could have them open up magically.

When prospects picked up at home, he would invariably apologize, saying that he didn't want to bother them at home. He would then immediately ask when the best time would be to call them in the office. Most prospects might find such a move coy. Others appreciate the enthusiasm. The caller has to be beguilingly charming to pull it off. It's not recommended for the faint of heart.

Should you do the same? Believe me, it's tempting. Reaching out to a prospect in an office a dozen times with no response is punishing.

Calling at home, though, is off the field, so to speak. There are rules to the game, rules of engagement. Reaching out to a family's home is almost like violating someone's privacy or at least ambushing them. Do it all inside the wheelhouse, within the confines of a business setting.

The same colleague wrote heartfelt notes to prospects and addressed the envelope to their homes. In the letter, he would express to the prospects how hard he's been trying to reach them. Oftentimes, wives open the mail at home. He found that letters of this sort might elicit a wife's kind sentiments and help sellers get in the door.

Do weekend cold calls violate any code of communication?

The truth is marketing, advertising and sponsorship heads who toil at retailers like Lowe's, Home Depot and Leslie's will occasionally be in on Saturdays when their stores are open.

Selling doesn't have to be staid. Make it fun!

Can I go over an ad agency's or marketing agency's head?

Going over an agency to a client can be risky. Yet, it's easier to ask for forgiveness than ask for permission.

Are there figures of speech to avoid?

Be circumspect. One day in Memphis, I was at an ad agency and we were talking about a particular sponsorship and how it can be packaged. I said, "There are different ways to skin the cat." The buyer's face turned colors. She stopped me abruptly and almost threw me out of her office. As it turned out, she was Memphis' number one cat lover and on the board of the Memphis Humane Society. I said, "Oops!" That was that. Learn quickly.

Are there better times of day to cold call?

Sometimes, your enthusiasm and creativity will be appreciated early in the morning. If you catch the prospect, great! If not, leave a message, "Last night, I was thinking about you. Wouldn't it be great if every morning the thousands of people who drive near our stadium see a bright sign touting your product? What a way to start the day!"

You never know when targets might pick up their own phones. Years ago, Eric Kahn, Honda's ad director, was partial to those who called early. He appreciated hard workers. If a seller phoned before 8:00 a.m., he was more likely to take the call.

When should I not call a prospect's cell phone?

If you contact prospects by landlines and their voicemail boxes provide a cell phone number for those requiring immediate attention, don't call unless it's absolutely necessary. You'll win the battle but lose the war.

Other than yes or no, what else can I learn from a prospect?

When you do have the privilege of talking with clients, get them to talk about their competitors. You never know what you'll glean. Something said might trigger a lead or a unique way to position your entity. You might find out that a prospect's competitor is about to launch a new product or that it made a personnel move. These generally result in additional budgets or thematic shifts in marketing. These heads-ups can sometimes be priceless. Be prepared with good questions. Do so by first understanding product nuances between top competitors in the prospect's space.

How does sports' seasonality play into the equation?

Timing is everything. Pitch when the sport is on the minds of the American constituency. So when the baseball postseason hits the calendar, viewers are watching the World Series. Fans are engaged. It's a perfect time to pitch next season. Advertisers are saying, "Hey, this is something that we should consider for next year."

Do I start at the top of a prospect's org chart?

New ideas should be pitched to those on top rungs. When you get pushback and wind up with functionaries, bureaucrats and assigned agencies, try to maintain dialogue with top management. Invite them to team and sponsor functions. It won't hurt. If you have to ask for forgiveness from the functionary for doing so, it's fine. But be careful. Brad Barnett at Nationwide described what he would consider irritating, "It's when a seller emails every contact he has at one time in the same company, starting with the CMO or CEO on an opportunity vs. day-to-day leaders, going around the agency when told no, or continuing to contact after being told 'no.'"

If the head of marketing pawns you off on someone else lower in the chain of command, whether internally or at the sports or marketing agency, always ask for a friendly introduction. It's best when dots are connected warmly. Be honest. Tell the marketing director that you're concerned of the anticipated reaction by the person to whom you're being referred because you started at the top.

If indeed you are asked by the person to whom you were switched why you went to the top, sheepishly say you were unfamiliar with the roster of employees and as such started with the head of marketing.

Thank the marketing director and say you'll be in touch. The goal is to keep the boss in the loop. In this case, after the conversation with the person suggested, send the marketing head a note of thanks and cover the outcome of your call with the underling. Try to encourage everyone you're communicating with in the buying hierarchy to take ownership of the process.

When should I avoid overnight deliveries?

Don't overnight letters, trinkets or anything that can wait. It's wasteful and will be viewed as such by the prospect. If it can be scanned or sent snail mail, do so.

When do I begin with a prospect's local or regional head as opposed to going to corporate headquarters?

If you're selling a local program to a national account, begin locally (e.g., University of Central Florida to Regions Bank. Client is in Alabama).

Interest begins locally at the grassroots level. Locally is where the accounts' personnel appreciate the value and power of the sports property being presented.

Oftentimes, you'll get more satisfaction from a regional head or local sales manager. It's they who profit most from the benefits of local sponsorships and advertising programs. Corporate ad directors and the higher-ups in marketing maintain good relationships with these managers in the field. After all, it's the ad director's global goal to enhance brand value and increase visibility so that the regions can produce more revenue in the field. Marketing provides the tools that the regions need. The decision maker is constantly consulting the area manager.

If the sponsorship you're selling is endorsed at that level, there might even be a local budget to push it through without engaging out-of-town upper-tiered hierarchy. If it does need to be cultivated through a super-regional level or through the corporate marketing department, let the local people take up the cause. They'll know the inner-working internally and help shepherd the program through the internal process.

Because the marketing department serves as the regions' advocates and there's support by management in the field for a particular sports package, marketing might be prepared to open its purse strings to satisfy regions' requests.

Even nationally, if the client's sales' head does no more than get your proposal in front of the powers that be in marketing and does so with a strong endorsement, you're ahead of the game. Remember, it's the clients' sales staff that often takes advantage of whatever merchandising and hospitality are provided as part of the deal you're proposing.

I've reached wits' end with a prospect, What should I do?

General Dwight Eisenhower was quoted as saying, "If you can't resolve a problem, make it bigger." In other words, if your calls to sponsorship or advertising heads are unreturned, go to the prospect's top executive. It might create a fuss or commotion, but it will get attention, something you've failed to do until this point.

Going to a boss or to a president is sometimes the only alternative you have. Top executives or their administrative assistants will help navigate your way through the red tape and get you a hearing.

While going over someone's head is unappreciated, whether at the client or at the marketing or ad agency, always ask yourself what are your alternatives? Unfortunately, if you weren't getting satisfaction, your choices are limited. Once in a while, you might get lucky. The boss or big kahuna might have an affinity for what you're selling and will shepherd you along through marketing.

What kind of small talk should I make with a prospect as I develop a relationship?

Always keep a list of generic characteristics you can talk about with your prospect. They might include a spouse's name, likes and dislikes, hometown, prospect's favorite sports team, former employer, college attended, children's name, unique interests, major in college and hot buttons about media and sponsorships. (Stay away from politics.)

If I'm fortunate enough to catch a prospect on the phone, what should I remember?

If you want a meeting, which is why I assume you are calling, it's probably best to tell the prospect exactly that. State how long you'll need and what you'll cover. One way to get the date is to assure the target that you'll be mindful of his or her busy schedule. It's a nice way to say I won't be a pain in the butt and I'll be in and out quickly.

So when you're trying to get an appointment and you caught a decision maker at his desk, flaunt a 30-second success story. If you're a local team's seller, you might say, "You might have heard about our promotion with Domino's Pizza. It generated huge sales of pizza one night last week. Yes, when our team scores 100 points, fans get discounted pizza at Domino's. We can do something similar, and I would love to come over to brainstorm ideas." It might be enough to have the decision maker pencil in a date.

Whatever it is you're selling, whether it's radio, TV or a sports promotional house, always have snippets of case studies that you can spew quickly and cogently. You'll want to do so successfully on an introductory phone call to earn a face-to-face meeting. Marketers will meet with you only if you can help them. People are busy. Be brief, get to the meat of the story and the reason you're calling. You want an appointment.

Set expectations. Don't make a cold call like you were trying to hit a hole-in-one. The cold call is to trigger interest and secure an appointment. The visit then stimulates new sets of expectations all with the goal of an order. If it's a par 5, play it that way. Don't go for a hole in one.

How do I use a sports asset to demonstrate that we would really love having a prospect as a sponsor?

Scoreboards or blimps can be used to personalize messages. Team sellers oftentimes post messages on their scoreboards when the stadium is empty. They entice advertisers, making them feel loved. "The Blazers would love Kia on their team. Mr. Anderson, we would love to see you make it happen!" Everyone loves to see their name in lights. It can sometimes get them to act. Make sure that the 8" x 11" photo of the scoreboard message is neatly framed. Do it right!

How do you cash in on a prospect returning your call?

One day, I answered the phone, and believe it or not, it was a major prospect returning my call within hours of my message. I was so surprised and uplifted that I sent him a handwritten note telling him how grateful I was and how much his return call meant. "Life is measured not by what you do but what you do for others."

Establishing a relationship with prospects will give you the edge when the spending opportunity presents itself. It is then, when prospects have budgets, that they will feel more comfortable doing business with you rather than a stranger. I was representing a television network several years ago and pitched Snyder's Pretzels. Nothing eventuated for months. One day I got a call from the Snyder's prospect. He said, "I have some extra money in my budget, show me what you have." I did and we got a small order.

How do I find out how I'm doing?

Early in your career, while you're still wet behind the ears, ask your boss for constructive criticism, feedback and regular reviews. (Remember New York's Mayor Ed Koch. He would stand in front of subway stations and ask the constituency, "How am I doing?")

Yet there's no greater reassurance than closing a new piece of business. You'll feel like a million bucks and will know that you're doing just fine.

Does it hurt to be different?

Pick your spots to throw off advertisers. West Coast seller David Rubinstein walked into Chevron headquarters in California to see the marketing executive, the late Jim Gordon. This was a conservative and stodgy oil company in the 1980s—suits, ties and polished shoes.

Rubinstein, an iconoclast who at the time represented the Oakland A's, eased the tension by kicking off his shoes and stretching out on Jim's office couch. He would then proceed to pitch and negotiate packages. I can imagine the reaction of stuffy Chevron executives walking by and catching that scene. Some sales characters can get away with anything. In fairness, Gordon and Rubinstein knew each other at that point.

What happens after I crack my first cold call sale?

Never rest on your successes. Yes, an order after a long gestation feels heartwarming. But the oldest line in sales is, you're only as good as your last order. Don't look back. If yesterday seems so big to you, it means you did nothing today.

Is imitation allowed?

Honda wasn't buying sports radio. Westwood One came up with the idea of selling Honda the broadcast booth to its NFL broadcasts. "Welcome back to the Honda Broadcast booth at the Meadowlands." Kraig Kitchin had done the same thing earlier at Premiere Networks, selling AutoZone the studio title to Jim Rome's talk show. Imitation is the best form of flattery.

Do you stop selling once you've been promoted to management?

As your career grows and you're promoted to management, stay on top of your accounts, stay invested in day-to-day selling. Never think that as a manager or as an executive you don't have to sell. Know all your clients, stay engaged in the sales process and never feel that you're removed from it. It will help you throughout your career.

Remaining current will always enable you to find a sales job if and when you need it down the road. You'll then feel comfortable taking a step back and digging into the day-to-day sales trenches.

What's the best way to take ownership of your early sales career?

One phrase is always top of mind. My first boss, Ken Swetz at Katz Media, used it often. "Excuses serve those who make them." Get the job done. Ken was magnificent at turning a word. When he was pitching something and a decision was imminent, he would call the decision maker and say that he felt "like an expecting dad!"

Provide an example of being respectful of a prospect.

When you take the Visa client or a member of one of its agencies to lunch, don't pay with American Express. The thought hit me too late, while I was eating my meal. Frankly, I almost regurgitated my lunch right then and there at the table. At the time, I wasn't a Visa subscriber. Luckily it wasn't a real fancy joint, so I opted to pay by cash. I suspected though that the client wondered whether I owned a Visa card. Thankfully, he never asked.

***

At Katz years ago, I had the president of my company with me at an Anheuser-Busch dinner. He was smoking, which back then was allowed at many restaurants. In fact, one of the AB clients was smoking too.

For a number of minutes at the restaurant, one of the AB executives stared right at me somewhat angrily before motioning me off to the side. We walked away unnoticeably and off in a corner he said, "Would you tell Dick to quit. Did you see what he's smoking?" I said, "Got it, Joe."

It turns out Dick, my president, was smoking Marlboro, a product of Philip Morris, which at the time also owned Miller Beer, AB's major competitor. People are sensitive. AB and Miller were and still are archrivals.

***

Tomorrow you might be taking a client to lunch, and to your surprise, the prospect picks up the check. Years ago, Peter Allerup, a beer client, insisted that he pay for our lunch because, in his view, our lunch discussion benefited him, the client, more so than it did me, the seller. He said that learning of the latest developments in media and what his beer competition is doing was of great advantage to him. It's these uplifting experiences that are an inspiration to keep moving.

How do you sell the sizzle of sports at the outset of the conversation with a prospect?

It's sizzle that sells sports. While ultimately the numbers do have to add up, it's the sizzle that will get the seller in the door. Capture it. "How would you like to have your company's name up in big lights at the stadium all season?" It's a quick, enticing email that's a short enough bite to grab attention and merit an appointment.

In media too, there's something that's particularly exciting about a company enjoying the limelight in sports.

So mention the sport and talent on the phone as quickly as you can to get the prospect to listen. If you're selling broadcasting, mention the personality whether it's Bob Costas nationally or Bob Davis in Kansas, who's the voice of the Jayhawks.

After the conversation, mock up a make-believe newspaper story with a headline. "Michelin buys a piece of the Terps." This would be followed by the story of how Michelin bought a sponsorship and what components it included. Send it to everyone in the decision-making process. It should include mocked pictures of client and team. Also draft a copy of a prospective press release. Demonstrate the enthusiasm for the idea. Show your optimism. Keep whetting prospects' appetites. It will catch some attention!

How do you handle malaise?

Never feel self-pity. Work harder and with greater determination. Charlie Weis, Notre Dame's one-time football coach says, "It's one thing to hope you'll win and another to believe you'll win."

You're at the controls. Stick with it, ride the waves of the sales vicissitudes. You'll be better off for it. Don't give into despair. Everyone goes through tough times. Good sellers survive through thick and thin.

Self-pity is an anathema in sales.

Where else can you come up with ideas on what and how to pitch a prospect?

Don't be afraid to bounce ideas off your manager, co-sellers, family members or your drinking buddies. Two heads are better than one. We're not talking about the Manhattan Project. This doesn't require an understanding of atomic science. It takes perception of consumer behavior. Buddies consume products daily and can lend thoughtful advice. A guy in a bar might have a compelling idea on how men's deodorant might better appeal to him. You can use these anecdotal suggestions in presentations.

What's the key theme in selling sports?

When selling sports, it's important to keep stressing the fact that it's not news, sex or violence.

The sports team is a piece of the rock, part of the community. The pro franchise or the college institution is viewed as a quasi-governmental entity. You're representing the gold standard. Be proud!

How do you handle recessions and financial headwinds?

When times are bad, big events become difficult to sell. In the depth of the Great Recession in 2009, FedEx and the domestic cars determined that it wouldn't be prudent to be visible on the Super Bowl when companies were introducing severe retrenchment programs.

But there's always a silver lining to serve as an oasis of prosperity. There are industries that excel through thick and thin. For that matter, GEICO showed growth during the forgettable years of the recession because consumers were in saving mode and GEICO promised discounts at the price of a phone call. Retailers known for their thriftiness like Sam's Club often prosper. Subway does well as do parts and services retailers that extend the life of expensive investments like automobiles and appliances.

Focus on targets that fit the financial climate of the day. When times are good, pursue luxury items.

In good times, too, don't rest on your laurels. Times won't always be good. Work on your backups when things are good so you'll have backups in harder times.

What examples can you provide of effective listening?

Years ago, FedEx told us that it was keeping an eye on UPS, a traditional bulk shipper, getting into the overnight mail business. Good sellers then pounced on the opportunity with UPS, which was indeed increasing its budget to take share from FedEx.

In a discussion with University of Phoenix, it was learned that its head, Brian Mueller, was leaving the school's presidency to head up Grand Canyon University. It had 'lead' written all over it. Mueller was behind the University of Phoenix naming rights purchase of the Glendale football stadium.

A seller of sports on network radio got wind through a financial client that CapOne, traditionally a television exclusive advertiser, was using radio for the first time in bigger Northeast markets. Would CapOne now consider a national network radio sports program? It is certainly worth trying!

GEICO is the poster child for effective ROIs on advertising. Warren Buffett's Berkshire Hathaway bought GEICO out of bankruptcy in 1975 and continually approved enormous increases in advertising budgets year after year. In 1995, GEICO spent $20 million. By 2009, the budget was up to $800 million. It now exceeds a billion dollars annually. Has the investment worked? In a 16-year period, GEICO quadrupled its share!

The conversational, storytelling and entertainment-themed commercials, called a "whimsy and wit" marketing approach, have now been mimicked by competitors and non-competitors alike.

Sellers with vision saw changes coming among insurance competitors. Stodgy companies like Allstate and Progressive embraced unconventional marketing too. Now the entire category is a huge sports spender with GEICO leading the charge.

Do you befriend competitors?

Don't operate in a vacuum or silo. Competitors of your own team, property or broadcast entity share mutual problems, and you folks can occasionally help one another.

Your friendly competitors might pass along something innocuous enough that might help you generate another lead or helpful idea.

You might hear that a prospect or client had a child. It gives you a chance to send a congratulatory note. You might get wind of personnel changes at a sports marketing or advertising agency. Keep your ear to the grindstone.

Networking, of course, is the fuel that also keeps the engine of a career moving. If one job doesn't work out and you're looking for another job, friends within the industry will be allies. Remain friendly with your competitors.

This isn't Pat Riley's Knicks' team unwilling to extend a hand to help an opponent off the floor.

What nuances should I read into dialogue with my sales manager?

In the movie *The Express*, Syracuse football coach Ben Schwartzwalder repeatedly heaps praises on Ernie Davis to motivate him to go the extra yard. It's a Pygmalion technique that some sales managers use for inspiration too. A comment like, "I know you can do it. That's why I hired you. I'm absolutely confident that you'll be a star," often brings out the best in people. The ongoing praise promotes a self-fulfilling prophecy. Sellers just don't want to let down someone who believes in them and will as such work tirelessly until they make their budgets.

Through these repetitive reassurances, sales managers might ask you to hit an unattainable budget. "You're good. You can get it done." It might be music to your ears, but think hard before you commit to a budgetary number that is unachievable.

Do concepts ever emanate from the prospect?

Many of the great sports and media sales started with concepts completely concocted by clients themselves. For instance, Heinz created the Red Zone in football. They introduced it at Heinz Field in Pittsburgh. Now so many college and pro teams have their own red zone sponsor. So, when you're with prospects, encourage them to come up with tie-ins of their own wishes. It will give them a sense of authorship. It will enable you to work with them symbiotically to create partnerships to their liking.

Marketers recognize big names. They value charisma. Many will also appreciate the value of engaging with a worthwhile community charity. If so, include it as a promotional element in the framework of the proposal. Capture the top line of the idea in a 20-second tease. Spit it out enthusiastically and ask for an appointment.

Tom Murray, who runs Perio, manufacturers of Barbasol, fostered a charitable relationship with Boomer Esiason's Cystic-Fibrosis Foundation. It's a win-win. For every made field goal on Monday nights, Perio makes a contribution to the foundation. It's a worthwhile cause and is easily promotable on NFL broadcasts.

How do you show your prospect that you want to foster a true partnership?

Prospects have to feel that you're proposing a mutually beneficial agreement. If they feel you're looking for a quick sale, they'll dismiss the offering.

Keep focusing on the word 'partnership.' The client should feel partner and symbiosis, not sale. If the prospect thinks this is a hit-and-run pursuit, there will be immediate distrust that will be hard to overcome. Talk of an embedded product, of indulging yourself in the success of this partnership, of an intrusive campaign for the good of the prospect's products and services.

As John Macdonald at Enterprise Car Rental says, "Because a seller who does not have a relationship with me or my business will not know my particular needs, the first communication should be attempting to start a relationship. In order to start a relationship, the seller has to convince me that he/she or his/her properties can have the potential to meet my needs/issues. Listening not selling is required."

How do we use our coaches, players or broadcasters to sign sponsors?

Deputize visible faces or respected personalities in your organization to take up your cause. Have these popular figures spend time regularly, every few weeks, reaching out to prospects by phone, email, and letters. Customize something special for them to say so that it's somewhat personalized and that it addresses the status of each particular situation. Let them allot time each few weeks to reach clients you're trying to cultivate or move the sales process closer to the finish line. You will provide them with names of the prospects and the status account-by-account that you would like them to reach.

Any special dress code for certain calls?

Always check the dress code before you head out on a call. At Enterprise, for instance, white shirts and ties are the order of the day. If you go on Fridays, it's a blue shirt. Even those behind the counter who will usher you to your rented vehicle wear a shirt and tie. Jack Taylor, a military man founded Enterprise. He believed in structure. When in Rome, do like the Romans.

How do I show the prospect I don't hold grudges if I lose a deal?

If after a long gestation, the deal falls through, show your prospect that you understand. Respond like the UPS team does when it loses a piece of business to a competitor: send a boxed lunch. Tomorrow is another day. Nothing is forever. More opportunities will surface.

How have corporate scandals and the demise of banks affected sponsorship sales?

It's a new world. Enron and other derelict directors of publicly traded companies forced Congress to tighten rules. Congressional legislation, Sarbanes–Oxley and Dodd–Frank, has handcuffed expenditures. Under the microscope, executives think twice before committing to college sponsorships if they are alumni of the school. They fear potential repercussions.

These days, teams, networks and rights-holders oftentimes struggle to even get clients to accept trips. Companies, particularly those publicly traded, don't want to be vulnerable to criticism and potential investigations.

How do I use an asset like the broadcast booth?

Entertaining in the broadcast booth and down on the field is a magical element that's almost unique to sports. Bring a prospect's child. The client will be indebted to you forever. It's great to reach a dad through his child. Nothing beats it.

I'm starting out cold calling and have been placed in a pit with other sellers. There's no privacy. It's a little intimidating. Any suggestions?

The difficulty of cold calling is much harder when doing so in a pit with fellow sellers, in a Macy's window so to speak. It's tough enough leaving creative messages or pleading for a return call in the privacy of a closed room. Doing so within an earshot of a floor full of colleagues is a bitch.

I would often suggest to my cold callers that they schedule time in a conference room for their own use so that they have freedom to say what they wish without other ears on the wall. It's tough to be yourself in an open office setting. You might be able to write email freely, but phone conversations are restraining.

How important is rest?

Be rested and have energy! Verne Harnish who heads up Gazelles Inc., an executive search firm, wrote an instructive story for *Fortune*. He covered a broad range of advice, like improving internal communication, maintaining an unbending focus and remaining steadfastly organized. Harnish underscores the need to protect your sleep. He goes so far as to suggest not to read from smartphones at night because the blue light that's emitted disrupts sleep. "Blue blocker" is even suggested. One thing is for sure, you'll want to feel pumped every morning. To do so, it's imperative to feel rested.

Any tips on staying focused?

Harnish talks in the same *Fortune* article about steering away from exogenous distractions. It's easy to digress when a computer is on or when a smartphone is handy. Discipline yourself. Don't go to sports sites or other areas of interest. Focus on your work. Try shutting off your phone and staying off social media for a few hours each day.

The Internet should be used for the sacred mission of gathering and crystallizing information covering leads you are chasing, industries you might want to explore as targets and the like. Yes, it's easier said than done. One way to achieve this is to simply quantify your goals every day for the number of new calls you make, the number of follow ups and the time you spend to investigate new prospects.

What is your advice on camaraderie and conviviality in offices?

When something good happens in the office, such as another seller getting an order, congratulate your colleague enthusiastically and sincerely. Management looks for team players. Salute your peers. It shows goodwill and promotes staff camaraderie.

When you get an order, be humble about it around the office. The explosion of happiness should be channeled to your confidence, not demonstratively in the view of others in your office. Understand that others might have had bad days.

Victory forges community, but when you're going through a tough stretch and it feels like the world is out to get you, fight harder. Don't ever allow setbacks to erode confidence among your peers. It's infectious at any level.

When you get an order, yes, it's a 'bullhorn' moment, but don't forget the underlings. Always thank the sales planning and promotions department, administrative assistants and others who helped you along the way. At the Super Bowl in 2009, when Sully Sullenberger was honored for landing a doomed US Airways flight in the Hudson, he was introduced with the entire crew, his co-captain and flight attendants. No man is an island. It's a team effort. Your management is not only judging your sales ability but also gauging your camaraderie and maturity.

How do you deal with morose buyers?

You will run into them too often during your career. They're incorrigibly gloomy and will occasionally take out their frustrations on sellers.

Light up the room. Whether it is in person or on the phone, try to remain disarming. Try to bring a smile to the person on the other end of the phone. Remain an oasis of happiness and optimism.

What are the advantages of selling for a company that represents a number of properties, say the Olympics, golf, the NFL and the NHL?

When selling a variety of sports products, break up the daily monotony by occasionally focusing on one product at a time instead of a broad menu. When you're part of a team that sells a handful of media packages, mix it up. Say to yourself, "Today, I'm going to reach out to all golf leads and tomorrow the NFL." Doing it this way can sometimes keep things moving more interestingly.

If you work for a multi rights holder like IMG or Learfield that sell a menu of teams, any caveats?

If you're trying to sell Notre Dame to an Irish fan or alum, don't walk in with a Boston College shirt, even if you're in New England and also represent the Eagles. This is the prospect's proud moment. Don't be insulting. It's happened. The seller was told in no uncertain terms to think before he comes back next time.

Any better time of year to sell sports?

Oddly enough, although the sponsorship business slows down around the Christmas holiday, it's not a bad time to attempt a cold call. People have a little more patience and are a little more generous and prepared to share a moment with a fellow human being. It's also yearend bonus time, and after getting their bonuses, prospects are in cheery moods. As Charles Dickens wrote, "I have always thought of Christmas time as a good time; a kind, forgiving, charitable, pleasant time."

It's a particularly good time to sell baseball in the cold climes of the North. In cold December when spirits are uplifted by the joy of the holiday season, baseball and warm weather are indeed welcoming thoughts.

How do prospects feel about being texted?

Tom Peyton HONDA	Text should only be used during an existing dialog or deal negotiation...never for a cold call.
Anonymous AUTO-RELATED MARKETER	Absolutely not, unless I engage texting first.
John MacDonald ENTERPRISE	I find that overbearing.
Drew Iddings HERSHEY'S	Text messages are meant for familiar social communication, not business. Please don't. Ever.
Noah Syken IBM	No (inappropriate)
Rex Conklin HOME DEPOT	No!
David Lim AMTRAK	I feel they have invaded my personal space...unless I have an existing relationship with someone.
Julie Lyle HHGREGG	Absolutely not. That is my personal space for urgent matters.
Stephen Quinn WAL-MART	My family texts me, and I never want to get a text from someone I won't be eating dinner with this week.

Phil Wang WELLS FARGO	Too intrusive. You should not text me. That's a channel that you need to get permission to use.
Ed Gold STATE FARM	Never, ever text me, unless I tell you it is OK.
Betsy Wilson UPS	I would only accept / respond to a text from someone I'm already doing business with, and have a strong working relationship. A cold contact via text is not acceptable.
Paul Hodges REGIONS BANK	I don't care for texts unless they are from partners/sellers that I have an established relationship with.
Mark Eckert EDWARD JONES	You've just entered my personal space, and will never be responded to or considered for anything in the future.
Tim Sullivan WENDY'S	Not acceptable unless I give permission.
Ellie Malloy JOHN HANCOCK	Please, no. It's invasive.
Brad Barnett NATIONWIDE	Too intrusive for first line of communication. I would suggest sellers never take this approach. After a relationship is established, this can be effective, but not initially.
Michael Robichaud MASTERCARD	On a cold call? I'll ignore. When I worked at Nextel, I was the only employee in the company that didn't put his Nextel phone number on his business card to avoid cold calling to my phone. If I know you well enough, you have my mobile.
Jack Hollis TOYOTA	Texting is absolutely not an appropriate method of communication for cold calls. Texts do not help me get to know a person, their service or business.

Chapter 11

Anecdotal Experiences

You Never Know

The NFL's senior vice president, Brian Lafemina, will tell you, "In the next decade, in the past decade, or in any decade, the lifeblood of any professional sports franchise is new business. Since I was a kid, I have collected yearbooks from various teams going all the way back to the 1950s, and one of the things I noticed early on is that 90% of the sponsors change within any 10-year period. So, if you are not looking for the next sponsor and always filling that pipeline, you are putting your business at risk."

In that pursuit, as Linda said of her husband, Willy Loman, in the classic *Death of a Salesman*, "A small man can be just as exhausted as a great man."

When you fall off a bike, just get up and try again.

Wrangler
Pop off the mat resiliently and go for it!

In downtown Greensboro one afternoon, after a disappointing face-to-face sales presentation at Jefferson Pilot (now Lincoln Financial), I headed dispiritedly to the airport.

I knew that the best cure for a disappointing sales call is to make another one immediately. Never end the day on a discouraging note.

Looking out the window of my rented car, a bright marquee appeared unexpectedly from atop a downtown office building. It read Wrangler. Shame on me that I didn't know Wrangler was housed in Greensboro. I thought that I had scoured the marketplace for prospects to make the trip efficient. I obviously missed a big one.

So I said to myself, "what the heck." Let me walk in on the company and see what damage I can do. I was at a terrible disadvantage. I had no idea for whom to even ask. I had no access to directories or informational resources. Mobile devices in the early 2000s weren't quite as sophisticated as they are today.

I drove to the Wrangler building, got out of the car and walked toward the receptionist. To mask the awkwardness of the moment, I marched in confidently with a military-like posture. Thankfully, the receptionist, a polite North Carolinian was accommodating.

I told her that I was in the neighborhood and hoped to track down Wrangler's marketing director. The woman asked whether I had an appointment. And I'm thinking, "I can't even come up with a name, a meeting, forget it!"

So instead of doing a Jackie Gleason "homma, homma, homma," I was honest and admitted who I was and what I was trying to accomplish. "I need a little of your help." So she phoned upstairs and reached out to an administrative assistant. I was able to overhear only one side of the conversation, the receptionist's. I watched and listened. Her grim facial expressions weren't promising. After hanging up, she politely told me that Mark Clift, the company's marketing director was behind closed doors and would not see me.

Well, I say to myself. "Look, I won't be in Greensboro again, so let me pleasantly persist." Overbearing won't get it done.

I proceed to give the receptionist a beseeching look of despair, one that I hoped would earn her empathy. I said, "Please give Mr. Clift's assistant one more try. Should he give me an audience, I will be mindful of his busy day and won't be long. Promise!"

She gave me an uncomfortable but acquiescing look and redialed Clift's office. After engaging in a short conversation, she tells me that Clift's assistant will ask him whether he can make some time for a short visit. I take a seat in the reception area and wait and wait. After some thirty minutes, the receptionist's phone rings and I hear, "OK, I'll tell him."

"Mr. Clift will be down in a few minutes," she shares with a taut smile of relief.

"Wow, how about that!" I say to myself.

Half an hour later, Mark Clift arrives in the lobby with a warm smile, wearing what he peddles: Wrangler jeans. He politely tells me that he doesn't take meetings without appointments. "But if you want to join me outside, I'm taking a cigarette break."

It was a bone-chilling rainy day in Greensboro. Clift was probably annoyed that I barged in on him against the usual protocol. He wasn't about to apologize for having me bellow a shortened pitch on the Wrangler porch.

His accent was redolent of the South, but I couldn't quite put my finger on exactly where. Instead of plowing right into my pitch, I first asked Clift about his geographic background. He told me that he is from Tennessee and a fan of the Vols' football team. Being a radio play-by-play nut, I immediately asked if he ever listened to John Ward. I asked because I knew what he would say. "Of course, which Vols' fan doesn't know John Ward?" he tells me proudly before impersonating the venerable broadcaster's touchdown call. The brief diversion loosened him up a bit.

Unlike many others I met, he had no biases against radio play-by-play. I told him about our Westwood One programming and he said that he was vaguely familiar with the sports coverage, or at least he said so to be polite.

After some fifteen minutes, I wasn't sure who wanted to end this impromptu meeting first, Clift who had to get back to his office or me, standing in a polluted haze of cigarette smoke. I asked him for his card, and he began poking around his pockets before digging into his wallet and apologizing for giving me a mucky and bent one.

Clift expressed some mild interest in our NFL property and gave me a couple names with whom to follow up. We did as he prescribed, pitching the agency and later his ad director, Craig Errington.

After a few months we secured a small order, and through the years, we grew the business into a healthy annual six-figure commitment. Within ten years, Wrangler was spending a few million dollars in network radio.

In the world of sales development, you never know. I had flown to Greensboro to see Lincoln Financial and failed. I had no appointment with Wrangler, walked in cold and enjoyed a fruitful beginning!

Today, had I used a smartphone to log into any number of advertising or sponsorship directories, I might not have been as ill prepared walking through the door at Wrangler. Then again, by appearing self-assured, would I have evoked the sympathy of the receptionist? I guess I'll never know.

Getty Oil
Do you have the personality to pull this off?
How will the prospect respond?

When I started in this business at Katz, I worked for an iconoclastic character, an irreverent, unforgettable chap. His name was Gil Miller, may his soul rest in peace. Jimmy Dolan, Madison Square Garden's head honcho, later gave Gil a virtual lifetime contract at Cablevision. He was that good.

Gil was one of the most unpredictable characters you could meet. Among other things, he belonged to a nudist colony. That alone tells you a little about his offbeat persona. He would often have no idea what he was selling, but he was mesmerizing. Gil was a little guy, probably no more than 5'3". Wow could he sell.

As a young salesperson, I was pitching Getty, an account handled by Air Time, a major media buying service in the 1970s and 1980s.

One day, I got an appointment to see Air Time's president Bruce Fogel, and I took Gil, my supervisor at the time, with me to the meeting.

It was an ice cold New York day. We both bundled up and walked over to see Fogel. When we arrived, we announced ourselves to the receptionist who showed us to the guest closet where we hung our coats. Shortly afterward, Bruce's secretary warmly greeted us and walked us down to his corner office.

When we walked in, Bruce was on the phone, but he motioned for us to take seats. Media buying services then were like city rooms of local daily newspapers—chaotic and noisy.

As we settled in his stifling office, I noticed that Gil was still wearing his scarf and gloves. I'm embarrassed beyond belief. What in the world is he doing with his scarf and gloves on in the stuffy office of the agency president?

Bruce shortly gets off the phone and the meeting begins. There were some pleasantries, followed by our presentation. Through it all, members of Bruce's staff are poking their heads through his office door, eager for a minute of his time. Believe me, these disruptions often take precedence over a rep's pitch. Not then. Despite the bevy of activity, Bruce never interrupts us, not once. Meanwhile, I'm thinking, What is Bruce thinking of Gil's indoor garb, scarf and gloves?

When the meeting ends and Gil and I are in the elevator, I said, "Gil, why in the world were you wearing your scarf and gloves in the man's office?" He took a deep breath and looked me straight in the eyes, a harbinger of a lesson that the veteran seller was about to share. Gil took command of the moment with a didactic tone and a deliberate pace. "Bruce Fogel is a busy man, isn't he?" I nod my head, yes. "Did you notice that he never took his eyes off me, did he?" I concurred. "Not once! He listened to every word," I said. Gil goes on, "Do you think that would have been the case had I sat there like every other run of the mill salesperson?"

Lesson learned. Create a niche. Be memorable.

Buyer #1: An innocuous ruse. One day I'm sitting in my office and the phone rings. Gil says, "Sal?" I said, "No, Gil, you dialed me, David." As it turned out the whole thing was a ruse. Gil was in the office of an agency buyer pretending he was calling the president of our company to get approvals for additional accommodations that the buyer insisted be included in a package she was considering. Gil made it sound like the requests were third-rail issues.

"Well, if Judy is to approve this sponsorship, we'll have to provide the client a trip to the all-star game." Gil carried on, begging and pleading for added sponsorship elements. I was young, and it took me a minute to catch on. Although he knew all along he could provide the extras, he was showing the buyer whose office he was in while on the phone that he was fighting on her behalf. It worked. Gil demonstrated to Judy that he secured the impossible, he went to the top to get it and she should now approve the deal. She did.

Buyer #2: Dig into a bag of tricks. I watched Gil in my early days and remember seeing him struggle at times to reach particular clients. He tried over and over. These were pre-email days, of course, and before voicemail messages were available everywhere. Secretaries screened calls then.

After he had suffered all the frustration he could handle trying to get through to a prospect, he reached out one last time and told his secretary to promise her boss good news if the prospect took his call. Using this approach, a beleaguered prospect grudgingly picked up the phone. "Mr. Hall," Gil starts, "I promise you good news if you give me 60 seconds to tell you about the Kansas City Royals." Gil then proceeds to generate enough excitement with the prospect and earned an appointment. Afterward, Hall, almost anticlimactically says, "So, what's the good news you promised?" Gil answers, "Mr. Hall, had you not given me an appointment, I would have promised you that I would never ever call again. You and your patient secretary would never have to put up with me again." Hall chuckled, appreciating Gil's unconquerable spirit.

Again, the idea is to get in the door and use the opportunity to maintain dialogue and communication.

Super Bowl Suites
Taking advantage of a fertile setting

At Westwood One, our deal included a cherished suite at the Super Bowl. Stadia today generally have a couple of levels of suites that ring the building. It's the high rent district, especially on Super Bowl Sunday. The suites are well represented by Fortune 500 companies.

While I had responsibility for entertaining clients in our own suite, I would work the scores of other suites each year. I kept my laptop or iPad with me in the stadium so that I could research the top executive names of one company after another. Each suite had a label. I would walk into Kellogg's suite, for instance, and ask for an executive by name. If he or she wasn't there, I would throw out another name. Each Super Bowl produced a ton of good leads, appointments and eventually new business. But believe me, it takes audacity to walk into these suites cold. We generally had personalities in our suite, whether Bill O'Reilly or Dennis Miller. So I would ask these executives if they wanted to come down to meet them. At the Super Bowl, executives are relaxed and patient, so they're more open to unsolicited greetings.

Buyer #3: Cold calling frustration manifested itself unintentionally, and it worked. I kept calling this one target, but the secretary was cold and stoically unhelpful. I tried two or three times, and she was impervious to any reason. So I called one more time, and I began stuttering out of complete frustration.

"I keep calling and I've gotten nowhere," I told her and began to stammer with halted breath. "Ple, Ple, Ple, Pleeease, I would love to get a minute with Mr. Hudson." Anyhow, Hudson was simply compassionate or must have thought that I was a lunatic. He got on the phone with me.

After the experience, I began to wonder whether I should stutter on purpose. The truth is that stuttering is better with an airline reservation agent on the phone or a waitress in a restaurant. It demonstrates a sense of urgency for service, attention or sympathy. It's a tactic at best, not a strategy on a sales call.

Kodak
Be ready at a moment's notice

Still fueled by innocence two years or so into my first sales job, I was peddling three radio baseball franchises that Katz Media represented nationally, in other words, outside the teams' locales.

The Royals were beginning to improve but the sphere of excitement for selling team sponsorships is in teams' regional radiuses, not outside of them where it's difficult to taste the indigenous excitement they generate. We had the Dodgers on radio too when radio garnered bigger audience shares than they do today. Yet for all the history, beginning with the incomparable Vin Scully, selling Dodgers' radio packages outside of Southern California is trying to find a pin in a haystack. But I was too young, awestruck and, like a lot of young people, just happy to be in the game.

One winter day, I reached out to Kodak in Rochester and I got the runaround. In those days, marketing and advertising people still had assistants who most often screened incoming calls. Sometimes by warming up an assistant, you would get a target on the phone.

The Kodak administrative assistant (called a secretary back then) insisted that I contact Bill Campbell at J. Walter Thompson, the company's ad agency in New York. Although I wanted to reach the client directly, there seemed to be no recourse. I would have to start with the agency.

I did a little homework and found out that Campbell was a former college football player who later served as head coach of Columbia University's football team. He didn't have much coaching success. He was let go after six seasons in 1979 after a 1–8 record. Campbell popped himself off the mat immediately and pursued a career in marketing. He landed at Thompson managing the Kodak account. Business was not foreign to him. While playing football, he earned his Columbia degree in economics.

Bill Campbell picked up the phone on my first attempt. He didn't say much but let me give my spiel. I wanted to sell him the Red Sox' play-by-play broadcasts, in addition to the Dodgers and Royals. I finished my intro by asking him for an appointment. He said, "Can you come over now?" Wow! I didn't waste any time. By the time I hung the phone up, I had my jacket on and rushed over to Thompson. I grabbed a couple off-the-rack presentations on my way out, the best I could do given the immediacy of the opportunity.

In the office, Campbell was a man of few words. He was a busy man.

I told him what I had. He asked a couple of questions, made a couple of requests and said, "You have an order." He bought three packages on the spot. I was so stunned that, had I been hit with a feather, I would have fallen off my chair. I had never experienced anything like it.

The feeling was eerie. I felt like I was given the keys to the kingdom. For that matter, I was so leery that I didn't immediately call the three franchises to share the good news. The entire development was that implausible.

How real can this guy be? Generally, even if an ad agency has interest in a package, it will be eyed over and analyzed by a litany of people in the media department before it's sent to the client with a recommendation.

It taught me a lesson that I didn't appreciate until I was a veteran seller. Bright minds and bold executives are more confident about making impulsive decisions. Intuitively, Campbell felt that Kodak should have a presence in a family game like baseball, when the outdoor season is in full swing. What better than the sport that then was arguably the country's pastime?

He could have had the proposals float around the agency's media department where the gremlins would have scrutinized all elements until the season came and went. He didn't. Campbell went with his gut and reached out on a limb. His instincts said do it and he did.

Placing the order a couple of months before the season allowed him to market the program internally, to plan some product placement or what in today's vernacular is called experiential marketing.

The Campbell story will happen to a seller once in a decade or two. The Bill Campbells of the world don't surface every day.

In getting to watch Campbell, I said to myself that this man will either be fired shortly for operating against the grain or will run the place in due time.

By the time the baseball season that year was up and running, Campbell was promoted to head of marketing at Kodak corporate in Rochester. He was a man on a fast track. From Rochester, Campbell went to California to become marketing head for Apple. It was then run by John Sculley and Apple didn't have the cachet it has today.

Over his thirty years in Silicon Valley, Campbell has become somewhat of an icon, a mentor and coach to CEOs of several major corporations, 17 years on the Apple board and today he is chairman of Intuit.

There's an interesting twist to my cold call. In 2009, 30 years after we met, I reached out to Bill with the cooperation of Chris Simko at CBS Television to see whether Intuit would have an interest in becoming an official NCAA sponsor. Intuit is a visible leader in tax and small business accounting software.

So Bill and I had a phone conversation about a customized package. After all, it made so much sense. NCAA basketball is played in the heart of the winter, the early part of the calendar year, when America's rank and file are beginning to file their tax returns, the core of Intuit's business. He asked that I send him a proposal, which I did.

When I got him on the phone to follow up, he didn't beat around the bush. He said no as quickly as he said yes 30 years earlier. That was that. You win some and you lose some.

Corona
Share a personal experience

There's nothing like sharing a story with a prospect that hits home. It's so much more compelling. For years, category exclusivity was critical to marketers. Anheuser Busch, as a beer for example, didn't want Miller to have any part of the team broadcasts it sponsored. Cars were the same way until the influx of foreign autos broadened the marketplace into a sellers' market. With more demand against their inventory, television entities had to guarantee no more than import, luxury or domestic exclusivity. As auto ad demand continued to grow, local television stations provided even less separation. Keeping two autos out of one commercial cluster was about the best the stations guaranteed.

We were visiting with Corona one day, and I talked about the Friday when my dad, not a big beer drinker, brought home a six pack of Ballantine, not Rheingold. Back then, when local breweries dominated beer consumption, Ballantine sponsored the Yankees and Rheingold the Mets. I was a Mets' fan growing up, and I bristled at my father for bringing Ballantine into a Mets' household. An announcer like the Yankees' Mel Allen was as associated with Ballantine as he was with the team. Sponsors considered it a privilege to associate their brands with local sports institutions. It was a magical connection that reaped great benefits, tangible and intangible.

Today, in a commoditized world amidst an ever-fragmented media landscape, the osmosis and symbiosis of team and sponsor is a cherished relic that is still so precious.

An 'announcer's read' still has great value whether it's Vin Scully singing the praises of a Farmer John hotdog in Southern California or Bob Uecker touting Miller Beer in Milwaukee. In the day, the Knicks' first voice, the iconic Marty Glickman, enthusiastically bonded team and sponsor inextricably. Made Knicks' baskets were "Good, like Nedicks!" The phrase became so popular that it echoed through the New York schoolyards. Nedicks, the New York orange drink, became part of the local nomenclature. It's this power that you hope to translate and communicate in a pitch.

UPS
Double check the vendor with which you're sending a shipment

Never take anything for granted. The road to hell is paved with good intentions.

It's easier said than done. If you're about to send UPS a pitch, tickets or anything overnight, be sure not to send it by FedEx. Please. You would be surprised how often it happens. So much can get lost in translation. Between messages to assistants and their instructions to a diminishing breed of mailroom employees, a lot can go wrong!

Make sure it is delivered with the vendor you're pitching. There's a heated rivalry between the two competitors. When a package arrives by FedEx at UPS, the FedEx driver trumpets victoriously by honking rhythmically a few annoying times as he cruises around the circular driveway. UPS will most certainly not even open the package.

Clients are sensitive about reciprocity. A little quid pro quo!

Buyer #4: Reach out by cashing in on a prospect's passion. We were trying to do more business with a client who shall remain nameless (to protect the innocent). I came to learn that the advertiser was raised in Cleveland and had fond memories of the "Miracle of Richfield," the great Cavaliers' playoff run in the mid 1970s. I happened to know the legendary voice of the Cavs, Joe Tait. I asked Joe to send a tape to this client with highlights of that unforgettable Cleveland season. When the client received it, he was quite excited. He was a great fan of the Cavs and Tait, and the recording triggered innocent memories of his youth in Northern Ohio. We got the order!

Undisclosed Prospect
Be tastefully irreverent

I was meeting a couple of stiff prospects for lunch and was joined by another one of our sellers. That morning, I wasn't sure which tie to wear. My wife suggested one and I had my eye on another. So when I arrived at lunch I wore one tie, and after a few minutes left the table, went to the bathroom and changed ties. When I got back, I told the prospects the story and asked them for their opinions on which tie worked best. It eased the tension at the table. It triggered some conversation, and we had an enjoyable lunch. It won't work very well today. Ties are becoming things of the past.

Office
Nothing you hear should surprise you

Funny things happen that you will remember forever. When I was selling radio sports, I came back from a lunch date and my new assistant gave me a quizzical look. "Kathy from Y&R [major ad agency] called and said she wants the floor mats immediately." I'm thinking, Does our broadcast company now also sell floor mats?

I said to my assistant, "No, Judy. Y&R wants a list of the stations' formats—the programming they run; news, country, sports. You get it? Not floor mats."

I knew my assistant didn't have a long future in office work when a few days later I heard her shout across the hall to another assistant, "How many Ls in Dallas, two or three?"

Undisclosed Prospect
Perceived manners at the lunch table

In the late 1970s, as a young New York based Katz Media seller, I took a prospect to lunch in Dallas and was joined by Katz' Texas sales manager. I thought the meeting went well, but as I came to learn, it didn't really. The prospect was slighted by what he deemed were my improper table manners. I was young and learning every day, but this encounter would stand the test of time.

Growing up, my dad always insisted that I keep my elbows off the table and that I eat with proper manners. He looked at me nefariously whenever I didn't.

Although I'm a righty, I hold the knife and cut the food with my left hand and hold the fork and eat the food with my right hand. Apparently, most righty Americans switch utensils from one hand to the other after every bite so that they cut their food and eat, both with their right hand. Although I didn't slobber at the Texas table that day and there were no crash landings of food from mouth or plate, the prospect dubbed the practice European. That was that. No order. I accepted it as a regional bias. America is a great country.

Some twenty five years later when I was running Westwood One's sports division, I called Exxon's head of public affairs, Ken Cohen, to talk about the Masters, which we were carrying on radio. He generously invited me to Dallas for lunch to discuss particulars. When I arrived at Exxon's sprawling campus, I was ushered into the corporate dining room where we were served nobly in a private location. I was introduced to Exxon's CEO, Rex Tillerson, who happened to be having lunch in the dining room at the same time. It was a fleeting moment, but one I will always savor.

As I sat comfortably but humbly among corporate royalty, I remembered the prospect who disparaged my manners 25 years earlier. How would he have reacted to seeing me dine in the majestic Exxon dining room?

Media Edge
Losing a tooth on the way to a sales call

I was coming off a root canal on an upper front tooth and the temporary crown fell off while I was rushing to an appointment at Media Edge. I couldn't get the crown back in on my own. I was late for an appointment. I didn't look pretty, but heck, I went for it. I figured if there's any way to be disarming on a sales call, this was it. Actually I was very self-conscious and talked without moving the top of my mouth. Do what you have to do!

Undisclosed Agency
Watch what you say

You never know. Be careful what you say and where. One day in Minneapolis, I was talking with a buyer at an ad agency. We made some early small talk, chatting about exercise regimens. Before segueing into the pitch, I said to the lady, "Whatever you're doing, keep it up. It's working. You've got a girlish figure." I came to learn later that she found the comment offensive. One person's compliment is another's insult.

Entertaining Clients
Nothing you hear should surprise you

In my years doing St. John's basketball, I invited a client's daughter to sit with me at the broadcast table before a game. While I was preparing for the broadcast, she watched the players shoot around.

To keep her occupied, I gave her a copy of the St. John's roster so that I can continue to work undisturbed. At a pause, she sheepishly turned to me with the look of someone who experienced an epiphany. Confidently pointing to the roster, she says, "I discovered something interesting. Look, almost all the St. John's players were born in June. See, it says, 6-7, 6-9, 6-8, 6-5, 6-2." I stopped her and warmly put my hand on her wrist. "Not really, Maddy; those are the heights of the players. Most basketball players are above six feet."

Necco
Going over the head of an elusively stubborn prospect

I noticed a feature story in the local newspaper on Necco Candies. As a matter of courtesy, I sent it to the company's marketing director. I was hoping that she would appreciate it. There was no way she would have seen it 1,500 miles away.

When I didn't get the common courtesy of a thank you, I called the woman. When she didn't get back to me for weeks, I fumed. This one really annoyed me to no end. I was tempted to unleash a verbal attack, but I bit my tongue and maintained measured restraint. After some eight weeks elapsed and no response from her, I researched the company and came to learn that the company had been bought by a venture capitalist in Washington. So, of course, I called. After a few days, I began a dialogue with the executive of the VC firm that hired the marketing director, who was absolutely discourteous. The venture capitalist was a gentleman. The marketing director of Necco is still nowhere to be found.

Chapter 12

Great Cold Calling Sports Sponsorship Success Stories

Sports have come a long way!

In 1956, the football Giants couldn't nail down a single sponsor for their radio broadcasts, and the first two games of the season weren't carried at all. In a desperate measure, colorful announcer Les Keiter went on-air over WINS in New York and publicly asked his audience for sponsor leads. The *New York Times* responded. The newspaper sponsored the broadcasts that season, making the games available on New York radio. Television in those years blacked out home games.

You might say that Les cold called on air!

Sports inventory the last forty years or so has grown exponentially. Consider this. Until the 1980s, the dasher boards at NHL arenas were pristine, the NBA had no floor signage and baseball ran only one minute of commercial time between half-innings. Today, in-facility signage is littered and baseball broadcasts run as many as two minutes of spots between half-innings.

Beginning in January 1971, cigarette commercials were banned from television and radio, wiping out a productive revenue category that broadcasters had to replace. By the 1970s, the standard length of network television spots decreased to 30 seconds from 60 seconds. For all intents and purposes, this development doubled broadcasters' overall inventory. Add the advent of cable television in the 1970s and 1980s. It, too, resulted in a massive explosion of advertising inventory both locally and nationally.

In sports, the four major leagues lustily added new franchises and built new buildings with rich trappings, like luxury boxes and hospitality suites. The pros added playoff games, and the NCAA significantly expanded the basketball tournament field. As a result of this massive explosion of supply, there's an unending exigency to find and sell new advertisers and sponsors.

Longtime NBA executive and now prominent industry consultant Ed Desser pointed out in an opinion column in *SportsBusiness Journal,* "Sports organizations have transformed into multifaceted media and entertainment enterprises. No longer do they just stage and administer events, sell tickets and sponsorships and license media rights to legacy network platforms, handing over control of their brands and valuable content. Rather, today's modern sports property has evolved into one that systematically captures, processes and distributes its own content, strategically integrating its interrelated businesses."

The NFL's senior vice president of Club Business Development, Brian Lafemina, points out, "With the advent of the digital age and a seemingly insatiable appetite for sports, there is almost no limit to the inventory that can be created. In addition to the content, there are more platforms that you can deliver the content on—web, mobile, social and more. On each of these platforms there are multiple channels—YouTube, Facebook, Twitter, Instagram, Apple TV, Netflix and so on. All of these allow for greater segmentation of sponsor messages, creating opportunities for sponsors that may never have used sports as a marketing tool to become a part of the ecosystem. All of this will lead to more sponsors and has already redefined the skill set that a successful sales executive will need to possess."

By 2018, Pricewaterhouse projects the sports sponsorship business to grow to $17.6 billion. By then, PwC also expects sports media rights to hit $19.3 billion, a jump of 30% from 2014. The report states, "Stronger economic conditions and the industry's continued relaxation of prior brand category restrictions should grow the funds available for sponsorship commitments and mitigate, to a certain extent, the net impact consideration related to the industry's rollout of new sponsorship inventory." The company also notes that the revenue gap between media rights and the industry's largest segment, gate revenues are projected to close to within $500 million (2 percent) by 2018.

To reach these lofty numbers, it will be critical for governing bodies, team owners, leagues, athletic directors and others charged, to propel sponsorship revenue by nailing down fresh corporate dollars. In other words, there will never be a shortage of effective sellers who creatively break down new doors. Remember, the backbones of both media rights and sponsorship are successful sellers, particularly the ones who drum up new business.

This concluding chapter is a sampling of relevant sports cold calling successes, big and small, those that took creativity and ingenuity and those that required an acceleration of outbound phone calls and pleasant persistence.

Whole Foods
Finding a common past and passion

Because cold calling is not only a crucible in the sports field, we'll begin with this applicable non-sports example. Crain's New York ran a front page story on the difficulty food purveyors have, cracking distribution at the upscale Whole Foods chain. Tim McCollum is founder of Madecasse, a Brooklyn-based company that produces chocolate in Madagascar to help the island's impoverished citizens. He fruitlessly spent two years sending email, making phone calls and visiting individual Whole Foods stores.

But persistence paid off when McCollum learned that, like him, the president of a Whole Foods' Foundation, was an alumnus of the Peace Corps. The connection helped McCollum get bars of Madecasse chocolates in Whole Foods' Northeast outposts. The chocolate was a hit. Now it is available in all the chain's 400 locations. From just $250,000 in sales in 2010, Madecasse's sales were on track to do $4 million in 2014. McCollum dug and found the personal common denominator, the Peace Corps. It worked, just as it might when you pitch a college package to an alumnus. Embedded bonds are difficult to break.

Find that special connection. Never stop digging.

The Bowl Games
The crossword puzzle of naming rights, from the popular to the obscure

Bowl games were steeped in tradition. The Rose Bowl, the grand daddy of 'em all, was first played in 1916. For years, the Orange, Sugar and Rose Bowls remained pristine, distancing themselves from corporate ownership. In 1988, a parade of bowl game naming rights began. Mobil (now ExxonMobil) sponsored the Cotton Bowl, Sunkist, the Fiesta Bowl and FedEx, the Orange Bowl.

Naming rights to bowl games had not quite blossomed when the Independence Bowl became the Poulan-Weed Eater Bowl in 1990. Poulan wasn't Sunkist, a household name, and fans deridingly called the game the "Weedwhacker Bowl." The sports world wondered whether organizers of sporting events were selling their hearts and souls for corporate cash.

It was no joke. The bowl landscape sprouted. With its continued appetite for football programming in December, ESPN fills the month televising bowl games from cities big and small, from New York and San Francisco to Boise and Albuquerque.

There are now some 40 college bowls played across the country. Many of the smaller ones, especially those with little heritage, are challenged every year to generate revenue. The Gator Bowl, Sun Bowl and Citrus Bowl have been around for scores of years and are fixtures in their communities. But bowls played in places like Shreveport or St. Petersburg, Florida, are relatively new.

Brett Dulaney steers revenue for the St. Petersburg Bowl that's now sponsored by Bitcoin, a company so young it was born only a year after the game itself, in 2009. The game has deals for school participation with the ACC, the American Conference and Conference USA.

The bowl's first sponsor, magicJack, pulled out after just one year. So, through an internal contact, the St. Petersburg Bowl reached out to Nick Vojnovic, the CEO and founder of Beef O'Brady's, a locally headquartered restaurant chain. At the time, the bold Vojnovic, an active member of the National Restaurant Association, was considering a commitment to a corporate partnership with two of the areas pro teams: the Rays and Bucs. But Dulaney and bowl management convinced him that the chain is better off being a big fish in a small pond and Vojnovic agreed to lend the Beef O'Brady's name to the St. Petersburg Bowl for a period of five years.

Beef O'Brady's enjoyed healthy responses from its commitment to the St. Petersburg bowl game. As its television spots ran during the game broadcast, Google hits for information about the chain were off the chart, including franchisee inquiries from out west and areas outside Beef O'Brady's footprint. But as the five-year deal was winding down in 2013, there was a sense that the restaurant chain would not renew.

So the next development was a cold call in reverse. Tony Gallippi and Stephen Pair were co-founders of the financial services company, BitPay. The company, based in Atlanta, is the largest Bitcoin checkout processor in the world.

By reading a blog, Gallippi and Pair got wind of the fact that the St. Petersburg Bowl's sponsorship might be available. Biased somewhat to the game because of its ACC connection, the two Georgia Tech alumni, reached out to the St. Petersburg Bowl to express interest in sponsoring the game. But Dulaney and his cohorts were engaged in talks with other established sponsors and didn't immediately get back to BitPay. "I knew nothing about BitPay and the Bitcoin industry," Dulaney said. "But once we engaged in discussions, I did my due diligence and studied the mechanism of this fascinating industry." The St. Petersburg Bowl and Bitcoin came to terms on a three-year deal through 2016.

Earlier in his career, Dulaney, a former golf pro, spent time selling sponsorships for the University of South Florida. For two years beginning in 2003, he cold called Steve Scott, the chief marketing officer of the Caspers Company, which is the largest franchisee of McDonald's in the Tampa-St. Petersburg area. For two years, he didn't get a return call.

In 2005, Dulaney's phone rang. It was Scott. Shocked, Dulaney almost dropped the phone. Scott explained that the recent death of Casper CEO, Joe Casper, brought a new direction to the franchisee. Scott elaborated that Casper had a falling out with South Florida years earlier and would do no business with the school.

Dulaney was told that Joe Casper's son, Blake, who had just taken over the company's reins, was looking at the opportunity through a fresh lens. One man's demise had turned into another's chance. Dulaney's two years of cold calling finally paid off. He and Scott cut a sponsorship deal. McDonald's was in the University of South Florida Bulls' camp.

The Holiday Bowl was born in San Diego in 1978. By 1986, it sold its naming rights to Sea World. By 2013, 27 years later, it had seven separate naming rights' sponsors, from Chrysler's Plymouth to Thrifty Car Rentals and from Culligan Water to Pacific Life Insurance. In 2010, the San Diego Bowl was once again hunting for a new partner. Mark Neville, the San Diego Bowl's fearless associate executive director, again began chasing a new corporate partner to adorn the marquee.

Leaving no stone unturned, Neville reached out to Bridgepoint Education, a for-profit educator. The target's industry wasn't out of the box. Competitor University of Phoenix is active in sports, on radio and television broadcasts and has its name etched on the NFL Cardinals' stadium in Glendale, Arizona.

Bridgepoint didn't wink at the first, second or third pass. Neville stayed on them assiduously. "They were promotionally active in the community," he said. After many unreturned calls and email messages, Neville sent Bridge-point one running shoe in a shoebox with a note that said, "Now that I have one foot in the door, would you be open to a presentation by the bowl game?" His creativity paid off. "I got a call back almost immediately, and it ultimately led to the title sponsorship."

Reflecting on his success with Bridgepoint, the San Diegan adds, "This was nothing too unique. Persistence sometimes pays off – as does a lot of patience. There's a lot of competition out there for the sponsorship/advertising dollar, so it pays to be creative and confident."

Jeff Ditmer heads up sales for the Independence Bowl, which is housed in Shreveport, Louisiana. The game started in 1976 as the Independence Bowl and has had its funky lineup of title sponsors, beginning with Poulan, later Sanford, Mainstay Investments, PetroSun, Advocare and most recently, Duck Commander, beginning in 2014.

When Advocare bailed out of the Independence Bowl in 2013, the Shreveport folks were on the prowl again for a new title sponsor. With the help of Bill Glenn of the Breakout Group, Ditmer and bowl management focused its efforts on Duck Commander, the company and brand behind the best-selling duck call. Duck Commander is based in West Monroe, Louisiana, a little more than an hour from Shreveport.

Duck Commander had sports in its roots. The company was founded by ex-Louisiana quarterback Phil Robertson, and it had engaged in sponsorship activity with NASCAR. The cold call to Duck Commander got attention and the first meeting got traction. Within six weeks, the deal was done.

Ditmer has had success cultivating corporate support by first seeking endorsements of national accounts' local representatives. Going the local route, he got a commitment from American Airlines. The local people took up the bowl's cause and shepherded approvals through company head-quarters in Dallas. Detmer's attitude is "willingness." He tells prospects, "You think it, we can do it!"

"In this business, people are protective of their leads; you've got to do it on your own." In pitching new accounts he adds, "Yes is best, no is second best and maybe is the worst!"

Ditmer's gotten money from hospitals, bail bondsmen and funeral homes. He attends chamber of commerce meetings after hours, where he hobnobs and beefs up his capital of contacts. Doing so, he befriended decision makers at Shreveport Federal Credit Union and has had the company as bowl sponsors for more than a decade.

In addition to corporate sponsorship and hospitality, Ditmer also sells group tickets for the game. One day, he was smiling and dialing when a prospect answered the phone by first name only. Jeff confidently introduced himself and passionately spewed a 30-second pitch suggesting that the organization buy a couple dozen tickets to the game. Unbeknownst to Ditmer, he had reached the city morgue. After a slight pause, the woman on the other end said, "I don't think the bodies here can make it to the game." After that call, Ditmer knew he had lost it and called it a day.

Steve Ehrhart, executive director of the AutoZone Liberty Bowl, tells the story about one of his sellers who walked into a Dunkin' Donuts trying to sell the manager a dozen tickets to the game. The manager was so sold on the bowl that he called Dunkin's corporate office and got the marketing office to buy spots on the game's national telecast. In the early days, before companies like AXA and AutoZone sponsored the Liberty Bowl, Ehrhart cold called Piggly Wiggly, a southern supermarket chain, and secured a sponsorship commitment. When Ehrhart brought the news to the athletic directors of the conferences associated with the game, they were uncomfortable with the association. The chain, they felt, was too provincial, almost un-American, too southern. Ehrhart was discouraged from doing the deal.

Ehrhart, the first general partner of the Colorado Rockies, is a natural seller. In Memphis, he was invited to attend the annual Blues Ball. "It was a Saturday night and I went reluctantly. I had to dress up. It was a weekend but I knew it was the right thing to do. It's the largest ball in the nation and it raises money for local charities. It means a ton to the city.

"At the event, I introduced myself to Nick Jebbia who was running Powertel, one of the early cellular companies that confined its distribution to Tennessee and Georgia. We talked about the Liberty Bowl and he said, 'Count me in!'" Because the Powertel network covered only a limited region, Ehrhart presented a local sponsorship package. But Jebbia insisted on buying the bowl's national telecast too. He told Ehrhart, "I want to get our name out there. You never know who's watching." That he did. A few years later Powertel was bought by T-Mobile, and no one had to throw Jebbia a fund raising dinner.

Wise Potato Chips
Knowing where the chip will crack

Larry Rothstein can employ the motto of the Great One, Wayne Gretzky, "I skate where the puck is headed not where it is now." Like Gretzky, Larry's ahead of his game.

A successful radio seller early in his career, Rothstein and Barry Bluestein launched their ad agency in the 1980s with just their small personal savings, no investors, no guarantees and a ton of confidence. Within a number of years, they landed big names like HP, a stable of local Subway franchisees, Fuji Film, Sony's digital imaging business and others. Rothstein's energy is unsurpassed. He has a knack for knocking down new doors and winning new business. By the early 2000s, Rothstein developed a sports arm, dubbing it Source 1 Sports. He quickly won the Amtrak business, an account the agency still has in its stable today.

In 2004, he got wind of the fact that Charles Chips, which owned signage at Shea Stadium, was not planning to renew its Mets deal.

Rothstein smelled opportunity. If he could sell the sign to another potato chip company and build a catchy sponsorship around it, his agency, Source, would land the assignment of running the partnership. Rothstein had to be selective on which potato chip company to pursue. Competitor Utz already was embedded at Yankee Stadium, so it was not in play. Frito Lay, a major national brand with a roster of its own ad agencies, would unlikely hire the smaller and then unknown Source to represent it even if it had an interest in the Mets.

So the savvy Rothstein had a plan. He knew that Wise Potato Chips, an iconic New York brand had recently been acquired from Borden by venture capitalists. The company was based in Atlanta and was in need of fresh ideas to protect its New York franchise. Rothstein had done his due diligence. He visited stores, chains, convenient stores and bodegas. He learned, among other things, that the Hispanic market was critical to Wise.

Unbendingly self-assured, Rothstein cold called Wise's vice president of marketing Jordi Ferre, who took Rothstein's call and listened assiduously. Part of Rothstein's charm and allure is the excitement he portrays, one of a kid in a candy store.

With halting breath, Rothstein enthusiastically told Ferre that Charles Chips was unlikely to renew its Mets deal and that the Mets could potentially generate enormous visibility for Wise in key summer months when families picnic and enjoy the outdoors. Rothstein unhesitatingly said that a partnership with the Mets would galvanize Wise's channel of distribution in the country's largest city.

He tantalizingly shared skeletal concepts on the phone and promised to put the flesh on the bare ideas if they could get together in Atlanta. Ferre said come on down.

Rothstein traveled to Atlanta and made an inspiring pitch to the Wise executives. He presented a resourceful program, one that would cash in on the growing popularity of shortstop Jose Reyes. He and his Source colleagues mocked up Reyes' image on make-believe Mets' signage. Rothstein reminisces, "We had Reyes sliding into a base with bags of Wise chips coming out of his hip pocket. They loved it.

"We were chock full of ideas, showing Wise how the signs at Shea would look and how the program would work at point of purchase. To serve the Hispanic constituency, we suggested Mets' Spanish radio. On the ground, we developed creative tentacles from incentive opportunities to softball games at Shea for the trade. We came up with fantasy programs too and showed the execs how the Mets' logos would look on Wise trucks. They were pumped.

"I left the meeting telling them that if they let us do this for them, 'Wise would own New York.'"

The cold call worked. Rothstein and Source got the green light. "Eleven years later, it's still working and it's grown tremendously," says Rothstein. Under Source's aegis, other franchises like the Red Sox have been added to Wise's sponsorship programs.

Wise didn't have big budgets. Larry said, "It was a leap of faith at the start. They were spending a few bucks here and a few bucks there. We not only had to convince them to embrace the Mets as a major program. We also had to have them agree to give up a number of these other smaller programs."

On behalf of Wise, Source engineered a "Big City Crunch" at Citi Field in the hope that it would set a world record for the most crunches of potato chips at one time. The event was monitored by officials of Guinness, who flew in from London to gauge the record-setting attempt.

At the end of the third inning at a Reds–Mets game, fans were asked to open bags of potato chips, which were distributed to them free when they entered the stadium. There was a countdown to begin the contest and at the magical moment, Citi Field was filled with the sounds of thousands of fans crackling their potato chips simultaneously. Later in the seventh inning, Guinness officials came out on the field to confirm that indeed a world record was set for the most potato chips ever crunched at one time.

"The number of dollars that Wise originally committed has more than tripled," Rothstein says. Yes, it all started with a cold call and a well thought out idea.

Benjamin Moore
Painting a patchwork of success

In his early years, Rothstein pursued accounts from Source's New Jersey base, reaching out by cold call to businesses, big and small, in proximity and out-of-town. Source's still-limited experience didn't deter him from reaching out to multimillion dollar entities.

One day, Rothstein picked up the phone and called Sal Rossi, the regional vice president of Benjamin Moore Paints. Rothstein knew that he could package radio inventory on Mets' and Yankees' radio broadcasts and give advertisers a pervasively rich experience.

Rossi invited Rothstein to his office and made it clear that there were no corporate dollars for any such undertakings. He did, though, encourage him to pitch Benjamin Moore's retailers and dealers in the New York area to build consensus for a co-op deal. Co-op pursuits are endlessly granular and there are no guarantees. But work didn't scare Rothstein. He knew that, if he could showcase Benjamin Moore, more name accounts would follow. He scratched and clawed, reaching retailers in the area one by one. Executing these co-op programs can be a nightmare. Spots have to be tagged (e.g., 'Visit your Benjamin Moore store, John's Paint in the Bronx on Grand Concourse and Fordham Road'). Rothstein pulled it off and used Benjamin Moore as a springboard. He concurrently expanded the Benjamin Moore program, doing the same radio baseball program in Philadelphia with the Phillies. Success with these franchisee programs helped Rothstein get McDonald's, Subway and others.

Nowadays, like many others, Rothstein uses LinkedIn. "Tom Coba is a guy I knew when he was at Dunkin' Donuts, and I then worked with him a bit at Subway. I saw that he landed at ServiceMaster in Memphis.

The company's services include home cleaning and maintenance, pest control and lawn fertilization. Terminix is part of ServiceMaster. I reached out to him via LinkedIn. He emailed me within an hour and we're getting together soon," spewed the always bubbly Rothstein.

Federal Mogul, ANCO Blades/Champion Spark Plugs, NHL
Keeping a deal after a work stoppage

Expensive league-wide sponsorship programs aren't nailed down every day. There are a lot of sticky details to which to agree. It's more complicated than simply buying the rights to a league's shield. Commitments are required to the leagues' media partners, and there's the issue of knotty, multi-leveled promotional activation on the ground.

Just ask Mike Callanan, the NHL's senior director of integrated marketing. He canvasses the sponsorship landscape every day.

In 2012, Callanan meticulously scouted a new business prospect, cold called the account, found the decision maker and presented an attractive proposal. After intensive months of work and negotiations, he finally nailed down Federal Mogul, a new league-wide corporate partner. It was a classic success story. But this one was undermined by one irreparable problem. The NHL couldn't deliver the goods to which it agreed.

How terribly frustrating! Callanan might have been tempted to head to the nearest tavern.

The former CBS Sports sales executive determined that the league was perfectly suited for Detroit-based Federal Mogul. Callanan studied one of the company's flagship brands, ANCO Wiper Blades. "I said to myself, 'wiper blades on windows look much like skate blades.' The NHL was perfect, a better match than NASCAR, one of the company's other sponsorship programs." Callanan and his NHL cohorts did their homework. Unlike other auto aftermarket suppliers that distribute through big chains like AutoZone, Advance Auto and NAPA, Federal Mogul sells its brands through mom and pops, thousands of smaller automotive parts stores.

"I had no contacts at the client and didn't know where to begin but I was very confident that our proposed elements would resonate." Mike's first telephone call was to Jessica Wynn, the company's media director, whose name he found in an industry directory but whom he didn't know. Wynn took his call and Callanan broached the opportunity. "She got it," Callanan recalls. "Jessica was sufficiently intrigued to help me move the idea up the chain." Wynn engineered a meeting for the league with Mike Proud, the company's marketing director. The league developed a driving proposal, full of execution, giveaways and executive promotions.

This was months before the NHL Winter Classic was scheduled for the Big House, University of Michigan's football stadium which seats more than 100,000 fans. "Because the Classic was scheduled for the Detroit area, we were pretty sure that we could generate interest in the NHL among businesses in the area. It made sense! Hey, Detroit is Hockey Town.

"The company loved the idea, the timing, the seasonality and the compatibility of its customer profile with our fan base," Callanan remembers. Details were negotiated, an agreement was signed and all was in place for the start of the season. Federal Mogul was chomping at the bit to implement the sponsorship.

Then the word 'lockout' reared its ugly head. A work stoppage began on September 15, 2012, and the 2012–2013 season didn't begin as scheduled in October. The dispute between players and owners dragged. On November 2nd, the league announced the cancelation of the Winter Classic that was scheduled for January 1st. The Classic was a large reason Federal Mogul bought the NHL sponsorship.

The game's fans, media partners and corporate sponsors suffered a season of thwarted expectations. No elephants, no circus!

After a new collective bargaining agreement was finally ironed out, the NHL season was shortened from 82 to 48 games. It was too late and too little for companies to fully cash in on activation that requires a lot of runway.

Federal Mogul, first-time NHL partners, planned a big splash. Its hopes were dashed. It didn't have the deep pockets of GEICO to fall back on other major sponsorships. It counted on its fresh NHL deal for much of its overall marketing program.

What now?

The league smartly rescheduled the Winter Classic for the Big House in 2014, giving at least Detroit-based sponsors something special to look forward to in January 2014.

Callanan still had a lot of hand-holding to do. Initial sponsorship commitments are somewhat fueled by leaps of faith. When plans backfire, trust can be shattered. Not easy! Callanan and his NHL cohorts pledged their best. Federal Mogul remained committed. Although it had to wait for its full taste of an NHL season-long sponsorship, the initial results were satisfactory and the company remained league partners. As for the Winter Classic, the one-year postponement didn't weaken fans' appetites. The game in the Big House drew 105,491 and the television coverage drew 8.2 million viewers in North America. It was the most watched NHL game ever.

Not all was lost. Callanan's good cold calling work was preserved.

The Callanan experience with Federal Mogul reminds me of a story shared by Eric Reid, the longtime television voice of the Miami Heat. In the mid 1980s, Eric was still the radio voice of the Providence College Friars. Sales were part of his responsibly. It wasn't something he enjoyed; it was a requisite of the job. One Friday, Eric knocked on the door of a business, asked for the owner by name and made a presentation. The owner embraced his pitch, committed to a sponsorship verbally and asked him to come back on Monday with a contract that he would sign. On Monday morning, Eric entered the same business and asked for the owner by name. The receptionist looked at Eric sadly and teary eyed. She told him that the owner died suddenly over the weekend. Sad story, no recourse, no order! Eric had paid his dues. He might not have made a sales call since.

York Air Conditioning and Heating/Johnson Controls
Finding a lead in the catacombs of the arena

Callanan works his cold calling efforts through paths of least resistance. He deputized Van Wagner, an effective New York-based sports marketing agency and giant outdoor signage company, to develop a proposed program for York Heating and Air Conditioning.

Callanan focused on three potential synergies:

1. Seasonality. The league's schedule starts during the heating season in the fall and ends during the beginning of the cooling season in late spring.

2. Connections already in place. Mike knew that ice trucks in the NHL included equipment of York's parent, Johnson Controls and that York itself served as vendors to many of the league's buildings, providing heating and air conditioning.

3. Environmental awareness was a focus of the prospect and as such a good target for NHL Green.

All the stars aligned. The deal came to fruition. In fact, when the program was announced, Melissa Marineau, director of marketing for Johnson Controls-Unitary Products, proudly said, "NHL Green shares our goal of raising awareness of environmental issues and helping to educate the community on ways to save energy."

Callanan's acquisition of York and Federal Mogul is an inspiration for sellers to go after the big and the small, the traditional and the non-traditional.

As it turned out, York, like Federal Mogul's ANCO Wiper Blades, had no television commercials in the can that it could use on-air. The league itself had to work with both companies to develop television creative. It's all part of the fun and the challenge of working with pristine first time sponsors.

Mazda
Using cute creativity as a command to action

One of the more imaginative tactics I remember was used by Damon Overholser, at the time a seller for the Los Angeles office of Westwood One. He couldn't reach the decision maker, John Lisko at Mazda's advertising agency. He tried day after day. Nothing. Message after message was ignored. One phone call after another. None returned. Frustrating!

Out of anger or creativity, or both, Damon figured he'd do something bold. He went to a local electronics store and bought an inexpensive portable landline phone. He then sent it to his elusive contact by overnight mail. A note was attached to the phone. "I've called you for weeks. Here's a phone that you can use to return the call."

It worked. The prospect, John Lisko, returned the call. And believe it or not, the seller and target established a dialogue. Mazda wound up buying the NCAA Tournament from Westwood One. By smartly maintaining a relaxed, yet creative pursuit, you'll eventually break down a target to meet with you.

Bose
Keeping your finger on the pulse

Mike Jaquet is the chief marketing officer of the U.S. Ski and Snowboard Association. He traces his roots through television where he worked for CBS Sports Network, the cable arm of the over the air network, and its forerunner CSTV. An avid skier, Jaquet had an opportunity to go to Park City, Utah, to drum up revenue for the USSA, so he jumped. Jaquet was a cross-country skier at the University of Colorado, and is originally from nearby Idaho.

Mike and the USSA team smartly concluded that the sponsor target is similar to golf. "We're counter seasonal. The profile of a skier is a high end earner who plays golf in the summer and skis in the winter. I keep a close eye on sponsor developments in golf and glean lots of leads doing so," Jaquet says.

LinkedIn and social media sites have made cold calling easier. "In today's day and age there's so much communication by email. A cute line in an email won't get you through the door." As an example, Mike says that sellers shouldn't expect to cash in on common fandom to elbow their way into a prospect's office. Invoking a mutual affinity for the Yankees won't do it. Jaquet suggests studying social media sites and researching Google to build reconnaissance. "The probability of a meeting and closing will then shoot from 5% to 60%. To cut through the clutter, you must present something beneficial and relatable. When you call Charles Schwab pitch something tactical to implement accepted strategy."

His cold calling GPS is his finger, keeping it on the pulse. Jaquet constantly works the phones networking with fellow sellers, old cohorts, sports agents, agency colleagues and more. By doing just so, Jaquet was able to sign Bose as a USSA sponsor in December, 2013. "I was on with an agent at CAA and he brought up Bose, telling me that CAA was consulting the company. He hooked me up with the right parties and we quickly agreed that we can help Bose reach teens and young 20-year-olds. They were trying to stave off competitors like Skullcandy and Beats."

Chick-fil-A
Cashing in on a client's passion

Jaquet reminisced about his earlier iteration, when CSTV (now CBS Sports Network) wasn't sufficiently distributed in cable homes to qualify for transactional buys. "We ran lengthy pregame shows as lead-ins to the games that were carried on the traditional CBS over-the-air network. Because of the lack of ratings, it was a challenging sale."

So, among other things, Jaquet urged his staff to research a prospect's likes, dislikes and profiles. "One day, we got in to see Steve Robinson at Chick-fil-A. The Richards Group, the company's ad agency, refused to buy the package. We needed Robinson's blessing." Jaquet and company established the fact that Robinson is an alumnus of Auburn. The CBS Network then customized a video to demonstrate the power of the SEC which it planned to present to Chick-fil-A. "In it, we had 'War Eagle' interviewed by his handler. We had fans emote. We had the fight song. We had a video of the chant. It was stirring!"

After brief introductions at the meeting, Jaquet and his seller dimmed the lights for the video presentation. Robinson had no idea what to expect. "He watched the video intensely. When it ended, we brought the lights up and Robinson had a tear in his eye."

Robinson turned to Jaquet and his seller and said, "That's a great video. I feel we'll do business because you understand the culture of the SEC."

Jaquet says that the Chick-fil-A deal at the time was the biggest for the fledgling network. "It was wildly successful; we did shows from the parking lots. It was lots of fun," Jaquet says proudly.

Acura
Bring a guitarist to the call

While at CBS Sports Network, one of Jaquet's sellers fought hard to get a meeting with the Acura agency in California. The seller told Jaquet that the agency had heard his pitch a hundred times, so to get the room's attention, he would have to do something different. "We came in there with a crazy looking acoustic guitarist. The seller then sang the whole pitch using rhythmically funny and entertaining words. The agency people were laughing hysterically and thought that it was inventive. We actually got a buy!"

Sheryl Swoopes
Selling an endorsement by an athlete

For close to 30 years, Tom George served as a senior vice president of Octagon's Athlete and Property Marketing Division. Tom is full of life. He's always up, always enthusiastic and always pitching. At Octagon, his responsibility was to market the Octagon-represented athletes to the corporate world. He worked the landline on his desk like a machine, soliciting endorsement opportunities and corporate representation programs. Through the years, Octagon clients have included Grant Hill, David Robinson, Anna Kournikova and Michael Chang.

In 1993, Sheryl Swoopes set a single game NCAA scoring record, pouring in 53 points against the University of Texas. She then led Texas Tech to the NCAA Tournament title that April.

Despite her dominance of the game, Swoopes was hardly a household name when her collegiate career ended. It was 1993, three years before the WNBA launched, a year before the World Championships were played in Australia and three years before the Atlanta Olympics.

To stay in the game, Swoopes' options were limited. But she took what she could get and headed to Italy to play international ball. She quit after ten games, though, because her salary was modest and hardly enough of an incentive to cope with her craving for home.

Back home in Lubbock, Texas, Swoopes accepted a job as a teller by day for $15,000. At night, she exercised and honed her basketball skills. It was then that Octagon had the 22-year-old under a representation contract.

George faced a challenging landscape in his effort to find Swoopes corporate engagements and endorsements. One day, Tom called Wilson to pitch Swoopes a ball deal. They expressed immediate interest and asked him how much. George suggested terms; cash guarantees plus royalties. The Wilson representative said okay, right then and there.

This might not sound overwhelmingly impressive today, but back then women weren't getting ball deals over the phone on cold calls. Swoopes, of course, went on to enjoy a glittering 11-year WNBA career and earn three Olympic gold medals in 1996, 2000 and 2004. She became the only woman to have a sneaker named for her. Today Sheryl Swoopes is sometimes called the 'female Michael Jordan.'

Ameriquest, the 2005 Super Bowl Halftime Show
Even the NFL sells last-minute inventory

Mike Callanan's boss at the NHL, Keith Wachtel, joined the league after selling the coveted shield of the NFL.

In early fall 2004, Wachtel was talking with Dean Bonham of the Bonham Group, one of the early third-party pioneers, consulting properties and sponsors on naming-rights deals. It was also at the height of the mortgage boom when privately held Ameriquest was the country's sixth largest mortgage lender. At the time, Ameriquest was significantly expanding its sports sponsorship portfolio and had interest in becoming an official NFL sponsor.

During the discussions in early fall 2004, the NFL's 2005 Super Bowl halftime sponsor dropped out and the league began scurrying for a replacement. It wasn't easy. The league faced two formidable challenges. The first was the clock. It was already the eve of the NFL season. The second was the lingering damage of the previous Super Bowl halftime show. In 2004, singer Janet Jackson's breast was briefly exposed in an episode remembered as the 'wardrobe malfunction.' The controversy was still fresh on the minds of the media, fans, consumers and prospects. America Online had sponsored the show in 2004 and bailed out.

To that point in his discussion with Bonham about the NFL, Wachtel hadn't raised NFL halftime. Wachtel remembers, "We quickly changed gear, demonstrated why halftime made sense and that it would be the only position we would consider." In an unusually accelerated period, Ameriquest bought in and committed for two years. CNN Money reported that Ameriquest paid $15 million while America Online had paid $10 million.

What Wachtel remembers most is not the sudden and effective call he placed to sell through the halftime show, rather a lesson about two key negotiating elements of a sponsorship: value and price. Shortly after Wachtel's pitch, Bonham called him and said, "The price is high but we will accept your price, but the value is not there." Wachtel and his boss Peter Murray flew to Denver, spent ten hours negotiating and came to terms. Key to Ameriquest was the integration of a blimp the company had purchased. Keith remembers, "Yes, the blimp. Ameriquest wanted to milk everything it could from it."

In summary, Wachtel concluded, "The part that still stands out for me of the Ameriquest deal, something that I respect and use all the time in negotiations is the value or price discussion. If it's value, we will make it work, if it's price it will be harder to get a deal done." (Especially the NFL. It has the acronym and has built enough demand to remain firm on pricing!)

ThermaCare, PGA Tournaments
Maintaining a relationship after the umbilical cord is cut

Sandy Diamond joined the PGA Barclays Open (once the Buick Classic) in 2002 after successful sales stops at Katz Media, WABC Radio and IMG. His mission at Barclays is to sell local sponsorships for the New York area tournament that was once played exclusively at the Westchester Country Club. The annual championship is now hosted by alternating clubs in suburban New York.

When Sandy joined the PGA stop in 2003, Proctor & Gamble was an official national marketing partner of the entire PGA Tour. The Barclays received a nice windfall from P&G locally, additional support dollars to strengthen its brand visibility in the area and to activate promotional programs on the ground. But by 2004, just a year later, P&G ended its PGA national partnership including the local support for the Barclays.

Because the local deal percolated from PGA's national office, Sandy had no contacts to help him resurrect any local support. He knew it would be a long shot, even if he knew someone, because there was no longer a natural P&G-PGA corporate program. It would not be easy for local P&G management in New York to foster any consensus of support corporately to undertake an independent local program. But Sandy wasn't deterred. He had something up his sleeve.

Sandy observed that golfer Rocco Mediate had a bad back and wore ThermaCare, one of the brands that P&G promoted through its PGA sponsorship. (P&G sold the ThermaCare brand to Wyeth in 2008.) He cold called the local P&G office in the New York area and tracked down Field Marketing Manager Tim Linehan.

The Mediate angle resonated with Linehan who found a way to at least maintain the P&G relationship at the Barclays in 2004. He didn't have a deep-pocketed budget, so the revived program began with a small commitment. As part of the deal, Mediate agreed to do a 'meet and greet,' and P&G was able to use tickets for buyers of the brand like BJ's Wholesale Club.

In time, Diamond cultivated a sufficiently strong relationship with the client that enabled him to grow the investment to include other tournaments that he was selling, The World Golf Championships - the Cadillac in Miami, the Deutsche Bank in Boston and the Travelers Championship in Hartford.

To quote Sandy Diamond, "Because of a cold call that I made to the field marketing manager back in 2003, P&G served as a longtime partner of several of the tournaments and invested over $3 million with the PGA TOUR over a nine year span."

You've got to love cold calls!

Grainger
Wet behind the ears, two young cold callers collaborate to nail down a multimillion dollar deal

In the mid-2000s, Jeff Katz and Brandon Berman were hired by Robin Carretta and Alexis Wirth of Westwood One's Chicago office. Westwood is a major American radio network. Jeff had a year's experience right out of college, selling financial products and services to wealthy investors. Brandon Berman was fresh out of the University of Iowa. The two were hired to canvass new advertisers in the Midwest.

Network radio's core inventory is a hodgepodge of cobbled national programming, station by station and market by market. As such, if an advertiser is targeting an 18–34-year-old demographic, it might seek a customized network that provides bulk advertising inventory across many hundreds of disconnected stations across the country that reach that young target. Because of its complex nature, buys are generally executed by advertising agencies that understand the complex inner workings of the medium.

There's little labeled uniformity, so advertisers might not immediately identify the Westwood One name.

In view of this, cold callers' greatest challenge selling network radio directly to advertisers is the industry's lack of brand recognition. Premiere Radio Networks, for instance, a division of iHeart (once Clear Channel), is the country's largest radio network, but few outside the ad agency world know the name. The company does better than half a billion dollars a year in revenue.

In addition to 'advertising networks' described above, Westwood One also has an impressive stable of play-by-play: the NFL, the Masters and the NCAA Tournament. The Westwood name is heavily branded on these sports broadcasts, which affords the company significant visibility among the thick landscape of American sports fans.

Early in their careers, Katz and Berman were asked by Carretta to cold call Grainger, an account that bought some local radio but no network radio.

Katz and Berman set out on their cold calling mission. They contacted Perry Novelli, Grainger's advertising boss, requesting a meeting. As Katz reflects, "Brandon and I went after Grainger pretty hard, yet being in the right place at the right time helped. To get the appointment we told Perry that we can save him many millions of dollars and increase the reach of Grainger's radio advertising exponentially. He agreed to meet."

An industrial supply company that sells goods like fasteners, plumbing tools and motors, Grainger's products are available through retail outlets nationwide, an extensive sales catalog and online. Over the years, Grainger's product line has expanded to more than one million products and repair parts. The Grainger branch network has grown steadily, and today there are more than 700 Grainger branches nationwide.

At their initial meeting, Katz and Berman listened assiduously to Novelli as he shared Grainger's strategy of advertising in only 20 radio markets. The young sellers described for him in broad terms the enormous reach of network radio and the exalting advantages of fostering an interchangeable partnership with Westwood's NFL and NCAA radio broadcasts. They asked him for a second appointment where they could propose a plan in granular detail.

The two sellers then studied Grainger's footprint and were convinced that, if Grainger shifted its 20 market budget to a national network, the investment efficiencies would skyrocket and the reach would be exponentially higher.

At the next meeting, the two precocious sellers proposed a smashing multimillion dollar sponsorship that was chock-full of ingrained on-air features around Grainger's logo of "For the ones who get it done." They also substantiated the numerical analytics, convincing Novelli that the network investment was fail-safe. Perry was a sports fan who had also played basketball at the University of Arizona. He appreciated Westwood's portfolio of sports programming.

Within a few months, the talks intensified and Katz and Berman had the ball in the red zone. To close the deal, they secured the sepulchral-voiced Harry Kalas to do the radio commercials. The two young sellers, not long removed from their days in college, locked down an exclusive $3.5 million dollar buy. Grainger spent its entire radio budget with Westwood One.

Over the next decade, both sellers would grow their careers, Berman to senior vice president at Westwood One and Katz to an account executive with NBC Sports.

Reynolds Wrap, Interstate Battery, Kubota Tractor and Ace Bandages
What's in a name?

Play-by-play broadcasts on radio have been more difficult to sell to sponsors and advertisers in recent years for a number of reasons. Virtually all games today are available on some form of video, whether over the air television, cable or through an online stream. If fans find it impossible to access games on video, there are multiple sites where real-time stats produce a running box score. Radio play-by-play is not as indispensible as it once was.

Because of this, local radio rights fees have declined and teams and stations have taken more liberties to drum up revenue. Several seasons ago, Aladdin Bail Bonds advertised on Los Angeles Clippers radio. I'm not quite sure what took more convincing, getting the account to say yes or getting team management to agree to run the spots. Advertisers on a University of Miami football broadcast included Gun World, a "state-of-the-art shooting facility" that pushed "firearm training" and "guns for rent."

There are pockets of teams and geography where play-by-play on radio is still hot! Baseball in New York is one. The Yankees continue to command exorbitant dollars for their rights. In 2014, WFAN Radio in New York paid some $14 million for Yankees' rights fees and production costs.

It comes with an additional price: the price of pressure placed on WFAN's sellers! The station's play-by-play sales staff is constantly under the gun to sell every last piece of real estate associated with the broadcasts. There are big expenses to be retrieved. WFAN's sales staff sells 60-second, 30-second and 10-second drop-in announcements wherever it can.

The commercial intrusiveness is so overbearing that the *New York Times* did a nice-sized piece on the issue in 2013, running an apt headline, "Here's the Pitch but first one from our sponsor.*" The Times* listed examples, including the one for the paint sponsor, "Phelps painted the corner. Painting at the corners is sponsored by CertaPro Painters because painting is personal."

In 2012, even the iconic consumer advocate Ralph Nader weighed in. He was so tired of being flooded with advertisements on Yankees' broadcasts that he sent a letter of complaint to team president Randy Levine. In it he said to Levine that the unending commercials "disrupt the flow and excitement of the game broadcast and undermine your responsibilities as a guardian of the national pastime."

Nonetheless, the charge of Steve Kalman, the play-by-play sales manager for rights holder WFAN is not to leave an airline seat empty. Sell anything that's not nailed down.

Tommy Edwards famously sang "It's All in the Game." Dizzily cashing in on semantic harmony, Kalman and his team might want to sing, "It's All in the Name." Sponsors' names are tied to related baseball activity from the first pre-game show through the last post-game show.

Four such cold call orders demonstrate Kalman's success:

1.   **Kubota Tractor** sponsored the *Farm Report*. Baseball and Kubota's selling cycle were a good fit. Kalman said, "By creating a program that tagged participating dealers, we were able to deliver a highly efficient

package. And because listener reach of the Yankees' Network carries well outside New York City, we were able to hit rural areas that they target."

2.   **Ace Bandages** had the *Injury Report.* Kalman faced a challenge. "This sale wouldn't have been possible because the account generally buys national packages only, not local programs. But we built a strong retail component that appealed to Ace as a vehicle to defend its New York area market share and please its retail partners." In other words, WFAN Radio effectively lobbied Ace's retailers whose endorsement of the sponsorship proposal percolated to the powers that be at Ace corporate and the deal was approved.

3.   **Interstate Battery** sponsored *Tonight's Battery.* Kalman had to get consensus of Interstate's participating New York dealers. He had several meetings in the company's local warehouse, assuring dealers and the rank and file that local tagging would run without a hitch. "It took several months to get sign-off on the deal several years ago, and it's still running to this day," says a proud Kalman.

4.   **Reynolds Wrap** is an impressive cold calling hit. The sellers proposed changing the name of the post game show to the Reynolds Wrap-Up Show. Using this rhythmic power and the heritage of the Yankees, the sellers sold a package to a company that's not even based in New York. Kalman and his group had to effectively convince a major corporate marketing department in Chicago hundreds of miles from Yankee Stadium whose mandate is to reach women to sponsor a show that appeals mostly to men.

Neat, cute and catchy and an unforgettable order!

Aaron's
The one million dollar napkin

In 2008, Rob Butcher was appointed executive director of the nonprofit U.S. Masters Swimming, a national membership that provides benefits to 60,000 Masters swimmers. A four-year competitive swimmer at Georgia Southern, Butcher was selected to this lofty position after years of success in the sales trenches and in marketing leadership positions with World Racing Group and International Speedway. He began building his credentials as a callow cold caller.

In the summer of 2001, Rob Butcher was hired as an entry-level sales executive for International Speedway Corporation. ISC owns Daytona International Speedway and twelve other speedways. In 2001, one flagship property, Talladega Superspeedway, suffered through the season without a title sponsor. Butcher says, "It was viewed as a failure for our sales team. Although Talladega is located in rural Alabama, which presented logistical activation challenges, it has great racing and the third-highest television ratings on the NASCAR schedule.

"As a young lad trying to earn my stripes, I made a pledge in fall of 2001 to find a title sponsor for our April, 2002 Talladega Busch and Cup races." Butcher's effort started with an eight-week cold calling barrage that left no local stone unturned. He personally called every company in Birmingham, Montgomery and Atlanta. He remembers identifying more than 150 prospects and cold calling every one of them, "looking for someone, anyone, who would listen." Butcher respectfully called them over and over and is likely understating his experience when he says that 'numerous' calls weren't returned. "I was told not interested, sometimes politely and sometimes not so politely, by nearly every company. With each call, I became more comfortable and natural in my elevator pitch," he says. It likely strengthened Butcher's character and prepared him for heightened responsibility down the road.

Butcher says that the one prospect that showed promise was Aaron's, the title sponsor of the NASCAR Busch race at Atlanta Speedway. Aaron's was unsure if it would renew its 2002 title sponsorship. Aaron's, at the time, also sponsored the #99 NASCAR Busch Series car driven by Michael Waltrip.

Remaining pleasantly persistent, Butcher kept tabs on the #99 car. When it finished in the top 10, he would send Rich Lamprey, Aaron's director of sports marketing a handwritten congratulatory note adding a 'subtle' comment, 'It would be great to see the #99 in victory lane of the Aaron's race at Talladega.'

"Rich and I agreed to finally meet at the 2002 Daytona 500, a mere eight-weeks before the 2002 Talladega races. Daytona is our Super Bowl attended by all the corporate powerbrokers. If we didn't have a solid commitment from a sponsor coming out of Daytona, in all likelihood the 2002 Talladega race would go unsponsored," Butcher said, underscoring the exigency of doing some business at Daytona.

Butcher and Lamprey met in the Daytona club. "After a few minutes of pleasantries, I slid a napkin to Rich. I told him, you may write in any number you want for 2002 so long as you meet me with our numbers shown for 2003, 2004 and 2005. I won't be offended, just put the ball in my court and let's see if we can make a win-win deal."

Two hours later, Butcher got a call on his cell phone. It was Aaron's Lamprey, asking if Rob could come to its #99 hauler to meet with him and Aaron's president, Ken Butler. "Ten minutes later, I was standing face-to-face with Ken Butler who has a larger-than-life personality and is the consummate dealmaker."

Butler asked Butcher if he could really name his price for the 2002 season. "I responded yes so long as he met me on my numbers for 2003, 2004 and 2005," Butcher remembers as though it happened yesterday. The Aaron's president then gave Butcher a number that, under any other circumstances, wouldn't have been in the realm of consideration. "I thanked Ken and asked, whether the offer was firm. He responded yes and that Kentucky Speedway was on their way to meet with him. Whoever responded first would get the sponsorship."

Needless to say, the parties came to terms on a deal, and they eventually locked in an Aaron's title sponsorship of the 2002–2006 NASCAR Cup race at Talladega.

Asked what it takes to be an effective cold caller, the affable Rob Butcher says, among other things, "a natural and intellectual curiosity." Agreed. Knowledge is power!

Konica
K for strikeouts and for Konica

Paul Asencio has the Mets in his blood. Through good times and bad, he has peddled team sponsorships to the corporate community in the competitive New York market. Going up against the Yankees the past 20 years hasn't been easy. Paul's mind is always conjuring up leads, and he's always chasing prospects.

The commercial architecture of the ballpark was quite different when Shea Stadium opened in 1964. At Shea then, the Mets had a big Rheingold Beer sign. The big scoreboard sign was pretty much it. The local brewery's name was as interchangeable with the team as were their first three beloved announcers, Lindsey Nelson, Bob Murphy and Ralph Kiner. But there was also a reserve clause, and baseball's payroll was paltry by today's standard. Expenses weren't nearly what they are today, inflation or deflation.

When the Mets packed their bags for adjacent Citi Field, some 45 years after moving into Shea Stadium, Asencio and the Mets' sales staff had inventory to sell. They had to pitch hard. The country was in the depth of the Great Recession, and companies were prudent about every dime they spent.

"We've had to be creative for years even before Citi Field," Asencio recollects. "We were trying to sell the K board where we posted the strikeout count. I racked my brain, thinking in elementary terms. Is there a company whose name begins with the letter K? I cold called Konica, landed the account and got to know Bob Striano, the company's president. The partnership has been mutually beneficial. Over the years, Bob and I became good friends," Asencio says.

Kozy Shack
For a cozy relationship

It's all about relationships. When Striano left Konica to run Kozy Shack, the Mets maintained Konica and Asencio added Kozy Shack. A doubleheader sweep! Kozy Shack, a company in the rice pudding business, isn't the prototype baseball advertiser. It's a product that's purchased for the most part by women. Asencio says, "We've been creative. We opened a Kozy Shack Gluten-Free Stand at field level outside the World's Fare Market. It features a full line of Kozy Shack puddings. Relationships are golden! Get to know people. Do a good job for them and they'll support you."

Gold's Horseradish
Spicing up a longtime relationship

Today at Citi Field, signage is visible almost everywhere. Those who watch Mets' games on television might have even caught a sign near the dugout for Gold's Horseradish, another company that targets women. But don't underestimate the power of sports. Mark Gold, who now runs Gold's, was a young Mets' fan in the 1960s and organized the team's first fan club. Passion is hard to suppress.

The lesson is simple. Find the connections, old and new; bat boys, ball boys and ball girls of yesteryear. These people are good prospects.

Safeway
Cultivating naysayers in the decision-making hierarchy

Lewis Schreck, an inveterate cold caller and vice president of the Washington Redskins Radio Network says, "There is nothing better than creating pieces of business from scratch, by finding decision makers, getting their attention, asking the right questions, forming a smart plan that solves their needs and finally getting the order. When the program is a success, it strengthens the relationship and the business will return year after year!"

Schreck cold called Safeway, a major American supermarket chain that has considerable presence in the Washington area. After being bounced around at corporate in California, he connected with the local person and began positive dialogue. At first, Schreck made team resources available to the chain to raise money for Muscular Dystrophy in the D.C. area, the charity to which Safeway is committed (e.g., autographed merchandise for silent auctions). He got local management to support a sponsorship proposal but the corporate media agency didn't buy into the idea. The agency's position was that advertising in the game broadcasts wasn't in line with objectives of reaching female supermarket shoppers.

"We had to circle away from a 'feel good' associative program and do something that would actually drive traffic. We built presence around our three hour tailgate show and our Football Friday Program to drive shoppers to Safeway to stock for game time munchies."

Safeway had a good four-year-run with the Skins.

Coopers & Lybrand
Cold call at odd hours

Vince Gardino is a legendary New York media sales executive whose experience has run the gamut. Street and people smart, he has spent time running sales for one-time radio juggernaut WOR and National Public Radio's WNYC. Vince also served as executive director of the American Classical Orchestra and is currently chief revenue officer for Straus News which includes longtime neighborhood papers like *Our Town* and the *WestSider*.

Through the years, Gardino sold a lot of sports, the Yankees included. He was one of the first to break a fast food account into radio play-by-play when he cold called and sold Kentucky Fried Chicken.

While running eastern sales for CNBC, in the network's formative years, Gardino's persistence paid off one night. Yes, one night, not one day.

One of the corporate accounts that Gardino and his seller Glenn Dolce targeted was Coopers & Lybrand, then the leading accounting firm in the world, headquartered in New York. Lee Pinkard was one of the principals of the firm and responsible for worldwide marketing.

Gardino homed in on his target. "I cold called Lee regularly for a month and always got his answering machine. I would dutifully leave my message each time, trying to set up an appointment. One night while working late for the cable upfront I was about to leave my office at 10PM when I said to myself, 'Can't let a day go by without calling Lee.' So I dialed his number and to my astonishment Pinkard picked up the phone! Expecting to get his voicemail, I was shocked to say the least. He apologized profusely for not getting back to me and explained that he had been crisscrossing the world visiting headquarters in Paris, Rome, Hong Kong, Tokyo, and Rio de Janeiro to name a few cities."

Pinkard granted Gardino an appointment to present the CNBC story. "When Dolce and I arrived at his opulent office I began wondering whether the presentation was too long and too time consuming. After all, Pinkard was a busy man and faced a hectic schedule every day. As I tried to speedily move along the presentation, he suddenly stopped me and said, 'Vince, take it nice and slow, I want you to take me through the whole thing. The presentation is well put together and I want to absorb everything I can about CNBC.' I of course dutifully complied."

The meeting with Pinkard lasted more than an hour. "He was as gracious as can be. We later secured a $250,000 order [big money then for a cable network still proving itself] through Coopers' agency in Boston, Hill Holiday. It took a month of cold calls but it was worth it!"

Southwestern Bell (now AT&T)
What's hot locally? In Texas, it's high school football

In 1999, when email communication was just beginning to pervade American businesses, Brian Corcoran still worked the phones peddling high school football in Texas. He diligently studied the profile of his prospects before dialing out.

Corcoran contacted Ed Whitacre, the CEO of Southwestern Bell, the company that eventually acquired AT&T, and at the time the regional carrier in Texas. Whitacre was a born and bred Texan. *Risk Management Magazine* wrote "Ed Whitacre is the Texan son of a railroad engineer. He grew up believing he would never leave his hometown, a little place called Ennis, about 30 miles outside Dallas." Whitacre was passionate about high school football. "He was an authentic connection," Brian remembers. Corcoran got the order! He sold Southwestern Bell the sponsorship for $250,000.

Ford
Get to the top

In 2001, Corcoran was selling 'official sponsorships' for the fledgling Arena Football League when David Baker was the league's commissioner. Baker and Corcoran agreed that the AFL should present a sponsorship to the Ford Motor Company.

Their thinking wasn't twisted. At the time, the NFL had an option to purchase 49% of the arena league. Ford owned the Detroit Lions. There were some natural ties.

Corcoran anchored the initial effort. He reached out day after day to Ford's chief marketing officer. "I must have made twenty painstaking calls into the CMO's office and explained my request to the gatekeeper. I never got a call back. Ford was engaged with the ESPN broadcasts of the arena league so there were some natural associations."

Getting no response to his onslaught of calls to the CMO, Corcoran placed a phone call into the office of Ford CEO, William Clay Ford, and explained to his assistant the reason for his call. "The next thing you know I got a callback from the CMO." Corcoran obviously applied the General Dwight Eisenhower ploy. If there's a problem that you can't solve through normal channels, make the problem bigger. Doing so triggers the attention that the problem requires.

"Within two months after our first conversation, the league signed Ford, its first blue chip sponsor," Brian happily remembers. On January 26, 2001, the *New York Times* reported that the deal was valued at $14 million. Commissioner Baker told *The Times* that the Arena Football League didn't elicit the assistance of the NFL to get the deal done.

Nextel (now Sprint)
Sports' best qualified cold call

NASCAR has always had an eclectic mix of sponsors. Between the tracks, the governing body and the drivers, the hodgepodge of logos are iridescently blinding. The names run the gamut. The traditional sports sponsors represent the industry staples, like auto, auto aftermarket, insurance and beer. The offbeat includes against-the-grain, eye-popping names like Boudreaux Butt Paste and Kim Kardashian Fragrance. In case you're wondering, Boudreaux is an all-purpose diaper rash remedy and Kardashian Fragrance, honors "one of America's most famous dilettantes," as one writer described the oft-photographed television and social media personality.

Yes, Boudreaux. To quote team owner Junie Donlavey, "It seems to be the biggest thing going for all these young mamas with their babies." Maybe, but anyone who took a basic advertising class in college knows that Boudreaux is hardly the demographic fit that the head of a media department would approve for a male-driven NASCAR buy.

In 2004, NASCAR had a bigger headache. Winston Cigarettes abdicated its incumbent seat, pulling the plug on its title sponsorship after a 33-year run. The world had changed drastically since Winston launched its NASCAR sponsorship in 1971.

As Steve McCormick blogged after Winston didn't renew, "NASCAR has reached the point where being associated with Winston is holding it back. For a number of years now tobacco advertising has been severely restricted. There are strict limits on where the Winston brand can be shown. These limits have affected NASCAR's ability to market and strengthen its primary product."

NASCAR needed a fresh breath of air, so to speak.

Enter Brian Corcoran. His mindset and stomach are perfectly woven to cold calling. "Most people don't know or understand the trials and tribulations of a cold caller on the prowl," Corcoran emotes. He talks about the all-consuming job of cold calling, what keeps him up at night, how his mind races at midnight to conjure up ideas and how thinking up leads always taxes his brain. "It's about connecting dots," he says. "You're always asking yourself who's trying to reach the *fansumer*? What are the hooks that can align the parties?"

When the sponsorship opportunity opened, Brett Yormark, who headed up sales for NASCAR, took the lead on active clients and the usual cast of well-known sports sponsors. Corcoran was told to pursue 'new blood.' He followed marching orders, making hundreds of calls. But there were no real bites.

"I identified Nextel because it had accelerated its sponsorship effort, working at the time with MLB and with an Indy car team. Nextel had a growing sports portfolio."

It just so happened that Corcoran had earlier dealings with Nextel's director of sports marketing, Mike Robichaud and interaction on an unrelated manner with Robichaud's boss, Mark Schweitzer, Nextel's senior vice president of marketing.

As the NASCAR sales team feverishly worked the landscape of prospects to build demand for a replacement for Winston, Corcoran sent Robichaud this email:

> *Michael,*
>
> *I hope all is well. I thought I would check in.*
>
> *The entitlement is heating up big time to replace Winston. I have not been able to keep my feet on the ground with all the travel.*
>
> *I will be down in DC the week of March 24th. Perhaps we can get together?*
>
> *Would it be worth the time to present the entitlement and/or NASCAR to you and perhaps Mark?*
>
> *Regards, BC*

To be successful, cold callers must work hard and smart. They also need lucky breaks every now and then. For Corcoran, Nextel was a fortuitous call.

Robichaud took the meeting, at which he told Corcoran that Nextel's CEO Tim Donahue had just been a guest of Motorola at the Daytona 500. Corcoran was told that Donahue was completely impressed, 'blown away' by the crowds, the enthusiasm for the sport and the interest in the merchandising. When he got back from Daytona to Nextel headquarters outside Washington, Donahue encouraged his marketing staff to foster a relationship with NASCAR.

After several presentations and spirited discussions, the top executives of both NASCAR and Nextel dined in Reston, Virginia, outside of Washington. The participants included all major decision makers, Nextel's Donahue and Schweitzer and NASCAR's Brian France, Mike Helton and George Pyne.

At the dinner, Donahue told the NASCAR group, "I want this, I like this and it will be good for our business."

Officials from both sides had all day meetings in New York in July 2004. They hammered out details of the deal that included agreements with NASCAR and with the tracks where the NASCAR Nextel Cup series was scheduled.

Shortly afterward, Corcoran received an email from Nextel that all the papers had been signed. It was a done deal. The qualified cold call turned into $750 million over ten years!

"The stars sort of lined up," said Brian France, NASCAR's executive vice president.

They certainly did for Brian Corcoran. He said that "Closing the Nextel deal was 'sweat equity of sorts' for all the other cold calling work that might not have panned out."

After six years at NASCAR, Corcoran spent two years with Fenway Sports and then opened his own sports marketing agency, Shamrock, in 2010.

As for Nextel, it merged with Sprint in 2005. As such, the Nextel Cup became the Sprint Cup. In late 2014, the winds of change gusted again. Sprint announced it would not renew its title sponsorship with NASCAR when the agreement ends in 2016. For NASCAR, it was back to the sales drawing board.

Barclays
Sports' richest real cold call

By 2006, the New Jersey Nets determined that they would move to Brooklyn. Their owner, realtor and developer Bruce Ratner, had grand plans for decrepit downtown Brooklyn. They included housing, a shopping center, a park, a promenade and a world class arena. The Nets might have been the face of the mammoth project; these larger tentacles, though, were what stimulated Bruce Ratner.

There was an incumbent. The Nets at the time were still playing in the Izod Center in East Rutherford, New Jersey. Phillips-Van Heusen owned the Izod brand, and its management engaged the Nets in spirited discussions about extending the naming rights across the harbor to Brooklyn. But the Nets, it appeared, had their sights on bigger corporate names—those with deeper pockets, broader core competencies and strong community resources. In 2012, Phillips-Van Heusen generated some $433 million in net revenue, hardly the target to consider a $400 million naming-rights deal.

The sellers faced major hurdles right from the outset. When the naming rights were first marketed, the team was still working feverishly on a basket of approvals: politicians, variances, financing, environmental issues, community boards and more.

It's one thing to sell a name to a sports facility that's full of life and another to peddle one that's still on its blueprint. The move was hardly a done deal. So, at worst, the Nets were selling a wild dream, and at best, a leap of faith.

Nonetheless, Brett Yormark, the Nets' energetic CEO, and Neil Davis, the team's chief revenue officer, were impervious to the cacophony of vocal objections and expressions of doubt by naysayers on both sides, New York and New Jersey.

Yormark is a master seller. In an earlier iteration, he headed up sales for NASCAR and was a member of the team that landed a $750 million naming-rights deal with Nextel. The road to Brooklyn, though, would be lined with more twists, sharp curves and pitfalls than Yormark ever experienced on a NASCAR track. The construction of the arena was fraught with lawsuits, financial challenges and political uncertainties.

Yormark and Davis immediately did two things. They first listed and dressed up all the selling features of the rights to the marquee. They then targeted a dozen or so potential naming rights holders, made up of the usual stable, from Chase to Verizon and other banner names in between.

There were quite a few unique attractions. By moving to Brooklyn, the Nets would be the first professional franchise in the borough since the Dodgers bolted fabled

Ebbets Field in 1957. As such, the Nets' move would be historical. The facility was to be built with all imaginable amenities, retail shops, restaurants, a hotel and a luxury high-rise.

The arena project was considered a developmental springboard for a much-needed gentrification of down-trodden downtown Brooklyn. By osmosis, the title owner would be deemed a good corporate citizen.

In the vicinity, the sponsor's name would appear in bright lights on highway signs and on busy streets. Up-grades were planned for adjacent subway stops and the Long Island Railroad station where the sponsor's name would adorn the sparkling new signs.

The new arena would be just a few subway stops from the heart of the financial district, known to the world simply as Wall Street, the citadel of capitalism. Wall Street, for that matter is almost equidistant to the Brooklyn arena as it is to Madison Square Garden.

In other words, as Davis put it, "The Nets were im-portant but only one component of the deal." There was real estate, goodwill in the community and a variety of non-basketball events in the building.

Brett Yormark had developed an interesting way to cold call, something that only he as CEO could pull off. Yormark deputized his administrative assistant, Jeanette Neary, to call a host of core CEOs and introduce herself to their administrative assistants. When she reached these assistants, she requested meetings of their respective bosses to talk about the move of the Nets to Brooklyn.

In the summer of 2006, Neary, at Yormark's behest, contacted the assistant to the chief administrative officer of Barclays Bank in the United States, Gerard LaRocca. Neary requested a meeting between Yormark and LaRoc-ca. Some days later, LaRocca's office notified Neary that the bank was open to meet. The Barclays' chief adminis-trator assumed that the meeting had something to do with a suite or a hospitality package.

Barclays was an intriguing prospect. It had tons of branches in England, where it was born centuries earlier, but it had none in America. As such, it was an against-the-grain cold-call.

Yormark is one of the most accomplished sponsorship sellers in the history of sports and Davis, too, had glittering credentials, including some 20 years at Madison Square Garden in its golden years of growth.

When LaRocca greeted the two of them at their first meeting, he likely expected a short PowerPoint covering suite and hospitality costs. What followed was mesmerizing.

Theatrically, the two protagonists painted a long-term vision of a deeply embedded partnership, replete with omnipresent visibility and pervasive goodwill. They talked 'partnership'—two organizations working in lockstep to end the malaise in downtown Brooklyn and doing so just a short distance from the powerbrokers of Wall Street. They portrayed a larger-than-life opportunity, one with unprecedented depth and unequaled presence.

The presentation knocked LaRocca's socks off, although he maintained his equanimity throughout the presentation.

Barclays is hardly a Johnny-come-lately regional bank. It traces its roots to 1690. Heritage weighs heavily. The decor of its offices, even on this side of the pond, is accented with thick wooden furnishings, redolent of its royal roots in the city of London. As such, what unsurprisingly caught LaRocca's eye was the artist's rendering of the proposed Brooklyn building. The architect was none other than the acclaimed Frank Gehry, who is globally renowned.

When the presentation wound down, LaRocca promised the Nets' brass that he would run the opportunity up the flagpole, the British flagpole. His boss, Rich Ricci, the bank's London based chief operating officer, was due in New York a few weeks later and LaRocca said he would ask Ricci whether he had sufficient interest to meet with the Nets when he was in New York.

Shortly afterward, LaRocca informed the Nets that Ricci indeed wanted to meet. In advance thereof, the Nets addressed a number of questions that Ricci had.

The meeting with both Ricci and LaRocca was also encouraging. Not long after, Yormark, Davis and owner Bruce Ratner were invited to London to present the opportunity to Bob Diamond, Barclays' president. Diamond had dual British and American citizenship and was an avid fan of the Red Sox and Celtics. He was later promoted to Barclays' CEO.

The meeting in Britain was a resounding success too. Everything about the proposal seemed to fit, starting with architect Gehry. Diamond bought into the value of the proposal, appreciating what the commitment would do for Barclays in the United States. It assured the bank of immediate recognition in a country where its visibility pales to indigenous competitors like Chase, Bank of America and Citibank.

On December 20, 2006, Barclays signed a letter of intent. It happened to be the same day that the Nets received approval to go ahead with the $4 billion Brooklyn Atlantic Yards project—the interwoven arena, community and retail undertaking.

At that point, the heirs to Arthur Brown who died in 1989 must have asked themselves, "What if?" Brown launched the Nets' franchise in 1967 as the New Jersey Americans of the American Basketball Association. The team first played in the dilapidated Teaneck Armory and often drew just hundreds not thousands. In their first season, the Americans qualified for the playoffs but were forced to forfeit the first round because the Armory was in disrepair, and the team had nowhere else to play. Brown moved the team to Long Island the following season, changed its name to the Nets and sold it in 1969 to Roy Boe for $1.1 million. Some 37 years later, the team that Brown originally owned signed a reported $400 million deal for 20 years of naming rights!

Over the next few weeks, lawyers from both sides dug in and the granular was churned out into an agreeable document. "There were so many deal points that it was mind boggling," Davis reminisced eight years after the announcement. "Remember, this was before ground breaking! We talked about naming rights to every which wall that meets the eye and came to terms on other points that only lawyers can think of."

By 2008, there were problems brewing as a result of the gusty headwinds of the crippling financial crisis. There were other issues, too, that further exacerbated the challenges, including disharmony over the project's potential environmental impact and resistance by the community due to the use of eminent domain. It all weighed on owner Ratner. By 2009, fighting multiple lawsuits and thinning financing for the project, Ratner was forced to sell a majority ownership of the team to Russian businessman, Mikhail Prokhorov.

Groundbreaking was delayed for years. Construction didn't begin until March 2010.

Through it all, the Nets held Barclays' hand. "There were some major bumps on the road," Davis remembered. "When Ratner ran into financial challenges he was forced to retrench. He economized by downgrading from the pricy Gehry to Ellerbe Becket/AECOM."

To Barclays, Gehry's signature meant much. The famed Canadian-born architect was to put his stamp on his first-ever designed sports complex. He proposed a unique rooftop park for area residents. All this appealed to Barclays.

"Going into Barclays, once we had a deal, to say that Gehry was no longer the architect was not a comfortable moment. It didn't sit well with the decision makers," Davis pensively remembers. As it turned out, the absence of Gehry and associated elements did indeed dull the luster. Deal points had to be vastly renegotiated. By 2008, Barclays itself was fighting the Great Recession that swept through the world economy.

Through lawsuits and dark economic clouds that were threatening the Nets' deal, the Yankees, football Giants and Mets were all planning new facilities of their own. Sports, like other businesses, can be cutthroat. These franchises have agendas of their own, and a number of them tried knocking on Barclays' door to switch pitch the bank's Nets commitment.

Bob Diamond, who put his signature on the original Nets deal, stuck with it through thick and thin, through changes in the agreement's components and through the greatest financial crisis since the Great Depression. When all was said and done, Barclays maintained its commitment although the original $400 million deal was pared to a reported $200 million.

Awkwardly, because Barclays does not have a single branch bank in the United States, it doesn't have ATMs in the Barclays Arena. The British bank uses the sponsorship for its wealth management services, philanthropic undertakings and online banking.

Funny, though, how things take twists and turns. Diamond never made it to Brooklyn in an official Barclays' capacity. He resigned under pressure as CEO in July 2012, just two months before the building's epochal opening.

When the building did open on September 21, 2012, Diamond at least didn't have to worry about the 200 or so protesters outside the arena who were objecting to the building's presence.

Still, Barclays remains one of sports' greatest cold calls ever!

Moda Health
Sports' biggest classic cold call ever

This book ends with the inspiring story of Uzma Rawn, who wasn't much different from many others launching their careers in sports.

When Uzma started in the business, she didn't know a soul and had no client contacts. She was passionate, confident, pounced on opportunities, soaked up knowledge, made the best of all experiences, worked indefatigably and made a glittering name for herself.

After spending her early youth in England and Saudi Arabia, Uzma Rawn moved to these shores and spent her formative years in North Carolina.

She loved being around basketball, a sport to which she first gravitated in high school. Later, at Ithaca College in upstate New York, Rawn always raised her hand enthusiastically volunteering to do whatever was required to promote the game or assist the basketball team on campus.

By her senior year, she sent her resume to Scott O'Neil of the NBA who headed up the league's team services department. After graduating with a degree in management and a minor in integrated marketing communication, Rawn was hired by O'Neil for a lower-rung job. For three years, she served under his tutelage and absorbed everything she experienced, from learning the ropes of team marketing to understanding the ins and outs of sponsorship sales. She was never afraid to ask questions and, as such, quickly developed her skills and grew her reputation.

When she saw what worked effectively for one NBA team, she eagerly shared it with another. Rawn earned O'Neil's trust. He began to send her on field trips to team offices where she helped and shared.

Rawn later caught the eye of Randy Bernstein, an accomplished sports marketing and management executive who, in 2010, recruited her to Premier Partnerships of which he is CEO. Premier consults sports teams and entertainment entities on sponsorship sales and marketing operations.

Among other responsibilities at Premier, Uzma was charged with landing a variety of new sponsors from naming rights to official brand sponsors. In other words, she spent lots of time working the trenches cultivating new business.

Uzma learned quickly, as she puts it, "that 75% or more of naming rights candidates are either moving to a building's locale or are rebranding.

"The minute I get a sponsorship assignment, I devour the local business press, whether local newspapers or independently published business journals. Information is precious. I subscribe to anything that will provide valuable intelligence."

The practice of 'knowledge is power' has served Uzma well. In Texas, where Premier represented the

Texas Rangers, she came across some invaluable intelligence. "CyrusOne is a global enterprise center. I read that they were leaving their Midwest headquarters and taking root in Carrollton, Texas. The article highlighted the amount of money CyrusOne was saving in corporate taxes moving to Carrollton. And there were some magical words. It said that CyrusOne wanted to be 'well known in the community.'"

Rawn reached out to Cyrus in cold call form and proceeded to sell the company a five-year corporate partnership with the Rangers. A cold call made good!

A Premier colleague of Uzma also pounced on a story that ecommerce retailer overstock.com was changing its name to odotco and immediately cold called the company's Utah headquarters and sold it the naming rights to the Oakland Coliseum.

The Moda deal in Portland might just be the *biggest classic cold call in team sports history*. The accomplishment exalted Rawn's reputation to unprecedented heights.

Steve Scott, who heads up marketing and sales for the Portland Trail Blazers hired Premier Partnerships to sell the naming rights to the Rose Garden, which the Trail Blazers opened in 1995. "We did so believing that Premier would cast a wider net. We needed an organization that could effectively bird-dog America to find a corporation with the breadth and willingness to make the commitment."

Premier focused on several categories, including health care, technology and financial services. The sales team at Premier Partnerships spent the first four months contacting more than 300 companies to gauge their interest in buying naming rights to the Rose Garden. It found no serious buyers.

One day in the spring of 2013, while on the prowl for the Blazers, Uzma was devouring local business news in Portland when she read that health care provider ODS was changing its name to Moda. She took note of the fact that the press release assured the people of Portland that it would be a *trailblazer* in the community. She noticed too that the company said it wanted to be *trailblazers* in health care. "The word trailblazer was used repeatedly in the press release," she remembers. "It was a no-brainer. The company was a prime target.

"The timing of my cold-call couldn't have been better. I emailed the company's president, William Johnson. He expressed interest. We met. The Blazers' brass demonstrated enthusiasm for embracing Moda. Dr. Johnson saw an opportunity to connect with the community at a time when he was trying to raise the company's brand awareness. The sales process was a 90-day slam dunk. Literally, the stars seemed to align. It seemed like the perfect fit."

By August 2013, Moda signed a 10-year contract for $40 million. Television, radio and digital advertising inventory were included in the sponsorship and naming-rights package. The company also received benefits with the Seahawks and MLS Sounders, which are also part of Trail Blazers' owner Paul Allen's Vulcan Sports & Entertainment.

Moda wanted to wrap things up quickly so that its name would be out there by the time that the health care open enrollment period started in October. It partnered with the Blazers in areas of health awareness, and it's been a mutually beneficial relationship.

Like politics, team sports are local. The company that made the commitment to the Blazers was right under the team's nose, right there in Portland. If the shortest distance between two points is a straight line, the effort went full circle. The team outsourced the assignment to Premier Partnership, a New York and California entity that ironically pitched and closed a company right in Portland. Yet all's well that ends well. Everyone was happy.

According to Scott, the purchase of the naming rights by Moda has worked brilliantly. He says, "Oregon is the most competitive state for health care insurance. The sponsorship has spiked the needle. Moda is now number one in the market after it was four or five." In fact, Scott proudly shares, "The Blazers won a silver award from Ad Age for the best integrated program in the health care category."

The business took note of the Moda deal. Uzma Rawn's name appeared in bright lights in 2015 when *Forbes* magazine selected her as one of the top 30 under 30 in the sports space. The preponderance of the top 30 list comprises competitive athletes. So not bad for a non-athlete who spent some of her formative years in England where basketball courts are hard to find. "I didn't feel as though I truly deserved it, but was so appreciative that there are others out there that felt as though I did, and who put my name in the hat to be considered," Rawn said of her selection by *Forbes*.

Once she cracked the list, Ithaca, her alma mater, extolled her feat featuring her in a media relations press release. "It's definitely one of the most memorable land-mark moments of my career so far," she says.

As Brian Corcoran of Shamrock, the prime author of the Nextel deal observed, "It's earned sweat equity. For every closed piece of new business, there are hundreds of unreturned calls and dismissive email messages." By the end of 2014, a year or so after cutting the Moda deal, Rawn was promoted to vice president at Premier Partner-ships. In 2015, she joined Major League Baseball in a sales executive capacity.

Reflecting on the Moda deal, Rawn says, "In its an-nual report, the company talked about how it will 'lead the way.'" She says Moda is derived from the Latin word 'modus,' which means 'the way.' As for quality cold call-ing, Uzma's work corresponds with the translation of her Arabic name, 'supreme or greatest!'

It begins with a cold call! Some take advantage of it and others don't.